FLORIDA

MORTGAGE BROKER'S GUIDE

Third Edition

Robert Smither, PhD

Dearborn™
Real Estate Education

President: Mehul Patel
Director of Product Development: Kate DeVivo
Managing Editor: Anne Huston
Managing Editor: Tony Peregrin
Director of Production: Daniel Frey
Production Editor: Samantha Raue
Senior Production Artist: Virginia Byrne
Creative Director: Lucy Jenkins
Vice President of Product Management: Dave Dufresne
Director of Product Management: Melissa Kleeman

Published by Dearborn Real Estate Education
30 South Wacker Drive
Chicago, Illinois 60606-7481
(312) 836-4400
www.dearbornRE.com

Printed in the United States of America

09 10 11 10 9 8 7 6 5 4 3 2 1

The Library of Congress has cataloged the previous edition as follows:

Smither, Robert.
Florida mortgage broker's guide / Robert Smither. -- 2nd ed.
p. cm.
Includes index.
ISBN-13: 978-1-4195-8466-4
ISBN-10: 1-4195-8466-9
1. Mortgage brokers--Florida. 2. Mortgage brokers--Licenses--Florida. 3. Mortgage loans--Law and legislation--Florida. I. Title.
HG2040.5.U6F67 2006
332.7'22076—dc22

2006027426

Third edition ISBN-13: 978-1-4277-8279-3
Third edition ISBN-10: 1-4277-8279-2

CONTENTS

FOREWORD

Congratulations on taking your first step toward becoming a Florida mortgage broker!

As you will see in the following pages, the mortgage industry plays a critical role in our nation's economy. Not only do mortgage brokers handle transactions worth trillions of dollars annually, but they also perform the very important service of helping many people buy their first homes.

The mortgage industry is a dynamic field that quickly adapts to meet the changing needs of homebuyers, homeowners, mortgage lenders, correspondent lenders, and investors. For this reason, knowledge of the laws and practices of the industry is a key factor in becoming a successful mortgage broker. The goal of this book is to help you pass the test that allows you to become a mortgage broker in Florida.

ACKNOWLEDGMENTS

Many people contributed to the success of this book. I particularly want to thank my associates in the mortgage business who provided input: David Hennon, Rick Shipp, Andrea ("Andy") Tolbert, and Paul Reich. I also want to thank my reviewers, whose helpful comments made this a much stronger book, especially

- Marty Bosy Newlon, Bob Hogue School of Real Estate; and
- Sandi M. Kellogg, Central Florida Community College (CFCC).

Industry reviewers who provided insight and direction on past editions include

- Mike Davenport, Bob Hogue School of Real Estate;
- Beth Hollingsworth, Ivanhoe Financial, Inc.;
- Sandi M. Kellogg, Central Florida Community College (CFCC);
- Marty Bosy Newlon, Bob Hogue School of Real Estate;
- Laurie MacDougal, Laurmac Learning Center, Oak Park, IL;
- Daniel J. Taddeo, PA, All Florida Real Estate Schools, Inc.; and
- Joe Schwartz, Bob Hogue School of Real Estate.

My associates in the real estate industry who contributed helpful suggestions also deserve thanks: Gail Bradford, Tom Clausing, Cindy Egeli, Brian Hammons, and Roger Rife. Others who helped along the way were Kent Akins, Frances Demetree, Diana Fink, Robert Miller, Marie Sevick, and Andrea Spainhour.

Finally, a special thanks to my editor at Dearborn Financial Publishing, Anne Huston, and my publisher, Kate DeVivo. Their support made the writing of this book a pleasure.

In the past decade, professionals in the mortgage industry have been part of a remarkable period of challenge and growth. Learning the material presented in this book offers you the opportunity to become a part of the industry's growth in the future.

I wish you every success.

Robert Smither, PhD

ABOUT THE AUTHOR

Robert Smither, PhD, is a licensed mortgage broker and real estate instructor in Orlando. He also teaches at Rollins College in Winter Park, Florida, where he served as dean of the adult evening and graduate programs. Smither holds an MA in Educational Psychology from San Francisco State University and a PhD in Psychology from Johns Hopkins University. A professional educator with more than 20 years of college and professional licensure teaching experience, he is the author of ten books and scored a perfect 100 on the Florida mortgage broker license examination.

CHAPTER

1 INTRODUCTION TO THE MORTGAGE BROKERAGE AND LENDING BUSINESS

LEARNING OBJECTIVES

After finishing chapter 1, you should be able to

1. understand the work of a mortgage broker;
2. explain the differences between mortgage brokers and mortgage lenders;
3. understand yield, discount points, and basis points;
4. explain the steps in the mortgage approval process;
5. understand the differences between second mortgages, home equity loans, and refinancing;
6. know the requirements for becoming a mortgage broker in Florida; and
7. understand the application process and state exam.

KEY TERMS

annual percentage rate (APR)
basis points
closing
discount points
equity
HELOC
home equity loan
loan originator
loan servicing
mortgage
mortgage broker
mortgage brokerage fee
mortgagee
mortgage lender
mortgage lending
mortgagor
refinancing
secondary market
second mortgage
underwriting
yield
yield spread premium

INTRODUCTION

Most people recognize the value of owning property, but not many realize that over one-third of the world's wealth is based on real estate. In the United States alone, almost 5 million people work in some part of the real estate industry, which includes homebuilding and construction, real estate sales and purchases, property appraisal, and mortgage brokering and lending.

Mortgage lending is the process by which individuals or institutions loan money to other individuals or groups who want to buy or finance property. In return for the loan, the borrower offers the lender a **mortgage,** which is defined as the pledge of real property as security for a loan. The party who offers his or her property as security for the loan—that is, the borrower—is the **mortgagor;** the party who grants the loan—the lender—is the **mortgagee.**

When buyers decide to finance the purchase of property with a mortgage loan, they often rely on the services of a **mortgage broker,** who is an individual who connects potential borrowers with potential lenders.

Figure 1.1 shows a brief time line of key events in the history of mortgage lending in the United States.

FIGURE 1.1 ■ Mortgage Lending Time Line

1800s	Mortgage lending business develops as a way to provide loans to farmers as the population of the United States moves west. The typical farm mortgage of that period covered 40 percent to 50 percent of the value of the property and required interest-only payments for five years and a full payment of the mortgage loan at the end of that period. As cities grew, financial institutions also began to make loans to urban borrowers under similar terms.
1920s	Real estate prices skyrocket, and lenders become eager to extend credit to as many homebuyers as possible.
1929	Stock market crashes, causing property values to drop to half of what they were the year before the crash. Borrowers begin to default on their loans, causing lenders to start selling properties at a loss. Many financial institutions with large loan portfolios fail.
1932	Congress creates the Reconstruction Finance Corporation (RFC), which is designed to provide liquidity to banks. In 1938, the RFC provides capital to create the Federal National Mortgage Association, today known as Fannie Mae. Fannie Mae has the mission of purchasing loans from mortgage lenders so as to provide lenders with a source of capital. In a similar manner, the Federal Home Loan Mortgage Bank is created with the mission of providing credit to savings and loan institutions.
1934	Congress creates the Federal Housing Administration (FHA) through the National Housing Act. Today, the FHA often sets standards that are eventually adopted by the entire mortgage industry.
1944	Congress passes the Servicemen's Readjustment Act—known as the GI Bill—which created the U.S. Department of Veterans Affairs (VA). VA loans allowed many veterans returning from World War II to purchase homes.
1968	Congress passes the Fair Housing Act of 1968, which prohibits discrimination on the basis of race, color, religion, sex, handicap, familial status, and national origin. Also in 1968, Congress creates the Government National Mortgage Association—Ginnie Mae—which establishes a secondary market for buying and selling mortgage-backed securities.
1970	The Federal Home Loan Mortgage Bank becomes the Federal Home Loan Mortgage Corporation—known as Freddie Mac. Freddie Mac is formed to purchase mortgage loans originated in savings institutions.
1974	Congress passes the Real Estate Settlement Procedures Act (RESPA) and the Equal Credit Opportunity Act (ECOA).
1993–2005	The mortgage lending industry expands as historically low interest rates cause a boom in home buying and refinancing.
2006–present	In response to new forms of financing developed by lenders, federal and state laws establish new standards and regulations for the mortgage industry.

THE WORK OF A MORTGAGE BROKER

Because most individuals or organizations who want to buy property cannot or do not want to pay for the property in full at the time of purchase, they look for institutions or individuals willing to loan them the money to make the purchase. Mortgage brokers serve a critical function in the mortgage industry by bringing together borrowers and lenders. Typical lenders include banks and savings institutions, life insurance companies, pension funds, real estate investment trusts, and wholesale lenders who specifically target the mortgage market.

For most borrowers, the process of finding a lender starts by contacting a mortgage broker who specializes in loans for the type of property the borrower wants to buy. Some mortgage brokers specialize in financing for individual residences, whereas others specialize in apartment buildings or shopping centers. Regardless of specialization, the goal of the mortgage broker is to find borrowers who meet the requirements of a specific lender and lenders who offer the best possible terms to the borrowers.

Because successful mortgage brokers have contacts with a large number of lenders—on average, 40 different lenders, according to industry reports—they know who has money to lend and under what conditions. Mortgage lenders not only make mortgage loans; many lenders also collect taxes and insurance on mortgaged properties—a process known as **loan servicing**—for their loans or the loans of other lenders, and they also sell existing mortgage loans to investors.

In contrast with mortgage lenders, mortgage brokers do not lend money. As *intermediaries* who bring together borrowers and lenders, mortgage brokers must keep abreast of all aspects of the mortgage business, including interest rates, discount points, fees individual lenders charge, the size of the loans different lenders offer, and what different lenders require to qualify for a loan. For the borrower, working with a broker who has such specialized knowledge makes the process of getting a loan much simpler, and often less expensive, than if the borrower approaches lenders directly. At the same time, relying on the mortgage broker to provide qualified borrowers also makes the process simpler, and often less expensive, for the lender.

Mortgage brokers typically earn income through a **mortgage brokerage fee** (discussed in chapter 2) paid by the borrower to a mortgage brokerage business that covers the expenses associated with submitting a loan application to a lender. In addition, lenders typically pay the mortgage brokerage business a commission known as a **yield spread premium** at the time the mortgage transaction is funded.

According to Florida law, the yield spread premium must be disclosed to the borrower as the maximum dollar amount the mortgage brokerage business may receive as part of the transaction. The exact yield spread premium must be disclosed to the borrower no later than three business days prior to closing. Also by law, mortgage brokers can receive compensation only from the mortgage brokerage business or lender where they hang their license.

Different states have different laws regarding licensure of mortgage brokers. In Florida, laws governing the mortgage brokerage business are found in Chapter 494 of the Florida Statutes (F.S. 494) and the rules are found in Chapter 69V-40 of the Florida Administrative Code. These Florida laws and rules can be found at the Division of Finance Web site

WEB LINK @

www.flofr.com/Finance/MBlist.htm

Under Florida law, an individual who performs the same work as a mortgage broker but who does not hold a mortgage broker license is known as **loan originator.** Although some states allow loan originators to be paid commissions or performance bonuses, in Florida, loan originators who work as mortgage lenders and correspondent lenders are paid salaries by their employers. The salary of a loan originator is reported on a W-2 form.

MORTGAGE BROKERS AND MORTGAGE LENDERS

Mortgage brokerage businesses do not make mortgage loans. Their role in financing the purchase of real property is to bring together potential borrowers and potential lenders. Mortgage brokers accept applications for loans, solicit loans from a lender on behalf of the borrower who submitted the application, and negotiate the terms of a loan between the borrower and the lender or the noninstitutional investor. After the closing, when the mortgage broker receives a fee for services, the broker is no longer involved in the relationship between the borrower and the lender, nor does the broker take responsibility for servicing the loan.

Mortgage lenders, unlike mortgage brokers, may fund the loans they originate, and they may continue to service the loan after the transaction has closed. Although a bank may lend money for mortgages, not all mortgage lending firms are banks. Rather, they are companies that use their own funds or borrowed funds to finance transactions related to real estate.

In addition to financing real estate transactions, mortgage lenders may fund loans originated by mortgage brokers or other mortgage firms. Sources of income for mortgage lenders include the interest charged, origination fees, discount points, servicing fees, and selling of mortgage loans in the secondary market.

For the most part, the duties of mortgage loan officers or loan originators are the same as those of the mortgage broker. Mortgage loan officers take loan applications, verify credit history, arrange appraisals and inspections, and negotiate terms of a loan. According to Florida law, however, any individual who works for a mortgage lending firm and is paid on commission as an *independent contractor* (discussed in chapter 2) is required to hold a mortgage broker license. Commission earnings are reported to the IRS on Form 1099.

YIELD, DISCOUNT POINTS, AND BASIS POINTS

Three of the most important concepts in the mortgage brokerage business are yield, discount points, and basis points.

Yield is the return to a lender or investor on a mortgage loan and is related to the interest rate the lender is charging. For example, a $240,000 mortgage loan made at an interest rate of 5.75 percent has a yield of 5.75.

Discount points are a form of prepaid interest on a loan, and they are used to increase the yield to a lender and possibly lower the monthly payments for the borrower. One discount point equals 1 percent of the loan amount, so two discount points on the $240,000 loan just mentioned would amount to $4,800 additional funds from the borrower at time of closing.

Borrowers and lenders can use discount points to "buy down" the interest rates on loans. For example, a lender may offer an interest rate of 6.75 percent on a loan, but if the borrower is willing to pay for two discount points, the lender will lower the interest rate to 6.50. For the borrower, this lower interest rate would result in a savings of $14,282.12 in interest payments over the life of the loan, an amount considerably greater than the $4,800 cost for the discount points:

	Loan with no points	Loan with two points
Loan amount:	$240,000	$240,000
Interest rate:	6.75%	6.50%
Total interest paid over 30 years:	$320,389.11	$306,106.99

Although paying points appears to save money for the borrower, it actually increases the yield to the lender by about 1/8 of 1 percent (0.00125) per discount point paid on a 30-year loan. In other words, eight discount points will add about 1 percent to the interest rate on a loan.

The yield to the lender is disclosed in the **annual percentage rate (APR)**, which is defined as the true cost of borrowing funds including the loan amount and any additional fees. In general, the highest yield for the lender comes from a mortgage loan with a combination of the highest interest rate, the highest discount, and the shortest term.

Lenders generally use percentages when calculating yield and interest rates on their loans. As mentioned earlier, a point equals 1 percent of the loan amount. Sometimes a lender needs to work with a fraction of a point and will use a system of basis points. A **basis point** equals 1/100 of 1 percent. So rather than a lender stating he or she charges a servicing fee of 0.35 percent, the lender may describe the servicing fee as 35 basis points.

AN OVERVIEW OF THE MORTGAGE LOAN APPROVAL PROCESS

The mortgage loan approval process begins with a buyer and seller agreeing on the terms regarding the purchase of a property. If the buyer plans to borrow money from a lending institution to finance the purchase, the sales contract will specify the number of days the buyer has to arrange financing. This date is important because if the buyer cannot arrange financing within the time specified, either the buyer or the seller can cancel the contract.

Once the contract is signed, the buyer may approach a lender and apply for a loan, or the buyer may ask a mortgage broker for help in finding a lender who offers loans at terms acceptable to the borrower.

The person who originates the loan at either the mortgage lending company or the mortgage brokerage business helps the borrower complete a detailed application form and assists in gathering all the information the lender requires to make a judgment about the creditworthiness of the applicant. In order to make this judgment, the lender asks for information about the applicant's current sources of income, assets and liabilities, and his or her record of borrowing and repaying loans in the past.

Sometimes the process of applying for a mortgage loan is not straightforward. In addition to all the information lenders require before they commit to making a loan, potential borrowers may be asked to explain any credit problems in their past or to provide justification for a loan amount that exceeds typical guidelines. In these cases, the mortgage broker serves as the intermediary who negotiates with the borrower and the lender.

In addition to bringing potential borrowers and lenders together and assisting with the loan application, the mortgage broker also facilitates the loan process by helping with other steps necessary to qualify for a loan. These include ordering credit reports on potential borrowers, arranging property inspections and appraisals, and estimating the expenses associated with obtaining and repaying the loan. These critical aspects of the application process help lenders evaluate risks associated with making the loan.

When the application package is complete, the mortgage broker submits the package to the lender, who then sends it for underwriting. **Underwriting** is the process of evaluating the risk to a lender associated with a particular mortgage loan. If the underwriter approves the application package, all parties involved in the transaction agree on a date for closing. **Closing** refers to the process of finalizing the transaction. At a typical closing, the borrower signs a promissory note for the loan amount and the mortgage. Funds are disbursed to the seller in the case of a new purchase, and to the buyer in the case of a refinance, in which the amount of the new mortgage loan exceeds the amount owed on the previous financing.

By signing the promissory note, the borrower agrees to make monthly payments of principal and interest, and perhaps taxes and insurance, to the lender. The lender may choose either to retain *servicing of the loan*—that is, to collect the borrower's payments and disburse payments to taxing agencies and insurance companies—or to sell the loan to another lender or investor on the secondary market. Loan servicing and the **secondary market,** which consists of investors who buy already existing mortgages and who do not loan money, are discussed in chapter 10.

Figure 1.2 illustrates the loan approval process.

The mortgage application, approval, funding, and servicing processes are, of course, more complex than described in this short explanation. The next chapters give a detailed look at all aspects of the mortgage brokerage business. Figure 1.3 explains three other aspects of mortgage lending—second mortgages, home equity loans, and refinancing.

FIGURE 1.2 ■ Loan Approval Process

Real Estate Transaction →	Loan Application →	Underwriting →	Closing →	Recording
• contract for sale and purchase	• employment verification • bank account verification • tax returns	• credit report • appraisal • employment/income verification • asset verification	• deed • note • mortgage • title insurance • survey • WDO report • final Truth-in-Lending	• legal notice

FIGURE 1.3 ■ Aspects of Mortgage Lending

SECOND MORTGAGES, HOME EQUITY LOANS, AND REFINANCING

In the typical real estate transaction, homeowners pay part of the sales price of their home and cover the balance by acquiring a mortgage loan. The value of their home that exceeds the amount of the mortgage is the **equity** the owner has in the property. Sometimes an owner wishes to use this equity as security for further borrowing through a second mortgage, home equity loan, or refinancing.

Second Mortgage

With a second mortgage, an individual borrows a certain amount that the lender advances in one payment. Most second mortgages have fixed interest rates and a set period—usually between 5 years and 15 years—for repayment. The payment amount remains constant throughout the term of the loan, and interest is tax deductible. Under Fannie Mae guidelines, second mortgages can be secured by owner-occupied primary residences only.

Home Equity Loan

A home equity loan, which is similar to a second mortgage, has several unique characteristics. First, the term on a typical home equity loan is open-ended; that is, the loan need not be paid in full on a specific date. Second, the home equity loan operates as a line of credit and is sometimes referred to as a **HELOC** (home equity line of credit). The lender sets the maximum amount the homeowner can borrow, and the borrower can use all or part of this amount as he or she chooses. Most home equity loans have a variable interest rate.

Refinancing

Refinancing refers to a borrower obtaining new financing on a property without transferring title. Homeowners typically use refinancing to lower the interest rate on a mortgage loan. Because there are closing costs associated with refinancing, a general rule of thumb is that refinancing is financially beneficial to a borrower if it lowers the mortgage interest rate by at least 2 percent and the borrower does not plan to sell the property in the immediate future.

Refinancing can also be a source of cash. If the owner's equity in the property is greater than the mortgage amount, the homeowner can refinance for a higher amount, pay the balance of the original mortgage, and use the extra cash as he or she chooses. This is known as a cash-out refinance. A limited cash-out refinance allows the borrower to pay off existing mortgages and liens affecting the property and to finance closing costs. The maximum amount of cash received at a limited cash-out closing is the lesser of $2,000 or 2 percent of the loan amount. In either case, interest payments on the loan are tax deductible.

BECOMING A MORTGAGE BROKER IN FLORIDA

According to F.S. 494.0033, to be licensed as a mortgage broker in Florida, individuals must

- be at least 18 years of age and have a high school diploma or its equivalent;
- have passed a written test adopted by the Department of Financial Services that determines competency in mortgage finance;
- have filed a completed application and paid a nonrefundable application fee of $200;
- have filed a complete set of fingerprints; and
- have completed 24 hours of classroom education on financing transactions and the laws and rules that govern such transactions.

The Application

Individuals who wish to be licensed as a Florida mortgage broker can obtain an application online through the Office of Financial Regulation. This application can be submitted to the state electronically or by mail.

WEB LINK @

www.flofr.com/Finance/Forms/mbapp.pdf

Soon after the application is received, DFS will notify the applicant of any deficiencies regarding the application—that is, information not provided, fee or fingerprints not received, required education not completed, or state exam not passed. Applicants have 90 days from the date their application is received to take care of these deficiencies before the application expires.

If any relevant aspect of an applicant's situation changes during the time his or her application is under consideration, the applicant has ten days to notify the DFS.

The Prelicense Course

Individuals may apply for their license before they take the 24-hour prelicense course, and they can also take the state exam. But before their application can be approved, they must provide evidence to the state that they have fulfilled this educational requirement. The prelicense course is offered through accredited mortgage business schools, colleges, universities, community colleges, and vocational-technical schools in Florida. Because the 24-hour mortgage broker prelicense course has no class test, individuals who finish the course and complete the other requirements can qualify to take the state exam. The prelicense course is based on a 50-minute classroom hour.

Within five days after the prelicense course ends, the school must submit electronically to the Office of Financial Regulation the full name and Social Security number of each student, the school's name and license number, and the completion date of all students who successfully completed the course. The mortgage business school must maintain student records for at least three years from the completion dates, and each school is responsible for confirming the identity of each student attending. Finally, the preclicense course instructor may use the course toward satisfying his or her prelicensing education requirement.

Like mortgage brokers, mortgage brokerage businesses, lenders, and correspondent lenders, mortgage business schools are subject to the requirements of F. S. 494. Violations of the law may result in revocation or suspension of the school's license, as well as a fine of up to $5,000 for each separate offense.

The State Exam

Applicants apply online to take the license exam. When an applicant is approved for testing, the DFS will assign the applicant the next test date in the month following the 15th day of the month in which the application is received. If the application is not received by the 15th, however, the applicant will be assigned the test date two months in the future. For example, if the application was received on February 15, the applicant will be assigned the March test date. If DFS received the application on February 16, the applicant will be assigned the April test date.

The DFS will notify the applicant of the date, time, and place of the test about two weeks before the test date. In Florida, mortgage broker license examinations are usually given on the fourth Tuesday—and sometimes Wednesday if there are more applicants than can be accommodated at the test site—of each month. In November and December, the test date is moved to the third Tuesday of the month due to the holidays.

The state exam for the mortgage broker license has 100 multiple-choice questions, each worth one point, that cover six areas of expertise: law and contracts, the application process, underwriting, the commitment and secondary marketing, the closing, and basic concepts of mortgage finance. Each of these areas has a specified number of questions on the state exam. Law and contracts, for example, constitutes the largest section of the test with 35 questions. The text box on page 10 lists the content areas of the Florida Mortgage Broker licensing exam and each content area's weighting.

Individual results from the exam are posted on the DFS Web site a few days after the exam and are mailed to the applicant as well. The minimum acceptable score on the state exam is 75 percent. Scores on the state exam are valid for two years from the date of passing the examination.

If the applicant has addressed all deficiencies regarding the application, the license is mailed and, upon both receipt and activation with a mortgage brokerage business, mortgage lender, or correspondent mortgage lender, becomes effective immediately. That is, a licensee can begin to operate as a mortgage broker upon receipt of a license.

License Renewal

Licenses issued by the DFS are valid for two years beginning September 1 of each odd-numbered year. Mortgage brokers who wish to renew their license must submit a renewal form and the required fee. Licenses that are not renewed become inactive and may remain inactive for up to two years. After two years, the license expires and is void. Mortgage broker licenses are issued in the name of the applicant and cannot be transferred or assigned to another person.

Mortgage broker licenses are renewed by completing a renewal form and paying a nonrefundable renewal fee of $150. Licenses of individuals who fail to renew within the designated period are moved from active to inactive status. Inactive licensees can reactivate their licenses by submitting the form and paying the $150 fee as well as a $100 reactivation fee. If a license is not renewed within two years of becoming inactive, however, it becomes void. The individual will need to requalify for licensure.

FLORIDA MORTGAGE BROKER LICENSING EXAM OUTLINE AND CONTENT WEIGHTING

Law and Contracts (35%)

Including definitions from Chapter 494, F.S., General Provisions Parts I-III, characteristics of the mortgage brokerage business, Florida Fair Housing Act, federal law, contracts, lien and title theory, mortgage documents, and the mortgage brokerage agreement. (chapters 1–6)

The Loan Application Process (15%)

Including completing the application, amortization, fixed-rate and adjustable-rate mortgages, credit reports and FICO score, different kinds of mortgages, debt-to-income ratio, lock-in agreements, loan transmittal, and Fannie Mae application and eligibility requirements. (chapter 7)

Underwriting (15%)

Including the three basic appraisal procedures, appraisal terminology, applicant's credit history, gift letters, resolving contingencies, adverse action, financial reserves, automated underwriting, and enhanced eligibility. (chapter 8)

The Commitment and Secondary Marketing (5%)

Including the loan commitment, locking in a rate, title impediments, secondary market participants, servicing a loan, and computing yields, discounts, and points. (chapters 1, 3, 7, and 10)

The Closing (20%)

Including title insurance, the survey, encroachments, hazard insurance, property inspections, payoff letter, preparation of closing documents, methods of funding the loan, and duties of the loan closer. (chapter 9)

Mortgage Financing (10%)

Including real estate taxes, homestead exemption, monthly payments, foreclosures, payoffs, and assumptions. (chapters 6 and 11)

Mathematical Computations

Math questions appear throughout the state exam. Important concepts include

- net loans and gross loans (chapters 2 and 11);
- discount points and yields (chapter 1);
- documentary stamps and intangible tax (chapter 11);
- interest calculations and prorations (chapter 11);
- principal and interest (PI) and taxes and insurance (TI) (chapters 6 and 11); front-end and back-end ratios (chapters 7 and 11);
- and converting income (chapter 11).

KEY POINT REVIEW

- *Mortgage lending* is the process by which individuals or institutions provide loans to other individuals or groups who want to finance properties.
- A *mortgagor* (borrower) is the person who offers his or her property as security for a loan; the *mortgagee* (lender or investor) is the party who grants the loan.
- *Mortgage brokers* connect potential borrowers with potential lenders but do not lend money. They typically earn income through mortgage broker fees and the *yield spread premium* paid by lenders.
- *Yield* is the return to an investor on a loan. *Discount points* increase the yield to the lender. In most cases, they lower the monthly payments for the borrower but add to the borrower's up-front closing costs. *Basis points* are used to express fractions of a point.
- *Underwriting* is the process of assessing the amount of risk associated with a loan. *Closing* is the process of finalizing financing or refinancing of real property and the homebuyer's signing of the mortgage and the promissory note.
- The *secondary mortgage market* consists of investors who buy existing mortgages.
- After the closing, the mortgage broker is no longer involved in the borrower-lender relationship.
- Second mortgages have fixed interest rates and a set repayment period. Home equity loans have variable interest rates and are usually structured as a line of credit. Refinancing refers to obtaining new financing on a property.
- The state exam for mortgage brokers has 100 questions that cover the following areas: law and contracts; the loan application process; underwriting; the commitment and secondary marketing; the closing; and basic concepts of mortgage finance.
- Mortgage broker licenses are valid for two years starting September 1 of each odd-numbered year.

REVIEW QUESTIONS

1. The process of evaluating the likelihood of a borrower defaulting on a loan is known as
   a. loan servicing.
   b. establishing the yield spread premium.
   c. closing a loan.
   d. underwriting.

2. Alvin wishes to apply for a mortgage loan on a new home by approaching an investor in the secondary market directly. Alvin
   a. is likely to get a lower interest rate by going directly to a secondary market investor.
   b. could probably get a lower rate from a mortgage broker.
   c. will not get a loan because secondary market investors buy existing mortgages and do not loan money directly.
   d. will need to meet the higher qualification standards of the secondary market.

3. Which most accurately describes a mortgage?
   a. Title to a property
   b. A pledge of property as security for a loan
   c. A promise to repay a loan
   d. All of the above

4. Mortgage Broker Johnson just closed a loan for Mr. and Mrs. Davis. After the closing, Mortgage Broker Johnson
   a. will no longer be involved in the loan relationship.
   b. must make sure that the Davis loan is serviced properly.
   c. will sell the loan on the secondary market.
   d. will continue to earn a commission on each loan payment by Mr. and Mrs. Davis.

5. The Platinum Mortgage Company takes applications but does not fund loans. Platinum Mortgage must be a
   a. loan servicer.
   b. mortgage brokerage business.
   c. mortgagor.
   d. secondary market participant.

6. The party who grants a mortgage loan to a loan applicant is
   a. responsible for connecting borrowers with lenders.
   b. the mortgagor.
   c. the mortgagee.
   d. the mortgage broker.

7. Which is NOT required for licensure as a mortgage broker in Florida?
   a. Passing a test that determines competency in mortgage finance
   b. Paying an application fee of $300
   c. Filing a set of fingerprints
   d. Being at least 18 years of age

8. Party A pays the yield spread premium to Party B. Party A is the
   a. lender.
   b. mortgage broker.
   c. borrower.
   d. mortgagor.

9. Alfredo's company collects payments from borrowers and forwards them to lenders. Alfredo's company
   a. handles loan underwriting.
   b. does loan origination.
   c. is a mortgage brokerage business.
   d. does loan servicing.

10. According to the information provided by the DFS, applicants who want to maximize the use of study time for the mortgage broker licensing exam would focus more time on reviewing
    a. law and contracts.
    b. underwriting.
    c. the commitment and secondary marketing.
    d. mortgage financing.

11. Mr. and Mrs. Homebuyer have a choice between working with a mortgage broker or approaching a lender directly. They decide to use a mortgage broker because
    a. working with a broker could give them more options.
    b. a mortgage broker will protect the homebuyers' interests throughout the life of the loan.
    c. mortgage brokers receive their fees directly from the federal government rather than from their customers.
    d. the mortgage broker they deal with is also likely to be a real estate broker.

12. Arthur signed a sales contract stating that he would find financing for a property he wants to buy by August 1. This date is important because
    a. the date he arranges financing affects the yield spread premium.
    b. not everyone will qualify for a mortgage loan and Arthur may need to find another lender.
    c. Arthur's written contract becomes voidable if he fails to find financing by that date.
    d. Arthur may be required to pay a 5 percent penalty if he doesn't find financing by that date.

13. Gloria would like to get a second mortgage on her primary residence. A second mortgage will
    a. allow Gloria to make variable payments during the term of the mortgage.
    b. most likely have a fixed interest rate and a fixed repayment period.
    c. allow Gloria to collect either $2,000 or 2 percent of the mortgage amount.
    d. lower the interest Gloria is paying on her first mortgage.

14. State Bank of Florida is offering loans at 6.75 percent with three discount points. If Stan gets a loan for $200,000 under these terms, Stan's discount points will cost
    a. $2,000.
    b. $2,025.
    c. $2,050.
    d. $6,000.

15. The yield to State Bank on Stan's loan will be
    a. 6.75 percent.
    b. 3.0 percent.
    c. 7.125 percent.
    d. 8.125 percent.

16. A deficiency refers to
    a. failure to quality for a loan because of bad credit.
    b. an inadequate yield spread premium.
    c. not having fulfilled all the requirements for a mortgage broker's license.
    d. being unable to make mortgage payments on time.

17. One reason HELOCs are attractive to borrowers is because
    a. they typically have lower interest rates than first mortgages.
    b. they allow borrowers to continue to borrow money as the debt is paid down.
    c. they do not require a second application.
    d. the term is fixed so borrowers can know when the loan will be paid off.

18. A lender charges a servicing fee of 35 basis points on a loan of $160,000. This amounts to
    a. 3.5 percent.
    b. $5,600.
    c. $1,600.
    d. $560.

19. Gary Wilson would like to get started in the mortgage business as soon as possible. One option for Gary would be to
    a. take a job as a loan originator with a lender or correspondent lender and apply to take the mortgage broker exam.
    b. take a job as a mortgage broker and take the exam within 90 days.
    c. become a mortgagor and not take an exam.
    d. arrange for a limited cash-out refinance on some of his investment properties.

20. The borrower signs the promissory note during the process known as
    a. loan servicing.
    b. underwriting.
    c. origination.
    d. closing.

21. The commission the lender pays to the mortgage brokerage business is known as the
    a. yield.
    b. basis points.
    c. discount points.
    d. yield spread premium.

22. Mr. Garcia is arranging a transaction regarding his primary residence in which he will receive the lesser of $2,000 or 2 percent of the loan amount. Mr. Garcia is probably doing a
    a. HELOC.
    b. cash-out refinance.
    c. limited cash-out refinance.
    d. first mortgage.

23. Which is NOT a source of income for mortgage brokerage businesses?
    a. Mortgage broker fees
    b. Commissions from lenders
    c. Loan servicing fees
    d. Yield spread premium

24. A basis point equals
    a. 1/10 of 1 percent.
    b. 1/100 of 1 percent.
    c. 1/1,000 of 1 percent.
    d. 1/10,000 of 1 percent.

CHAPTER 2

FLORIDA LAWS REGULATING MORTGAGE BROKERS AND MORTGAGE BROKERAGE BUSINESSES

LEARNING OBJECTIVES

After finishing chapter 2, you should be able to

1. understand the role of the Office of Financial Regulation in the Florida mortgage business;
2. explain the requirements for licensure as a mortgage broker;
3. understand the differences between employees and independent contractors;
4. identify the acts that require a mortgage broker license;
5. know what groups are exempt from licensure;
6. recognize the responsibilities of the principal broker and branch broker;
7. know the requirements for mortgage brokerage continuing education;
8. understand the requirements for licensure as a mortgage brokerage business;
9. know the requirements regarding mortgage brokerage fees and commissions;
10. describe the process for brokering a loan to a noninstitutional investor;
11. explain the fees associated with a commitment from a lender;
12. understand net loans and gross loans; and
13. understand third-party fee accounts, documentation, and transaction journal requirements.

KEY TERMS

associate
branch broker
brokerage fees
control person
controlling interest
employee
good faith estimate
gross loan
independent contractor
lock-in
mortgage brokerage fee
mortgage loan application
natural person
net loan
principal broker
Quarterly Report Transmittal Form
third-party fee account
usury

INTRODUCTION

As you learned in chapter 1, legal requirements relating to the mortgage business are found in Florida Statute 494 (F.S. 494) and Chapter 69V-40 of the Florida Administrative Code, and licensure is controlled by the Department of Financial Services. Chapter 2 takes an in-depth look at the laws and rules that govern mortgage brokers and mortgage brokerage businesses in Florida. Florida laws regulating lenders and correspondent lenders are discussed in chapter 3, and federal and state laws that affect mortgage lending and home ownership are covered in chapter 4.

THE OFFICE OF FINANCIAL REGULATION

In Florida, mortgage brokerage and lending are regulated through the Department of Financial Services (DFS). The Office of Financial Regulation (OFR) is responsible for administering and enforcing F.S. 494 and has the power to issue and serve subpoenas and subpoenas duces tecum (defined below) and to administer oaths. The OFR supervises various financial institutions and licenses and regulates nondepository finance companies and the securities industry, including mortgage brokering and lending.

LICENSURE AS A MORTGAGE BROKER IN FLORIDA

As explained in chapter 1, mortgage brokers are individuals who connect borrowers with lenders. When an individual wants to find financing and use his or her property as collateral for the loan, the individual can consult a mortgage broker who, for a fee or commission, will find a lender willing to finance the real estate transaction. The mortgage broker will ask the borrower to complete a **mortgage loan application,** which F.S. 494 defines as:

> *. . . the submission of a borrower's financial information in anticipation of a credit decision, whether written or computer-generated, relating to a mortgage loan. If the submission does not state or identify a specific property, the submission is an application for a prequalification and not an application for a mortgage loan . . . The subsequent addition of an identified property to the submission converts the submission to an application for a mortgage loan.*

As the definition indicates, an application for a loan does not become a mortgage loan application until a specific property is identified as part of the submission.

Florida Statute 494 defines acting as a mortgage broker as follows:

> *...for compensation or gain, or in the expectation of compensation or gain, either directly or indirectly, accepting or offering to accept an application for a mortgage loan, soliciting or offering to solicit a mortgage loan on behalf of a borrower, negotiating or offering to negotiate the terms or conditions of a mortgage loan on behalf of a lender, or negotiating or offering to negotiate the sale of an existing mortgage loan to a noninstitutional investor.*

In Florida, individuals who accept applications, solicit mortgage loans, negotiate the terms of a loan, or negotiate the sale of an existing mortgage loan—and who do so for a commission—must be licensed as a mortgage broker. Individuals who perform the same activities for a lender but who do so on a salary basis as an employee—known in Florida as *loan originators*—are not required to be licensed. Florida law defines *acting as a loan originator* as

> *...being employed by a mortgage lender or correspondent mortgage lender for compensation or gain, to negotiate, offer to negotiate, or assist any licensed or exempt entity in negotiating the making of a mortgage loan, including, but not limited to, working with a licensed or exempt entity to structure a loan or discussing terms and conditions necessary for the delivery of a loan product.*

Under this definition, account executives who work for lenders qualify as loan originators and must be listed in quarterly reports. In addition, these executives must also complete continuing education requirements.

A person whose job duties are mostly clerical, and may include quoting available interest rates, is not acting as a loan originator.

In contrast with a loan originator, a person who works for a mortgage brokerage business and holds a Florida mortgage broker license is known as an **associate,** which F.S. 494 defines as

> *...a person who is required to be licensed as a mortgage broker who is employed by or acting as an independent contractor for a mortgage brokerage business or a person acting as an independent contractor for a mortgage lender or correspondent mortgage lender.*

According to Florida law, no person licensed as a mortgage broker can be an associate of more than one licensed mortgage brokerage business, mortgage lender, or correspondent mortgage lender (lenders and correspondent lenders are explained in more detail in chapter 3). Florida law does not require mortgage brokers to be Florida residents.

Employees and Independent Contractors

One of the most important distinctions between mortgage brokers and other individuals who work in the mortgage industry is the nature of their employment. Mortgage brokers often operate as independent businesspersons, or they work for others solely on a commission basis. When mortgage brokers work for someone else, they are typically paid as an *independent contractor,* which means that they are responsible for paying their own employment taxes, unemployment insurance, Social Security taxes, and so forth. Independent contractors are not considered regular employees.

Florida law makes an important distinction between independent contractors and employees.

F.S. 494 defines an **independent contractor** as

> *...a person who contracts with another to perform a service where this person is not directed or controlled by the other person or is required to maintain separate records regarding his contract for services in respect to, but not limited to, accounting and taxes.*

In other words, independent contractors generally work without direct supervision and are paid on commission. An **employee,** in contrast, is defined as

> *...a natural person engaged in the service of another for salary or wages and subject to withholding, FICA, and other lawful deductions and under the control of an employer.*

A **natural person** is an individual, and not a corporation, general partnership, limited partnership, or other legal entity. As independent contractors, mortgage brokers can be paid on commission. Loan originators who work as employees of mortgage lenders do not need a mortgage broker license to perform their job duties, but if they do have a mortgage broker license, they can be paid as independent contractors (not as W-2).

ACTS REQUIRING LICENSURE AS A MORTGAGE BROKER

According to F.S. 494.001(3), acting as a mortgage broker means performing any of the following acts in expectation of compensation or gain:

- Accepting or offering to accept an application for a mortgage loan
- Soliciting or offering to solicit a mortgage loan on behalf of a borrower
- Negotiating or offering to negotiate the terms or conditions of a mortgage loan on behalf of a lender
- Negotiating or offering to negotiate the sale of an existing mortgage loan to a noninstitutional investor

WEB LINK @

Applications for the mortgage broker license, as well as for licensure as a mortgage brokerage business, mortgage lender, or correspondent lender, can be found at *www.flofr.com/Finance/Forms/mbapp.pdf.* Clicking on the type of license desired leads to the instructions for applying online or printing a form to mail.

Figure 2.1 compares the four types of mortgage licenses in Florida.

FIGURE 2.1 ■ Four Types of Licenses

License	F.S. 494 Definition	Initial Fee	Renewal Fee	Expiration
Mortgage Broker	An individual who accepts a loan application, offers to solicit a mortgage loan, negotiates the conditions of a mortgage loan, negotiates the sale of an existing mortgage to a noninstitutional investor, or offers to do any of the above	$200 + $42.25 fingerprint card fee	$150	August 31 of odd-numbered years
Mortgage Brokerage Business	A person acting as a mortgage broker	$425	$375	August 31 of even-numbered years
Mortgage Lender	Makes or services mortgage loans for others or offers to sell mortgage loans to noninstitutional investors	$575	$575	August 31 of even-numbered years
Correspondent Mortgage Lender	A lender that may make mortgage loans but cannot service a loan for more than four months	$500	$475	August 31 of even-numbered years

EXEMPTION FROM LICENSURE

Under the Florida Mortgage Brokerage and Lending Act and Regulations, certain individuals and institutions engaged in the mortgage lending business are exempt from licensure. These include

- a bank, bank holding company, trust company, savings and loan association, savings bank, credit union, or consumer finance company licensed under Chapter 516 of the Florida Statutes;
- a wholly owned bank holding company subsidiary or a wholly owned savings and loan association holding company subsidiary approved or certified by the Department of Housing and Urban Development (HUD), the Department of Veterans Affairs (VA), the Government National Mortgage Association (GNMA, commonly known as Ginnie Mae), the Federal National Mortgage Association (FNMA, commonly known as Fannie Mae), or the Federal Home Loan Mortgage Corporation (FHLMC, commonly known as Freddie Mac);
- Fannie Mae, Freddie Mac, any agency of the federal government, any state, county, or municipal government or quasigovernmental agency;
- any person licensed to practice law in Florida when such services are part of his or her practice as an attorney on occasion and not a major part of his or her income;
- an insurance company licensed in Florida when dealing with its clients in the normal course of its insurance business;
- a federally licensed small business investment company;
- a securities dealer dealing with clients in the normal course of its securities business;
- any person serving in a fiduciary capacity conferred by a court; and
- a wholly owned subsidiary of a bank or savings and loan association that solely distributes the lending programs of such institutions.

RESPONSIBILITIES OF THE PRINCIPAL BROKER

Florida law requires that each mortgage brokerage business designate a licensed mortgage broker as the principal broker. The **principal broker** is responsible for the operation of the mortgage company's principal place of business and all branch offices. To be a principal broker, an individual must have been actively licensed as a mortgage broker for at least one year *OR* be able to demonstrate to the satisfaction of the Department of Financial Services (DFS) that he or she has been actively engaged in a mortgage-related business for at least one year prior to being designated as principal broker.

Individuals who act as principal brokers also need to file the Principal Broker Designation form with the DFS within 30 days of designation or changes. Failure to do so within 30 days will result in a warning known as a Notice of Noncompliance. Subsequent failure to file the form will result in a fine of $500, but if the DFS determines that the failure to file the form is intentional, the fine becomes $5,000. In addition, if the mortgage brokerage business fails to notify the DFS of the principal broker, then all officers, directors, and ultimate equitable owners with 10 percent or more of the business are held responsible for the control the principal broker should be exercising.

Branch Broker Requirements

Mortgage brokerage businesses must also designate a licensed mortgage broker as the **branch broker** of any branch office and inform the DFS of this appointment. The branch broker, who is responsible for the branch office, does not need any prior experience.

As is the case with notifying the DFS about the principal broker, failure to notify the DFS about a branch broker may result in a fine of $5,000.

Other Requirements of Licensees

The DFS requires licensed mortgage broker businesses, mortgage lenders, and correspondent lenders to file the **Quarterly Report Transmittal Form** with the DFS listing each person employed with that firm during the immediate quarter of the year. This report states the name, address, Social Security number, date of birth, mortgage broker license number, date of hire, and, if applicable, date of termination for each person who acted as a loan originator or associate with the mortgage brokerage business during the quarter. Thereafter, a quarterly report is filed only if new associates or employees are hired or terminated during that quarter. The report must be filed within 30 days of the end of the quarter.

Licensees are also required to report any changes in business organization or persons named as officers or directors of the business within 30 days after the change occurs.

MORTGAGE BROKER CONTINUING EDUCATION

In order to keep their licenses in good standing, mortgage brokers must complete 14 hours of professional education every two years. According to statute, topics covered in continuing education classes must include handling mortgage financing transactions and the laws that govern mortgage finance. At least 4 hours of the 14 must be spent on the laws in Chapter 494 and the rules of Chapter 69V-40. In addition to mortgage brokers, individuals who hold licenses as principal representatives or mortgage lender associates (discussed in chapter 3) must also complete the 14-hour continuing education requirement within two years of the date of their employer's license renewal.

Licensees may complete their continuing education requirements through distance learning. However, Florida law requires that time spent in online courses be equal to the number of hours awarded to participants who attend classroom courses. Before a course participant can receive a certificate of course completion, the course provider must make certain that the participant completed the required number of hours for each timed module, passed a test covering each module of the course, and successfully completed a test covering all course content. Distance education providers are prohibited from providing answers to test questions to course participants. Passing the course requires a minimum score of 75 correct out of 100 questions on the exam.

Mortgage business schools that offer continuing education must submit evidence of a licensee's course completion within five days of the course ending, and records of course attendance must be kept for four years.

Individuals who receive their initial license between June 1 and August 31 of the license renewal cycle are exempt from continuing education requirements in that cycle only. Mortgage broker licenses are renewed by filing the appropriate form and paying a renewal fee of $150 before September 1 of odd-numbered years.

VIOLATIONS AND DISCIPLINARY ACTION

When a licensee is found guilty or pleads *nolo contendere* (no contest) to any crime or administrative violation that involves fraud, dishonesty, or other criminal action in any jurisdiction, the licensee must report this outcome to the DFS within 30 days. Licensees also have 30 days to report conviction of any felony to the DFS. When a licensee is involved in either a voluntary or involuntary bankruptcy, this must be reported within seven business days after the action is instituted.

Under F.S. 494.0041 and 494.0072, it is grounds for disciplinary action for a mortgage broker, brokerage business, lender, or correspondent lender to do any of the following:

- Plead nolo contendere to or be found guilty of a crime involving fraud or dishonesty or fail to pay any fee, charge, or fine imposed
- Commit fraud, misrepresentation, deceit, negligence, or incompetence in any mortgage financing transaction
- Misstate facts on an initial or renewal application
- Cause unauthorized disbursement of funds
- Fail to place immediately upon receipt any money received from a person dealing with him or her as a lender in a segregated account in a federally insured financial institution
- Fail to account for or deliver to any person any personal property that has come into his or her hands and that is not his or her property
- Fail to disburse funds in accordance with agreements or misuse personal property entrusted to his or her keeping or pay any fee, charge, or fine in a timely fashion
- Have a license to practice any profession or occupation revoked, suspended, or denied because of fraudulent or dishonest acts
- Violate other sections of F.S. 494
- Act as a mortgage lender or correspondent mortgage lender without a current, active license
- Fail to keep available for examination all books, accounts, or other documents required by law or rules of the commission or to refuse to permit an investigation or examination of books and records or comply with an office subpoena or subpoena duces tecum
- Consistently underestimate closing costs
- Commit fraud, misrepresentation, or other illegal act in any state, nation, or territory, or assisting any other person engaged in such misconduct
- Pay for a license or permit with a check or electronic transmission of funds that is dishonored by the applicant's or licensee's financial institution
- Be found guilty in a civil action of fraud, embezzlement, misrepresentation, or deceit involving a violation of any rule or regulation of any national securities, commodities, or options exchange or association
- In any mortgage transaction, violate any provision of the Real Estate Settlement Procedures Act, the Truth-in-Lending Act, or any regulations adopted under such acts

Penalties for any of the above include revocation or suspension of license, being placed on probation, issuance of a reprimand or fine, or denial of a license or registration.

Although Florida law now forbids disqualifying persons who have been convicted of a crime from licensure, licensure can be denied if the crime was a felony or first degree misdemeanor and related to the occupation related to the license. In other words, a person whose civil rights have been restored may be eligible for licensure as a mortgage broker, mortgage brokerage business, lender, or correspondent lender if the crime of which he or she was convicted was unrelated to the mortgage transaction business.

LICENSURE AS A MORTGAGE BROKERAGE BUSINESS

According to F.S. 494, the **controlling interest** of a mortgage brokerage or lending business means possession of the power to direct or cause the direction of the management or policies of a company whether through ownership of securities, by contract, or otherwise. Any person who directly or indirectly has the right to vote 25 percent or more of the voting securities of a company or is entitled to 25 percent or more of the company's profits is presumed to possess a controlling interest.

Along the same lines, a **control person** is "an individual, partnership, corporation, trust, or other organization that possesses the power, directly or indirectly, to direct the management or policies of a company, whether through ownership of securities, by contract, or otherwise. A person is presumed to control a company if, with respect to a particular company, that person is a director, general partner, or officer exercising executive responsibility or having similar status or functions; directly or indirectly may vote 10 percent or more of a class of voting securities or sell or direct the sale of 10 percent or more of a class of voting securities, or in the case of a partnership may receive upon dissolution or has contributed 10 percent or more of the capital."

Individuals who apply for a license to establish a mortgage brokerage business must submit the following to the DFS:

- A completed Application for Licensure as a Mortgage Brokerage Business (Form DBF-MB-201) and
- the nonrefundable application fee of $425, which covers the remainder of the biennial license period.

In addition to identifying the qualified principal broker who will be responsible for running the business, the mortgage brokerage business application must identify each person who will own 10 percent or more of the brokerage firm, along with the chief executive officer and each director of the firm. These individuals are required to submit fingerprint forms as well.

Any person who will own 10 percent or more of the brokerage firm—known as an *ultimate equitable owner*—and who wants to establish a mortgage brokerage business must also submit a set of fingerprints and Biographical Summary (Form MBB-BIO-1). As is the case with the mortgage broker license, applicants for a mortgage brokerage business license have 15 days to notify the DFS of any changes that affect their application. If any of the potential owners, officers, or ultimate equitable owners of the business have legal action pending against them, the DFS may deny the license.

The DFS has the right to deny a license to anyone who has violated any part of F.S. 494 or has pending any criminal prosecution or administrative enforcement action that involves fraud, dishonesty, or other act of moral turpitude. The DFS also reserves the right to cancel licenses issued because of *inadvertence*—that is, an error—on the part of

OPERATE, EXERCISE, AND CONTROL

The Florida Administrative Code makes an important distinction among the levels of authority or influence in managing a business.

Operate refers to exercising power or influence over business operations.

Exercise means fulfilling official duties or functions.

Control is having the influence and power to make decisions for a business.

Source: FAC 69V-40.001 (11).

the DFS. Finally, the DFS cancels licenses if the check accompanying the application is returned due to insufficient funds. However, in these cases, the license can be reinstated if the applicant sends a certified check for the specified amount within 30 days.

Licenses for mortgage brokerage businesses are renewed each September 1 of even-numbered years. Licenses that are not renewed revert from active to inactive status. Licensees can renew inactive licenses within a six-month period if they pay the renewal and reactivation fee and submit a reactivation form. If a licensee fails to renew an inactive license within six months, however, the license expires and becomes void. Branch office licenses that are renewed along with the principal mortgage brokerage business license are subject to the same time limits.

Any mortgage brokerage business—as well as mortgage broker, lender, correspondent lender, or mortgage business school—that changes its name or form of organization must notify the DFS no later than 30 days after the effective date of the change. The DFS must also be notified of any significant personnel changes no later than 30 days prior to the effective date of the change or within two business days after the date the licensee first received notice of the change.

Principal Place of Business Requirements

Each mortgage brokerage business must report a principal place of business to the DFS. The principal place of business does not need to be an actual physical location, but can be an address not necessarily located in Florida. If the address changes, the DFS must be notified within 30 days of the change. The DFS has no requirements with regard to signage.

Branch Office Requirements

Each branch office of a mortgage brokerage business must also be licensed by the DFS. The branch office license requires submission of a completed application and a nonrefundable fee of $225. The application must include the name and license number of the licensee, the name of his or her branch broker, and the office's address. A branch office license is required if the name of the mortgage business appears on any stationery, the office address is advertised, or the public is likely to assume that mortgage brokering activities are occurring at that location. In addition, branch office licenses are not transferable.

MORTGAGE BROKERAGE FEES AND COMMISSIONS

According to Florida law, mortgage brokers may not receive a fee unless they have a written, signed, and dated agreement with the person who applies for a loan. This agreement must describe the services the mortgage brokerage business will provide and explain the terms of any fees connected with the loan application process.

Brokerage fees refer to compensation paid for services performed by the mortgage broker on behalf of either the borrower or lender. According to F.S. 494, the definition of a **mortgage brokerage fee** is the total compensation to be received by a mortgage brokerage business for acting as a mortgage broker. The mortgage brokerage fee covers compensation paid to the licensee, a co-broker, an affiliate, or a third party.

This compensation can be received only after the mortgage brokerage agreement is signed and dated by both the borrower and the mortgage brokerage business, and only after the commitment has been received and accepted by the borrower and broker. Services that may result in compensation include

- arranging for a conditional mortgage loan commitment between a borrower and a lender;
- taking an application;
- preparing the information necessary for a conditional mortgage loan commitment;
- reviewing, analyzing, and evaluating a borrower's financial statements, income, and credit history;
- providing incidental services during the mortgage application process, including courier services, express mailings, and telephone charges; and
- arranging for premiums and other insurance charges related to the loan.

If the borrower is present at the signing, the initial mortgage brokerage agreement must be executed within three business days—defined as any calendar day except Sunday or a legal holiday—after the application is accepted. If the borrower is not present, the licensee must forward the mortgage brokerage agreement to the borrower within three business days after the licensee has signed the application. Under Florida law, the licensee has responsibility for documenting that the borrower received and approved the agreement.

If the terms of a loan change, the licensee must notify the borrower within three days of the licensee learning of the changes, but not less than three business days before closing. The licensee also has responsibility for proving that notice of the changes were provided to the borrower. If the borrower has a personal financial emergency—such as an imminent foreclosure—and receiving notice of a change in the terms of the loan will delay the closing, the borrower may waive the right to receive notice of changes. In this case, the borrower has the responsibility to provide a written statement describing the emergency and waive the right to the notice.

When the terms on an adjustable-rate loan change, the borrower must be notified in a form required by Regulation Z and the Truth-in-Lending Act (these laws are discussed in chapter 4). The licensee must be able to document that he or she provided such notice to the borrower.

As soon as the mortgage brokerage agreement is executed or forwarded to the borrower for execution, or at the time the mortgage brokerage business accepts a fee for an application, credit report, or property appraisal, the mortgage brokerage business must disclose in writing to the borrower

- that the mortgage brokerage business itself cannot make mortgage loans or commitments (such commitments can only be communicated on behalf of the lender when the lender provides a written commitment for the loan);
- that the mortgage brokerage business cannot guarantee the borrower will be accepted into any specific loan programs;
- the amount of fees associated with the good faith estimate, credit report, property appraisal, and any other documents, as well as fees earned by the mortgage broker business, lender fees, and official fees, and the procedure for obtaining a refund of such fees. Other than the mortgage broker business, recipients of fees may be described in generic terms, and any amount collected in excess of the actual cost must be returned within 60 days of rejection, withdrawal, or closing; and
- the maximum total dollar amount—and not a percentage range—of any payment from the lender, the nature of the licensee's relationship with the lender, how compensation is paid, and how the mortgage interest rate affects the compensation paid to the mortgage brokerage business.

As soon as the mortgage brokerage business becomes aware of the exact amount of any payment from the lender, that amount must be disclosed to the borrower within three business days, and no less than three business days before the closing. The licensee has responsibility of proving this notification was provided to the borrower.

Some mortgage brokers require potential borrowers to pay a nonrefundable application fee. In these cases, the broker must disclose to the borrower the amount of the fee and the exact services the broker will perform. The application fee must be a set amount based on the services provided; it cannot be based on a percentage of the loan amount or the amount of financing that the borrower is seeking. Also, mortgage brokerage businesses may offer other products and services for a fee or commission.

BROKERING A LOAN TO A NONINSTITUTIONAL INVESTOR

F.S. 494 defines an institutional investor as a bank, savings and loan association, savings bank, real estate investment trust, insurance company, real estate company, accredited investor, or other licensed business. A private individual is a noninstitutional investor.

To broker a loan to a noninstitutional investor, licensees must fulfill the following requirements:

1. The mortgage broker must provide an opinion of value from an appraiser unless the investor waives the opinion in writing and before the noninstitutional investor makes any payments. Also, the mortgage broker must inform the investor about any relationship he or she has with the appraiser.
2. The investor must receive a title insurance policy or an opinion of title (discussed in chapter 9) by an attorney licensed to practice law in Florida. The title insurance policy must insure the noninstitutional investor against problems related to the title and also identify any superior liens that exist against the property. In the case of an opinion of title, the opinion must include a statement about the marketability of the title to the property and also specify the priority of the mortgage being closed.

3. In cases where neither title insurance nor an opinion of title is available at the time of purchase, the licensee must provide a binder of the title insurance or conditional opinion of title that specifies any conditions or requirements to be corrected prior to issuing the final title policy or opinion of title.
4. In cases where the loan is not a first mortgage, the broker must provide a statement showing the balance owed by the mortgagor on any existing mortgages, as well as a disclosure if the licensee is directly or indirectly acting as a borrower or principal in the transaction.
5. The mortgage must be recorded before being delivered to the noninstitutional investor no later than 30 business days after the date of closing.
6. Any money from a noninstitutional investor for disbursement at a mortgage loan closing must deposited with and disbursed by either an attorney or a title company licensed in Florida. The mortgage broker may not have control of any money from a noninstitutional investor, but a licensee can receive a mortgage brokerage fee upon the closing of a mortgage loan funded by a noninstitutional investor.

FEES ASSOCIATED WITH A COMMITMENT FROM A LENDER

According to Florida law, mortgage brokerage fees that are earned are not considered interest or finance charges, nor can they exceed certain limits. The maximum fees that a mortgage brokerage business can charge a borrower on a **net loan**—that is, the amount of the loan proceeds received at closing—are as follows:

- On a mortgage loan of less than $1,000: $250
- On a mortgage loan greater than $1,000 but less than $2,000: $250 for the first $1,000 of the loan plus $10 for each additional $100 of the mortgage loan (or 10 percent of balance)
- On a mortgage loan greater than $2,000 and up to $5,000: $350 for the first $2,000 of the loan plus $10 for each additional $100 of the loan (or 10 percent of balance)
- On a mortgage loan of $5,000 or more: the net loan amount divided by 10 + $250*

The maximum fees on a **gross loan**—that is, a loan that includes additional costs or fees—are as follows:

- On a mortgage loan less than $1,000: $250
- On a mortgage loan of $1,000 but less than $5,650: the loan amount + $1,500, with the sum divided by 11
- On a mortgage loan between $5,650 and $5,750: the amount over $5,000
- On a mortgage loan over $5,750: the gross loan amount divided by 11 + 227.27†

Figure 2.2 shows the formulas for calculating the maximum fees on net and gross loans.

* An alternative method that closely approximates this formula is to add $2,500 to the net loan amount and divide the sum by 10.

† An alternative method that closely approximates this formula is to add $2,500 to a gross loan amount and divide that sum by 11.

FIGURE 2.2 ■ Calculating the Maximum Fees on Net Loans and Gross Loans

Maximum brokerage fee for *net loans* over $5,000:

Net loan amount ÷ 10 + $250

Maximum brokerage fee for *gross loans* over $5,750:

Gross loan amount ÷ 11 + $227.27

Usury Laws

Usury laws set the maximum lawful interest rate that can be charged on various loans. Florida's usury law is found in Chapter 687 of the Florida Statutes. In Florida, most mortgage loans under $500,000 face a usury law limit of 18 percent annual interest. The Florida Statutes define a *usurious contract* as follows:

> *All contracts for the payment of interest upon any loan, advance of money, line of credit, or forbearance to enforce the collection of any debt, or upon any obligation whatever, at a higher rate of interest than the equivalent of 18 percent per annum simple interest are hereby declared usurious.*

Under Florida law, a mortgage brokerage fee is not considered interest.

Good Faith Estimate

At the time the mortgage brokerage agreement is signed or the mortgage brokerage business collects any fee whatsoever, the mortgage brokerage business must provide the applicant with a **good faith estimate** (GFE). The good faith estimate, which is signed and dated by the borrower, discloses the total amount of the fees the borrower can expect to pay, including fees earned by the mortgage brokerage business, lender fees, third party fees, and official fees, including the cost of documentary tax stamps on the deed and mortgages, and the intangible tax on new mortgages. The GFE must also disclose the recipients of all payments charged to the borrower, along with the procedures for obtaining a refund of these fees. With the exception of the mortgage brokerage business—or the lender or correspondent lender when acting as a mortgage brokerage business—these recipients may be described in generic terms, such as appraiser, lender, and so forth. However, a GFE is not a substitute for a mortgage brokerage agreement.

Although the GFE is provided to the applicant at the beginning of the loan approval process, the mortgage broker is responsible for updating the GFE should closing costs or the yield spread premium change. The mortgage broker must provide information about the changes to the borrower, and the borrower must provide written acknowledgment of having received the information and agreement to proceed with the loan application. The mortgage broker must keep this acknowledgment on file for at least three years.

In addition, it is illegal for mortgage brokers to underestimate expected closing costs, and the final good faith estimate issued no earlier than three days before closing must agree with figures on the HUD-1 Uniform Closing Statement. Any fees collected in excess of the actual costs must be returned to the borrower within 60 days of rejection, withdrawal, or closing.

The mortgage broker must also disclose an estimate of the net proceeds to be paid directly to the borrower if the new mortgage will be affected by any outstanding liens on the property and by the number of days until the mortgage commitment expires.

The mortgage broker must also provide a good faith estimate of costs for services involved in securing a mortgage loan, as well as an estimate of the cost of other services that are not part of the brokerage fee. These services include a property appraisal, termite and other inspection fees, credit report, and attorney's fees.

The Florida Mortgage Brokerage Fee Agreement, along with the Good Faith Estimate, is show in Figure 2.3.

THIRD-PARTY FEE ACCOUNTS

Mortgage brokerage businesses can accept fees only for applications, credit reports, appraisals, or third parties prior to a lender making a written commitment. These fees must be paid to a mortgage brokerage business licensee and not directly to a mortgage broker.

Mortgage brokerage businesses are required to deposit all third-party fees and refundable application fees into a segregated escrow account in a federally insured financial institution within seven business days of receiving such funds. The financial institution the mortgage brokerage business uses must be federally insured and geographically located in Florida. This **third-party fee account** must be in the name of the mortgage brokerage business, and the business must maintain an updated and accurate record of account activity. Funds must be able to be withdrawn without notice.

Failure to maintain a segregated escrow account or keep accurate records of activity is a violation subject to a $500 fine per incident. Repeated violations of this provision may result in additional fines and suspension or revocation of the mortgage broker license. No profit can be made on third-party fees, and any funds not used for a service must be refunded to the borrower within 60 days after funding, denial, or withdrawal of a loan.

DOCUMENTATION

Licensees must keep records of their transactions, but such records need not be kept at the principal office of the brokerage business so long as the place where they are kept is stationary and secure and the DFS has approved their location in writing. Failure to notify the DFS where records are being kept will result in a Notice of Noncompliance for the first offense, but additional offenses bring a fine of $500. Intentional violations bring a fine of $500 and suspension of license. All records must be maintained for three years from date of original entry.

When the DFS wants to review a mortgage brokerage business's records that are kept somewhere other than the main office, licensees must present the DFS with a letter authorizing storage in another location, and they will have up to three business days from notification to provide such records. If a mortgage brokerage business refuses to comply with a DFS request to examine books and records, the DFS will revoke the business's license.

According to the DFS rules, mortgage brokerage businesses must maintain a separate file for each mortgage transaction. Each file must contain the mortgage brokerage agreement, a copy of the signed closing statement or documentation of denial or cancellation of the loan application, and a copy of the good faith estimate of costs and receipts for all services ordered for the borrower. In addition to these documents, all other documentation

FIGURE 2.3 ■ Sample Mortgage Brokerage Fee Agreement

Florida Mortgage Brokerage Fee Agreement

(Broker fee deemed to be earned upon obtaining a bona fide written lender commitment)

Integrity Mortgage Brokerage LLC is hereinafter referred to as "Licensee". Borrower(s) hereby engage Licensee to obtain a bona fide mortgage loan commitment for the loan terms identified below (or better) within 65 days from (today).

Borrower:	Mighty Hopeful Borrower	**Initial Interest Rate (fixed or ARM):**	6.250 %
Co-Borrower:		**Term of Loan:**	360 months/due in 360 months
		Loan Type:	☐ Fixed Rate ☐ GPM
Mailing Address:	4567 My Ave S.		☑ Arm: 5/.5 LIBOR ARM-IO
	Clearwater, FL 33992		☐ Other:
Subject Property Address:	1234 Any Street N	**Agreement applies to:**	☑ 1st Mortgage ☐ 2nd Mortgage
	Saint Petersburg, FL 33701		☐ 1st & 2nd Mortgage
Fair Market Value:	$ 350,000	**Loan may result in negative amortization?**	☐ Yes ☑ No
Sales Price:	$ 350,000	**Prepayment Penalty:**	☑ Yes ☐ No
Loan Amount:	$ 315,000	**Balloon Payment:**	☐ Yes ☑ No
w/MIP, FF:	$ 315,000	If yes, after	____ months

Additional Adjustable Rate Mortgage (ARM) terms - if applicable:

Your interest rate will be based on an index of 4.000 % plus a margin of 2.250 %. The index used to determine your initial interest rate and /or all adjustments is: Wall Street Journal LIBOR

Your initial adjustment period will be in 60 months and every 6 month(s) thereafter. The initial interest rate change can be higher or lower, but in no event will be more than 5.000 % at the 1st interest rate change date and no more than 2.000 % at any subsequent interest rate change date. The Maximum interest rate possible, subject to the interest rate caps previously stated, is 12.250 %.

Cash from/to Borrower(s) at closing after all settlement charges: $ 46,542.13 (see Loan Application)

Borrower agrees to pay a Total Mortgage Brokerage Fee to Licensee comprised as follows:
Borrower fees paid to Licensee: $ 3,600.00. This dollar amount represents the total of any/all fees directly being charged by licensee, including mortgage broker and/or loan origination fee points, processing fee, nonrefundable application fee and any other fee being charged by, and that will be paid directly to Licensee on final settlement statement.
Lender fee paid to Licensee: Licensee may also receive *additional compensation from funding lender, sometimes referred to as Yield Spread Premium,* depending on the loan terms and interest rate you accept. The amount of lender paid fee to licensee will be equal to, or less than $ 4,725.00 and is considered part of the total mortgage brokerage fee to be earned and received by licensee. *Both of these fees are deemed to have been earned by Licensee upon the date Licensee secures a written commitment to fund borrower(s) loan,* however, these fees may be deferred and paid to Licensee, at discretion of Licensee, at the time funding of Borrower(s) loan transaction occurs. However, if Licensee obtains a written loan commitment from the funding lender for the terms identified above and stands ready to close this loan transaction and borrower(s) do not close this loan transaction, then borrowers may be subject to paying all of these fees regardless of the loan closing not occurring. *See additional disclosure on page 2 of 2 directly above Borrower(s) signature line and separate disclosure describing relationship between Licensee and various lenders.*

Non-Refundable Application fee $ 250.00. If this fee is being charged, any amount received by Licensee as a nonrefundable application fee will be credited at closing against fees owed Licensee as a "paid outside of closing" itemization on your settlement statement and acknowledged as received prior to the closing of your loan. See Services Performed section below related to charging this fee.

THIRD PARTY FEES RECEIVED $ ________ payable to: ________.
Third-party fees are not refundable unless services were not actually performed by the settlement service providers (ex. courier, credit reporting agency, and/or appraiser).

SERVICES PERFORMED: Discuss loan products available to borrower, counsel borrower(s) as to amount and type(s) of loans qualified for, identify problems that may impair borrower eligibility for loan, assist borrower in completing loan application requirements, order appraisal, reports and required verifications to qualify borrower(s) for loan program applied for, package and submit loan application to any one or more lenders available to licensee, coordinate the acceptance of any loan approval or commitment by a lender, serve as liaison between borrower and lender for subsequent correspondence and communication and funding of loan.

Calyx Form - flmbbc.frm (11/07) Page 1 of 2

Source: Form provided by Calyx® Software.

FIGURE 2.3 ■ Sample Mortgage Brokerage Fee Agreement (Continued)

Florida Mortgage Broker Disclosures: Licensee may not make mortgage loans or commitments. Licensee may make a commitment and may furnish a lock-in of the rate and program on behalf of the lender when the licensee has obtained a written commitment or lock-in for the loan from the lender on behalf of the borrower for the loan. The commitment must be in the same form and substance as issued by the lender. Licensee cannot guarantee acceptance into any particular loan program or promise any specific loan terms or conditions. See page 1, paragraphs 4-5 disclosing third-party fee payment for other settlement service providers (ex. appraisal, credit report and/or courier fees) and application fee and the terms and conditions for obtaining a refund of such fees, if any). Any amount collected in excess of the actual cost of any third-party settlement service provider that Licensee has ordered in behalf of borrower shall be credited at closing or refunded to borrower(s) within 60 days after rejection, withdrawal or closing of your mortgage loan application with Licensee.

Time for Payment and Default: Unless otherwise agreed between Licensee and Borrower(s), all fees disclosed in Paragraph 3, page 1 of this agreement, shall be due and payable upon licensee obtaining bona fide mortgage loan commitment from lender/Investor, but may be paid at closing if agreed to by Licensee. If said commitment is secured and title is not found to be good, marketable and insurable by attorney or Title agency acting in behalf of the licensee or lender, or Borrower(s) refuse to execute and deliver the documents required by lender, or in any way fails to comply with this agreement, or if for any reason the loan referred to herein cannot be closed through no fault of Licensee, Borrower acknowledges that all fees disclosed in Paragraph 3 that constitutes the total mortgage brokerage fee amount of this Agreement has been earned by Licensee and agrees to immediately pay Licensee such fees and all costs incurred in Borrower(s) behalf. : In the event of any litigation arising out of this agreement, Licensee shall be entitled to all costs incurred, including reasonable attorney fees, whether before, at trial, appeal process should Licensee prevail in such litigation.

You are entering into a contract with a mortgage brokerage business to obtain a bona fide mortgage loan commitment under the same terms and conditions as stated herein (page 1 of this 2-page agreement) or in a separate executed good faith estimate form. If the mortgage brokerage business obtains a bona fide commitment under the same terms and conditions, you will be obligated to pay the mortgage brokerage business fees, including, but not limited to, a mortgage brokerage fee, even if you choose not to complete the loan transaction. If the provisions of s. 494.00421, Florida Statutes, are not met, the mortgage brokerage fee can only be earned upon the funding of the loan. The borrower(s) may contact the Dept. of Financial Services, Tallahassee, Florida, regarding any complaints the borrower(s) may have against the mortgage broker or mortgage brokerage business. The telephone number of the Department is 850-410-9805.

In addition, borrowers acknowledge receipt of the following additional disclosures

i. ☑ "Mortgage Loan Origination Agreement" describing relationship between interest rate & terms accepted by borrower and related lender fees paid to Licensee - if any
ii. ☑ Federal "CHARM booklet" disclosure on Adjustable Rate Mortgages (ARMS) - if applicable.
iii. ☑ Specific ARM rates, terms and conditions of ARM loan terms offered to borrower(s) - if applicable
iv. ☑ HUD settlement booklet
v. ☑ Good Faith Estimate of Settlement charges, dated and signed by borrower(s)

Licensee: **Integrity Mortgage Brokerage LLC**
9999 Compliance Lane
Tampa, FL 33617
(P)800-455-5566, (F)800-878-7700
License #: **MB0009888976**

Loan Officer providing this disclosure by Licensee
License #:

X ______________________________
Loan Officer: **Better Daise**

I/We acknowledge receiving a copy of this signed agreement and disclosures (i-v) referenced above as identified:

______________________________ ______________
Borrower **Mighty Hopeful Borrower** Date

______________________________ ______________
Co-Borrower Date

FIGURE 2.3 ■ Sample Mortgage Brokerage Fee Agreement (Continued)

GOOD FAITH ESTIMATE

Applicants:	Mighty Hopeful Borrower	Application No:	HBorrower08211
Property Addr:	1234 Any Street N, Saint Petersburg, FL 33701	Date Prepared:	05/10/2008
Prepared By:	Integrity Mortgage Brokerage LLC Ph. 800-455-5566 9999 Compliance Lane, Tampa, FL 33617	Loan Program:	5/.5 LIBOR ARM-IO

The information provided below reflects estimates of the charges which you are likely to incur at the settlement of your loan. The fees listed are estimates - actual charges may be more or less. Your transaction may not involve a fee for every item listed. The numbers listed beside the estimates generally correspond to the numbered lines contained in the HUD-1 settlement statement which you will be receiving at settlement. The HUD-1 settlement statement will show you the actual cost for items paid at settlement.

Total Loan Amount $ **315,000** Interest Rate: **6.250** % Term: **360 / 360** mths

800	ITEMS PAYABLE IN CONNECTION WITH LOAN:				PFC	S	F	POC
801	Loan Origination Fee	Paid To Lender	0.500 %	$ 1,575.00	✓			
802	Loan Discount	Paid To Lender	1.000 %	3,150.00	✓			
803	Appraisal Fee	Paid To Other		(325.00)				✓
804	Credit Report							
805	Lender's Inspection Fee							
808	Mortgage Broker Fee	Paid To Broker: IMB	1.000 %	3,150.00	✓			
809	Tax Related Service Fee	Paid To Lender		75.00	✓			
810	Processing Fee	Paid To Broker: IMB		450.00	✓			
811	Underwriting Fee	Paid To Lender		495.00	✓			
812	Wire Transfer Fee	Paid To Other						

COMPENSATION TO BROKER (Not Paid Out of Loan Proceeds):		
813	YSP (POC)	($4,725.00)

1100	TITLE CHARGES:				PFC	S	F	POC
1101	Closing/Escrow Fee:	Paid To Other	ABC Closers	$ 150.00				
1105	Document Preparation Fee			100.00				
1106	Notary Fees							
1107	Attorney Fees							
1108	Title Insurance:	Paid To Other	South Chicago Title	350.00				
	Endorsements	Paid To Other		287.50				

1200	GOVERNMENT RECORDING & TRANSFER CHARGES:				PFC	S	F	POC
1201	Recording Fees:	Paid To Other	Pinellas Co Clerk Courts	$ 185.00				
1202	City/County Tax/Stamps:							
1203	State Tax/Stamps:	Paid To Other	Intangible Tax	630.00				
	Doc stamps on Note			1,102.50				

1300	ADDITIONAL SETTLEMENT CHARGES:			PFC	S	F	POC
1302	Pest Inspection	Paid To Other	$ (175.00)				✓
	Survey	Paid To Other	300.00				

Estimated Closing Costs 12,000.00

900	ITEMS REQUIRED BY LENDER TO BE PAID IN ADVANCE:				PFC	S	F	POC
901	Interest	Paid To Lender	for 16 days @ $ 53.9384 /day	$ 863.01	✓			
902	Mtg Ins. Premium							
903	Hazard Ins. Premium	Paid To Other		4,374.96				
904								
905	VA Funding Fee							

1000	RESERVES DEPOSITED WITH LENDER:				PFC	S	F	POC
1001	Hazard Ins. Premium	Paid To Lender	2 mths @ $ 364.58 / mth	$ 729.16				
1002	Mtg Ins. Premium Reserves	Paid To Lender	1 mths @ $ 131.25 / mth	131.25				
1003	School Tax		mths @ $ / mth					
1004	Taxes & Assessment Reserves	Paid To Lender	3 mths @ $ 481.25 / mth	1,443.75				
1005	Flood Insurance Reserves		mths @ $ / mth					
			mths @ $ / mth					
			mths @ $ / mth					

Estimated Prepaid Items/Reserves 7,542.13

TOTAL ESTIMATED SETTLEMENT CHARGES 19,542.13

TOTAL ESTIMATED FUNDS NEEDED TO CLOSE:			TOTAL ESTIMATED MONTHLY PAYMENT:	
Purchase Price/Payoff (+)	350,000.00	New First Mortgage(-)	Principal & Interest	1,640.63
Loan Amount (-)	315,000.00	Sub Financing(-)	Other Financing (P & I)	
Est. Closing Costs (+)	12,000.00	New 2nd Mtg Closing Costs(+)	Hazard Insurance	364.58
Est. Prepaid Items/Reserves (+)	7,542.13		Real Estate Taxes	481.25
Amount Paid by Seller (-)	3,000.00		Mortgage Insurance	131.25
Earnest Money: Cash Deposit	-5,000.00		Homeowner Assn. Dues	50.00
			Other	
Total Est. Funds needed to close		46,542.13	Total Monthly Payment	2,667.71

☑ This Good Faith Estimate is being provided by **Integrity Mortgage Brokerage LLC**, a mortgage broker, and no lender has been obtained. **These estimates are provided pursuant to the Real Estate Settlement Procedures Act of 1974, as amended (RESPA). Additional information can be found in the HUD Special Information Booklet, which is to be provided to you by your mortgage broker or lender, if your application is to purchase residential real property and the lender will take a first lien on the property.** The undersigned acknowledges receipt of the booklet "Settlement Costs," and if applicable the Consumer Handbook on ARM Mortgages.

Applicant **Mighty Hopeful Borrower** Date Applicant Date

Calyx Form - gfe.frm (09/07)

originated, received, or related to the mortgage loan from the application through the final disposition must be maintained for three years from the date of the original entry.

If a mortgage brokerage business gives the borrower a written commitment for a loan on behalf of the lender, copies of both the commitment from the lender and the commitment from the mortgage broker must also be maintained in the file. If the mortgage broker gives the borrower a written **lock-in** (discussed in chapter 3) for the loan, the file must contain copies of the lock-in commitment from both the lender and the broker. This file must also contain a copy of the mortgage loan application, if applicable.

When a lender commits to funding a loan, the mortgage broker must provide the borrower with specific information about the loan. This information, which is disclosed initially in the broker/borrower agreement and revised with the lender's commitment, if necessary, includes:

- the gross loan amount;
- the note rate if the mortgage has a fixed rate and the initial note rate;
- the length of time for which the rate is effective;
- the frequency of changes;
- limitations on adjustments;
- potential for negative amortization (discussed in chapter 4) and margin interest rate differentials; and
- in the case of adjustable-rate mortgages, the nationally recognized index that is beyond the control of the mortgage broker, lender, or correspondent lender.

The penalty for not maintaining the documentation required by the DFS is a $300 fine. If a licensee fails to maintain documentation so that an audit trail cannot be provided, the fine rises to $1,000 along with a six-month suspension of the licensee. Failure to provide a good faith estimate, providing a commitment to the client without obtaining a written commitment from the lender, or missing documents in a file result in a fine of $250. On any one visit, the maximum fine for incomplete files or missing documents is $2,500.

Overall, fines per administrative complaint cannot exceed $5,000, although the penalty for serious negligence with regard to maintaining files can result in a license being revoked.

TRANSACTION JOURNAL REQUIREMENTS

Mortgage brokers are required to maintain a journal of their transactions. At a minimum, the journal should contain the name of the applicant, the date of application, the result of the brokerage transaction (that is, loan funded, loan denied, application withdrawn, or other), and the name of the lender, if applicable. The Mortgage Brokerage and Lending Transaction Journal must be kept in the principal or branch office where mortgage transactions are originated.

All transactions must be entered into the journal within seven days, and failure to do so will result in a Notice of Noncompliance for the first offense. Subsequent offenses carry a $500 fine, and, if the failure to maintain the journal is judged to be intentional, DFS will impose a fine of $500 and suspension of the license.

KEY POINT REVIEW

- Some of the acts performed by mortgage brokers include accepting or offering to accept an application for a mortgage loan; soliciting or offering to solicit a mortgage loan on behalf of a borrower; negotiating or offering to negotiate the terms or conditions of a mortgage loan on behalf of a lender; or negotiating or offering to negotiate the sale of an existing mortgage loan to a noninstitutional investor.
- An *employee* works for a salary or wages and is subject to withholding and other deductions. Annual compensation is reported on an IRS W-2 form. An *independent contractor* contracts to perform a service and is responsible for maintaining accounting and tax records. Annual compensation for an independent contractor is reported on an IRS 1099 form.
- Entities exempt from licensure include a bank; bank holding company; trust company; savings institution; credit union; consumer finance company; bank, savings institution, and holding companies approved by HUD, VA, Ginnie Mae, Fannie Mae, and Freddie Mac; and all governmental agencies.
- Lawyers, securities firms, persons acting as a fiduciary as appointed by a court, small business investment companies, and insurance companies that deal in mortgages as part of their regular business practice are not required to be licensed. However, lawyers are exempt only if they are not actively and principally engaged in the business of negotiating loans secured by real property.
- The principal broker is in charge of the operation of the mortgage company's principal place of business and all branch brokers. Each branch office must have a designated branch broker who is responsible for that branch.
- Licensees must complete 14 hours of continuing education every two years, but are exempt from this requirement if they obtained their initial license between June 1 and August 31.
- Licensees who are found guilty or plead no contest to any crime that involves fraud, dishonesty, or other illegal action in any jurisdiction must report the outcome to the DFS within 30 days. Felony convictions and bankruptcies must be reported within 7 days.
- Mortgage brokerage business licenses must be renewed before September 1 of even-numbered years. Licenses that are not renewed before September 1 revert to inactive status and expire after six months. Mortgage broker licenses must be renewed before September 1 of odd-numbered years.
- Change of address for a mortgage brokerage business must be reported to the DFS within 30 days.
- Mortgage brokerage businesses may charge fees for arranging a commitment, taking an application, evaluating a borrower's financial information, incidental services, and insurance premiums. Notice of any changes to the terms of a loan must be provided to a borrower no later than three business days prior to closing.
- The mortgage brokerage business must disclose any compensation paid by the lender to the business.

- When brokering a loan to a noninstitutional investor, the mortgage broker must provide an opinion of value as well as title insurance or an opinion of title, with a statement regarding the marketability of the property.
- A net loan is the amount of the funds provided by the lender at closing. Maximum mortgage brokerage business fees on a net loan equal the amount of the loan ÷ 10 + $250. A gross loan includes the total loan amount along with all mortgage brokerage business fees. Maximum mortgage brokerage business fees on a gross loan equal the amount of the gross loan ÷ 11 + $227.27.
- Refundable application fees and third-party fees must be deposited in a segregated escrow account in a federally insured financial institution located in Florida within seven business days of their receipt.
- Records of mortgage transactions must be kept for three years from date of origination. Mortgage brokerage businesses must keep a journal of their transactions for the principal office and each branch office location. Each mortgage transaction must have a separate file, kept either alphabetically or numerically.
- The mortgage brokerage business cannot make loans or commitments or guarantee the borrower will be approved for a loan. The business must also disclose all fees associated with the application process and a procedure for requesting a refund.
- Fees must be paid to a mortgage brokerage business and not to a mortgage broker. Fee amounts are determined by the size of the loan a borrower requests. Brokers are required to deposit all third-party fees in a federally insured financial institution in Florida within seven days of receiving such funds.

REVIEW QUESTIONS

1. An individual who solicits borrowers, lenders, or purchasers of mortgages and whose earnings are reported on a 1099 form
   a. requires licensure.
   b. is exempt from licensure requirements if serving as the principal broker in a mortgage brokerage business.
   c. is an employee and does not need a license.
   d. is acting solely as a salesperson and does not need a license.

2. William has accepted a loan application from Mr. Lee. William must enter this transaction in the transaction journal
   a. before the end of the quarter.
   b. the day the transaction occurs.
   c. before the end of the month.
   d. within seven business days.

3. Banks, bank holding companies, savings institutions, credit unions, and consumer finance companies licensed in Florida
   a. are required to be licensed as a mortgage broker.
   b. are exempt from licensure.
   c. can hold licensure as both a financial institution and a mortgage broker.
   d. are not permitted to deal in mortgages in Florida.

4. ABC Mortgage is handling Mrs. Martin's loan application. Mrs. Martin gave ABC $300 for an appraisal. How many business days does ABC have to deposit Mrs. Martin's money?
   a. 5
   b. 7
   c. 10
   d. 15

5. Attorneys are required to hold a mortgage broker license when they
   a. are actively and principally engaged in the business of negotiating loans.
   b. find properties for their clients and collect commissions from the sellers.
   c. lend their own money to clients who are buying property.
   d. help an elderly client arrange a mortgage on a smaller home.

6. The DFS requires that records of loan transactions be
   a. filed with the DFS.
   b. kept at the principal office.
   c. maintained for a minimum of one year.
   d. kept at any single site approved by the DFS.

7. Hardy Mortgages failed to notify the DFS that Joe White was appointed principal broker two months ago. Hardy Mortgages is likely to receive
   a. a Notice of Noncompliance.
   b. a fine of $1,000.
   c. a suspension of license.
   d. all of the above.

8. Government agencies are legally required to
   a. be licensed as mortgage brokerage businesses if they deal in mortgages.
   b. obtain a special type of license if they deal in mortgages.
   c. keep records of their transactions but are not required to be licensed to deal in mortgages.
   d. refrain from competing with mortgage brokerage businesses.

9. As the principal broker for Green Grass Mortgages, Jack has responsibility for
   a. Green Grass's principal place of business.
   b. Green Grass's branch offices.
   c. Green Grass's principal place of business and all branch offices.
   d. Jack's own brokerage business only.

10. An individual who is paid by salary, employed by a licensed lender, and offers to find a homeowner a mortgage at a lower interest rate than the homeowner is currently paying needs
    a. a mortgage broker license.
    b. a mortgage brokerage business license.
    c. either a mortgage broker or mortgage brokerage business license.
    d. no special license.

11. Dan is moving his mortgage brokerage business to an office park outside the city limits. With regard to this move, the DFS must
    a. be notified prior to the next renewal period.
    b. be notified within 15 days.
    c. be notified within 30 days.
    d. approve the new location before the business can move.

12. A person who applies to start a mortgage brokerage business will need to pay an application fee of
    a. $215.
    b. $300.
    c. $425.
    d. $525.

13. The mortgage brokerage business application must identify ultimate equitable owners who own at LEAST what percentage of the business?
    a. 10 percent
    b. 25 percent
    c. 30 percent
    d. 50 percent

14. When borrowers apply for mortgage loans, they can expect to pay an application fee that is
    a. based on the size of the loan.
    b. a set amount.
    c. based on either the size of the loan or a set amount.
    d. set by the DFS.

15. When a prospective borrower applies for a loan, the mortgage broker can legally charge the borrower for which of the following?
    a. Reviewing the borrower's financial statements
    b. Courier services
    c. Taking an application
    d. All of the above

16. The Quarterly Report Transmittal Form lists
    a. all transactions performed by the mortgage brokerage business.
    b. each branch office of the brokerage firm.
    c. names of individuals who have done business with the brokerage firm during that period.
    d. new or terminated associates of the brokerage firm during that quarter.

17. A mortgage brokerage business that makes a commitment to a borrower without first receiving a commitment from a lender may have to pay a fine of
    a. $100.
    b. $250.
    c. $350.
    d. $1,000.

18. ABC Home Finance was licensed as a mortgage brokerage business in 2007. ABC must renew its license
    a. annually.
    b. before September 1, 2008.
    c. before September 1, 2009.
    d. within two years of the date of the initial licensure.

19. Mortgage Broker John can tell the Jacksons their loan has been approved as soon as
    a. the mortgage brokerage business approves the borrower's application.
    b. he reviews and approves the Jackson's credit history.
    c. the Jacksons pay the brokerage fee and John completes his review of their application.
    d. John receives a written commitment from a lender.

20. Licensees who are found guilty or plead no contest to any crime involving fraud or dishonesty must report the outcome to the DFS within
    a. 24 hours.
    b. 7 days.
    c. 30 days.
    d. 90 days.

21. An individual who is employed by a mortgage lender and who negotiates the making of mortgage loans is a(n)
    a. mortgage broker.
    b. correspondent lender.
    c. loan originator.
    d. associate.

22. Full Value Mortgages appointed a new president after the former president retired. With regard to the DFS, Full Value
    a. need not report this change until the next license renewal period.
    b. must report this change within 24 hours.
    c. must apply for DFS approval before changing the company president.
    d. must notify the DFS of the change within 30 days.

23. The acknowledgment of a good faith estimate on a loan that has closed
    a. need not be kept by the broker once the transaction is finished.
    b. must be kept by the broker for 30 days.
    c. must be kept by the broker for two years.
    d. must be kept by the broker for three years.

24. Larry is applying for a loan of $142,000 after netting out all costs and fees. The maximum fee Larry's broker can charge him is
    a. $13,159.09.
    b. $13,136.36.
    c. $14,450.00.
    d. $14,427.27.

25. Licensure as a mortgage broker in Florida is controlled by the
    a. Office of Financial Regulation.
    b. Department of Financial Services.
    c. Financial Services Commission.
    d. Division of Mortgage Brokering and Lending.

26. If the terms of a loan change, the borrower must be notified within
    a. 24 hours.
    b. three business days.
    c. 48 hours.
    d. seven business days.

27. When third party fees collected by a mortgage broker are greater than actual costs, the excess must be refunded within how many days of closing?
    a. 3
    b. 7
    c. 30
    d. 60

28. Distance education courses for mortgage brokers
    a. are not legal under F.S. 494.
    b. do not require a course test.
    c. can be shorter than 14 hours.
    d. require a test on each module of the course.

29. For the Websters' purchase of a home on Marco Island, terms of the loan have changed. Mortgage Broker Bob was able to notify the Websters of the changes 24 hours before closing. This situation
    a. violates Florida law if the Websters do not have a financial emergency and waive their rights to notification.
    b. does not violate Florida law if the Websters have a documented financial emergency.
    c. is legal if the changes amount to less than $1,000.
    d. is illegal in any case.

30. Fees paid by the lender to the mortgage brokerage business
    a. must be disclosed on the good faith estimate.
    b. must be be disclosed but only if requested by the borrower.
    c. need not be disclosed in any case.
    d. must be entered into the transaction journal.

31. Mr. Munson would like to acquire controlling interest in Beachfront Mortgages. To do this, he needs to acquire what percentage of voting securities?
    a. 10
    b. 25
    c. 33
    d. 51

32. Broker Bob accepted $300 from an applicant to pay for an appraisal, but the borrower failed to qualify for a loan. Under Florida law, what action must be taken?
    a. Broker Bob may keep the $300.
    b. The appraiser may keep the $300 if he made a verbal contract with the broker to do the appraisal.
    c. Broker Bob must return the $300 to the loan applicant within 30 days.
    d. Broker Bob must return the $300 to the loan applicant within 60 days.

33. Joanne got her mortgage broker license on April 15. Joanne's license will expire
    a. on April 15 two years after the license was issued.
    b. before September 1 of the year the license was issued.
    c. on April 15 one year after the license was issued.
    d. before the next September 1st of an odd-numbered year from the date the license was issued.

CHAPTER

3

FLORIDA LAWS REGULATING MORTGAGE LENDERS AND CORRESPONDENT LENDERS

LEARNING OBJECTIVES

After finishing chapter 3, you should be able to

1. explain the requirements for licensure as a mortgage lender or correspondent lender and understand who is exempt from licensure in Florida;
2. explain the role of the principal representative;
3. identify the net worth requirements for lenders and correspondent lenders;
4. understand the rules that govern mortgage lenders and correspondent lenders that act as mortgage brokerage businesses;
5. understand other aspects of the mortgage lending business such as lender fees and servicing mortgage loans;
6. know record-keeping requirements, required disclosures, how to disburse insurance proceeds, and arbitration procedures;
7. understand the lock-in agreement;
8. know the grounds for complaints and investigations; and
9. understand what constitutes mortgage fraud.

KEY TERMS

annual percentage rate (APR)
arbitration
conflict of interest
correspondent mortgage lender
hypothecation
lock-in agreement
mortgage fraud
mortgage lender
mortgage lending process
pattern of misconduct
principal representative
prohibited practices
subpoena duces tecum

INTRODUCTION

The Florida Statutes identify four categories related to mortgage licensure. In addition to mortgage brokers and mortgage brokerage businesses, mortgage lenders and correspondent lenders also must be licensed. Chapter 3 looks at the laws regulating mortgage lenders and correspondent lenders.

Florida law defines "to act as a **mortgage lender**" as

...to make a mortgage loan or to service a mortgage loan for others or, for compensation or gain, or in the expectation of compensation or gain, either directly or indirectly, to sell or offer to sell a mortgage loan to a noninstitutional investor.

A **correspondent mortgage lender** is defined as

...a lender that may make mortgage loans but cannot service a mortgage loan for more than four months after the date the mortgage loan was made or acquired.

LICENSURE AS A MORTGAGE LENDER

Applicants who wish to be licensed as a mortgage lender must submit a completed application form and nonrefundable fee of $575 to the Department of Financial Services (DFS). In addition, the DFS requires that the applicant provide audited financial statements showing a net worth of at least $250,000 and a surety bond in the amount of $10,000 payable to the State of Florida. Both the net worth and the surety bond must be continuously maintained. Applicants must also document that they are duly incorporated or registered as a lawful business entity under the laws of Florida or other states.

Also, each ultimate equitable owner of 10 percent or greater interest, principal representative, chief executive officer, chief financial officer, chief operations officer, chief legal officer, chief compliance officer, control person, member, partner, joint venturer, and director must submit a completed fingerprint card and Biographical Summary Form OFR-494-01 to the Office of Financial Regulation.

If the applicant, principal officer, director, or ultimate equitable owner of more than 10 percent of the business has ever been found guilty of violating the mortgage lending laws or has criminal prosecution pending, the DFS may deny the application. The DFS also reserves the right to cancel the license if it was issued in error or if the check covering the application fee is returned for insufficient funds.

LICENSURE AS A CORRESPONDENT MORTGAGE LENDER

The requirements for licensure as a correspondent mortgage lender are somewhat different. Correspondent lenders must submit an application and nonrefundable fee of $500, along with audited financial statements documenting a net worth of at least $25,000 and a surety bond of $10,000 payable to the State of Florida. Both net worth and surety bond must be continuously maintained.

The applicant must also show proof of incorporation or other lawfully formed business organization. As is the case with the mortgage lender, the DFS can deny the license if there have been violations of mortgage lending law or there are pending cases against the applicant.

Similar to mortgage lender licensure, submission of a fingerprint card is required for each ultimate equitable owner, principal representative, chief executive officer, chief financial officer, chief operations officer, chief legal officer, chief compliance officer, control person, member, partner, joint venturer, and director is required.

The DFS may cancel correspondent lender licenses issued in error or if the check covering the application fee is returned for insufficient funds. Neither a mortgage lender nor correspondent lender license can be transferred or assigned.

EXEMPTIONS FROM LICENSURE

Under Florida Statutes (F.S.) 494.006-0077, the following institutions do not need a license to act as a mortgage lender or correspondent mortgage lender:

- A bank, bank holding company, trust company, savings and loan association, savings bank, credit union, or insurance company if the insurance company is licensed in the state of Florida
- Any person who holds fiduciary responsibility conferred by a court
- A wholly owned bank holding company subsidiary or wholly owned savings and loan association holding company subsidiary approved or certified by HUD, the VA, Ginnie Mae, Fannie Mae, or Freddie Mac
- Any person who receives a mortgage as part of a purchase-money transaction
- Any person who receives a mortgage as security for materials or services related to the improvement of real property
- Fannie Mae, Freddie Mac, an agency of the federal government or state, county, or municipal governments, or quasigovernment agencies
- A consumer finance company licensed before October 1, 1991
- A person who makes or sells mortgage loans for his or her own investment and does not represent himself or herself as being in the mortgage lending business
- A person who acts under contract as an agent for a governmental agency in the servicing of mortgage loans

People who are employed by a mortgage lender or correspondent lender are also exempt from licensing requirements when they act within their scope of employment—that is, they are paid a salary reported on a W-2 form. Other exemptions include sellers who are financing the purchase of their own property and persons who loan their own money, so long as they do not represent themselves as being in the mortgage business. This exemption also applies to individuals who have a lien against the property.

PRINCIPAL REPRESENTATIVE

Each applicant for a mortgage lender or correspondent lender license must designate a **principal representative** who manages the business. In addition, each ultimate equitable owner of 10 percent or greater interest, the chief executive officer, and each director of an entity applying for licensure as a mortgage lender must submit a Biographical Summary form. According to Florida law, anyone who is designated as a principal representative must provide evidence that he or she was originally licensed as a mortgage broker or has completed 24 hours of classroom education and passed the state examination. No prior experience is required.

The person who serves as principal representative must file the Principal Representative Designation form with the DFS within 30 days after accepting designation. Failure to file this form will result in a Notice of Noncompliance for a first offense. Subsequent offenses will result in a fine of $500, but if the offense is found to be intentional, the fine is $5,000. If the information contained in an Application for Licensure as a Mortgage Lender becomes inaccurate before the applicant becomes licensed, the applicant is responsible for correcting the inaccurate information within ten days of the change.

Also, the principal representative of a lender or correspondent lender can be held responsible for the actions of associates or employees that result in disciplinary action. However, the license of the principal representative can be suspended or revoked only if there is a pattern of repeated violations by associates or employees.

REQUIREMENTS AND RESPONSIBILITIES OF LENDERS AND CORRESPONDENT LENDERS

Licenses for lenders and correspondent lenders are renewed for two-year periods. Renewal of a mortgage lender license requires a completed application and payment of a $575 fee. Renewing a correspondent lender license costs $475, and the renewal fee for each branch office is $325.

When a lender or correspondent lender license is not renewed, it automatically reverts to inactive status. The license can remain inactive for six months and be renewed by filing a completed reactivation form and paying the appropriate renewal fee along with a reactivation fee of $100. If a license is not renewed within six months of expiration, it becomes void.

Net Worth Requirements

F.S. 494 requires that lenders maintain a net worth of $250,000 and correspondent lenders maintain a net worth of $25,000. If the net worth falls below the required amount, lenders and correspondent lenders must notify the DFS within 48 hours. Failure to meet the net worth requirements may result in a loss of license. If the DFS discovers that the net worth has dropped below the required amount, the lender or correspondent lender must immediately stop accepting loan applications. The lender or correspondent lender then has up to 60 days to satisfy the net worth requirements before the license is canceled.

However, if the licensee notifies the DFS that he or she no longer meets the net worth requirements, the DFS will allow the licensee 120 days to reach the net worth requirements. If the net worth requirements are not met within 120 days, the license is canceled. In either case, the licensee cannot resume operations without written authorization from the DFS.

Net worth requirements are verified by audited financial statements that are prepared according to generally accepted accounting principles (GAAP). Licensees must complete these audits within 120 days of the fiscal year-end date of the licensee, and have the audit available for review by DFS examiners upon request.

Lenders and correspondent lenders must maintain a surety bond of $10,000 payable to the State of Florida and issued by a company authorized to do business in Florida. A copy of this bond must be maintained in the principal place of business and made available for review by the DFS if requested. Any changes in bond status must be reported to the DFS. (Mortgage lenders who are licensed under the saving clause described in F.S. 494.0065, however, are not required to maintain a surety bond.)

Mortgage Lenders and Correspondent Lenders That Act as a Mortgage Brokerage Business

Florida law allows mortgage lenders and correspondent mortgage lenders to act as a mortgage brokerage business. When they act as mortgage brokers, however, lenders and correspondent lenders are required to follow the rules regarding mortgage brokerage business disclosures, fees, and other matters outlined in the Florida Statutes and the Florida Administrative Code.

Lender fees. In a mortgage financing transaction, lender fees or loan origination fees up to 4 percent of the face amount of the loan or line of credit are not considered interest or finance charges. If a licensee sells or assigns the loan to another person within 90 days after the loan was funded, loan origination fees up to 10 percent of the face amount of the loan or line of credit are not considered interest or finance charges.

Lenders and correspondent lenders are also subject to Florida's laws regarding usury. As you may recall from chapter 2, under most circumstances Florida law forbids interest rates on mortgages of greater than 18 percent.

Servicing Mortgage Loans

Servicing a loan refers to collecting payments and making disbursements of principal, interest, tax, and insurance (PITI) payments to the appropriate parties. Lenders and correspondent lenders who service mortgage loans must maintain at their place of business a segregated set of records for the accounts they service, as well as a separate account for receipts related to servicing. These records and receipts must be audited annually.

Record-Keeping Requirements

Lenders and correspondent lenders may keep all books, accounts, records, and documents related to their business at a location other than the principal office. However, licensees must notify the DFS in writing of where the records are being stored, and the DFS must approve storage at that site.

All records relating to the business must be available at a reasonable and convenient location within Florida and must be available for review within three business days from the date of a request from the DFS.

As mentioned earlier, each mortgage transaction requires a separate file. According to Chapter 69V-40.175 of the Florida Administrative Code, at a minimum the file must contain the mortgage brokerage agreement, a copy of a signed closing statement or documentation of the denial or cancellation of the loan application, and a copy of the good faith estimate of costs.

Disclosures and the Right to a Refund

According to F.S. 494, lenders must make certain written disclosures to borrowers before accepting a fee for an application, a credit report, an appraisal, or a reimbursement for third-party charges. The lender's disclosure must state whether all or any part of such fees or charges is refundable, as well as the terms and conditions of any refunds. The lender must also provide a realistic estimate of the number of days required to issue a commitment following receipt of the borrower's application. Lenders are also required to disclose to the borrower the name or title of a person within the lender's organization to whom the borrower can address written questions, comments, or complaints, and who is required to respond promptly to such inquiries.

The borrower must acknowledge that he or she has received these disclosures. The lender is responsible for keeping a copy of the acknowledgment and giving a copy to the borrower.

Borrowers may also withdraw an application at any time before receiving a commitment without penalty or responsibility for paying additional fees or charges. Should the borrower withdraw, the lender must refund any fees and charges to which the borrower may be entitled under the terms of the written disclosure form.

If the lender failed to provide the borrower with the written disclosure or failed to make a good faith effort to approve the loan, however, the lender is required to refund all funds paid to the lender.

Dispensing Insurance Proceeds

Sometimes lenders or correspondent lenders receive checks that are jointly payable to the lender and the borrower. Under Florida law, lenders or correspondent lenders must promptly endorse all checks or negotiable instruments jointly payable to the mortgagee and the insured. When a lender or correspondent lender receives compensation for property damage in which the lender or correspondent lender has an interest, the proceeds must be deposited into a segregated account in a federally insured financial institution, and the portion belonging to the borrower must be promptly disbursed. When the mortgagee or assignee has no interest in the property, the funds can be immediately disbursed to the insured.

Insurance proceeds related to additional living expenses for the insured must be promptly distributed if the insured can verify that the proceeds are for living expenses or loss of contents.

Arbitration

Sometimes mortgage transactions require **arbitration** between parties to the mortgage. When a dispute arises, parties may present their arguments before the American Arbitration Association or a nonindustry arbitration forum approved by the DFS. If the noninstitutional investor or borrower chooses, the arbitration can be held in the county where the investor or borrower entered into the agreement or at the business location of the mortgage brokerage business or mortgage lender or correspondent lender. Agreements reached under arbitration are binding.

Only borrowers or noninstitutional investors can decide whether to go to an arbitration board or to court.

The Lock-in Agreement

One of the most important considerations for both the borrower and the lender is the interest rate on a mortgage loan. For example, over the life of a 30-year loan of $100,000 with a 5 percent interest rate, the borrower will make monthly payments of $536.82, and pay a total of $93,256 in interest. If the same loan had a 7 percent interest rate, the borrower would pay $665 monthly, for a total of $139,511 in interest. The $129 difference in monthly payment amounts to an additional $46,255 in interest payments over the life of the loan.

Because interest rates fluctuate, and a small difference in an interest rate can make a significant difference in the cost of a loan, borrowers look for loans with lower rates. When a borrower applies for a loan, he or she may decide to wait to see if interest rates are trending up or down, or the borrower may request a **lock-in agreement**, which is an agreement where the lender guarantees the availability of certain loan terms for a specified period. The loan commitment does not require disclosure of the **annual percentage rate**, which is defined as the total cost of credit including the loan amount and any additional fees. Typically, the longer the lock-in period, the higher the interest rate or fees because this increases the lender's risk. Also, the higher the interest rate on a loan, the lower the origination fee discounts.

Because of the importance of interest rates, Florida has a number of laws regulating the use of the lock-in agreement. According to F.S. 494, each lock-in agreement must be in writing and must contain

- the expiration date of the lock-in, if any;
- the interest rate locked in, if any;
- the discount points locked in, if any;
- the commitment fee locked in, if any;
- the lock-in fee, if any; and
- a statement advising of the provisions of ss. 494.006-494.0077 regarding lock-in agreements.

Florida law also requires that any lock-in agreement received by a mortgage lender or correspondent mortgage lender by mail or through a broker must be signed by the mortgage lender or correspondent mortgage lender in order to become effective. Borrowers may rescind a lock-in agreement until the lender signs and mails a confirmation of the agreement to the borrower or to the mortgage brokerage business.

If the borrower decides to rescind, the mortgage lender or correspondent mortgage lender must promptly refund any lock-in fee paid. In addition, the fee is refundable if it is contingent upon approval by parties to whom the lender seeks to sell the loan. If the loan purchaser's requirements are not met due to circumstances beyond the borrower's control or the borrower is willing but unable to comply with the loan purchaser's requirements, the lock-in fee must be refunded.

COMPLAINTS AND INVESTIGATIONS

In Florida, the DFS has responsibility for the enforcement and administration of all laws and rules related to mortgage brokers, mortgage brokerage businesses, mortgage lenders, and correspondent lenders. The DFS may investigate any person suspected of violating F.S. 494, the Florida Administrative Code, the Real Estate Settlement Procedures Act, or the federal Truth-in-Lending Act (discussed in chapter 4). Any person who violates the laws or rules that regulate brokering a mortgage loan—or operating a mortgage business school as well—may face a fine of up to $5,000.

Although the DFS investigates formal complaints against licensees, it may also conduct investigations without a formal complaint. According to Florida law, investigations and routine audits must take place in a convenient location within Florida unless the investigation requires travel out of state. In those cases, the licensee being investigated or audited is responsible for paying the travel and per diem expenses of the investigators up to eight days per examiner per year. If the audit reveals fraud, however, there is no limit to the travel and per diem exposure.

Information from investigations is kept confidential until the investigation is completed or ceases to be active. F.S. 494 protects any person who furnishes information or evidence to the DFS regarding an investigation from civil liability. That is, people who cooperate with the investigation cannot be sued.

When it appears a licensee has violated or is about to violate F.S. 494 or the Florida Administrative Code, the DFS may ask the court for an injunction to prevent the licensee from engaging in the violation. In these cases, the court may issue a subpoena or a **subpoena duces tecum,** which requires the individual to produce any books, accounts, records, or other documents related to the action in question. The court also has the right to impound the property of the individual and appoint a receiver or administrator. Table 3.1 on the next page contains some other important definitions from F.S. 494 and Chapter 69V-40.

The DFS also has the power to issue a cease and desist order when it believes a licensee is violating, has violated, or is about to violate state law. The rules regarding cease and desist orders are governed by the Florida Administrative Procedures Act.

The DFS can also order the refund of any unauthorized or excessive fees charged by a licensee, and it can prohibit a mortgage brokerage business, mortgage lender, or correspondent lender from hiring a person who has been found guilty of misconduct. F.S. 494 defines a **pattern of misconduct** as three or more violations of the Florida Mortgage Brokerage and Lending Act and Regulations or the Rules Regulating Mortgage Brokerage during a one-year period or any criminal conviction for violating these laws.

Conflicts of Interest

Occasionally, a mortgage broker or employee of a mortgage brokerage business, mortgage lender, or correspondent mortgage lender will have a conflict of interest in a particular mortgage transaction. **Conflicts of interest** arise when

- a licensee or the licensee's relative provides additional products or services to the borrower;
- the licensee or the licensee's relative owns 10 percent or more of the firm that provides the additional products or services;
- the person providing the services owns 10 percent or more of any securities that benefit the licensee;
- a holding company owns 10 percent or more of any securities that benefit the licensee and the person providing the products or services;
- a person serves as an officer or director for both the licensee and the person providing the products or services; and
- a person serves as an officer or director for the person providing the products or services.

TABLE 3.1 ■ Important Definitions

IMPORTANT DEFINITIONS

Source: (F.S. 494 and Chapter 69V-40)

Branch office. A location, other than a licensee's principal place of business where: (a) the address of which appears on business cards, stationery, or advertising used by the licensee in connection with business conducted under this chapter [494]; (b) at which the licensee's name, advertising or promotional materials, or signage suggest that mortgage loans are originated, negotiated, funded, or serviced; or (c) which, due to the actions of any employee or associate of the licensee, may be construed by the public as a branch office of the licensee where mortgage loans are originated, negotiated, funded, or serviced

Felony of the first degree. A penalty for a violation of F.S. 494 in which the total value of money and property unlawfully obtained exceeded $50,000 and there were five or more victims

Institutional investor. A state or national bank, state or federal savings and loan association or savings bank, real estate investment trust, insurance company, real estate company, accredited investor as defined in 17 C.F.R. ss. 230.501 et seq., business licensed under ss. 494.001-494.0077, or other business entity that invests in mortgage loans, including a secondary mortgage market institution including, without limitation, the Federal National Mortgage Association (FNMA), the Federal Home Loan Mortgage Corporation (FHLMC), and the Government National Mortgage Association (GNMA), conduits, investment bankers, and any subsidiary of such entities

Noninstitutional investor. An investor other than an institutional investor, such as a private individual

Loan commitment. A statement by the lender setting forth the terms and conditions upon which the lender is willing to make a particular mortgage loan to a particular borrower

Mortgage loan. Any: (a) residential mortgage loan; (b) loan on commercial real property if the borrower is a natural person or the lender is a noninstitutional investor; or (c) loan on improved real property consisting of five or more dwelling units if the borrower is a natural person or the lender is a noninstitutional investor

Net worth. Total assets minus total liabilities pursuant to generally accepted accounting principles

Relative. A person's spouse, father, mother, children, brothers, and sisters; the father, mother, brothers, and sisters of such person's spouse; and the spouses of children, brothers, or sisters of such person (but not, according to F.S. 494, uncles, aunts, cousins, or grandparents); relatives can be related by blood, half-blood, or adoption

TABLE 3.1 ■ Important Definitions (Continued)

IMPORTANT DEFINITIONS (continued)

Substantial fault of the borrower. Situation in which the borrower: (a) failed to provide information or documentation required by the lender or broker in a timely manner; (b) provided information, in the application or subsequently, that upon verification proved to be significantly inaccurate, causing the need for review or further investigation by the lender or broker; (c) failed to produce no later than the date specified by the lender all documentation specified in the commitment or closing instructions as being required for closing; or (d) failed to be ready, willing, or able to close the loan no later than the date specified by the lender or broker. For purposes of this definition, a borrower is considered to have provided information or documentation in a timely manner if such information and documentation was received by the lender within seven days after the borrower received a request for same, and information is considered significantly inaccurate if the correct information materially affects the eligibility of the borrower for the loan for which application is made

Writ of ne exeat. A court order restraining a person from leaving the jurisdiction of the court

Mortgage brokerage businesses, lenders, and correspondent lenders must disclose to borrowers that they have a conflict of interest and that they may receive a financial benefit as a result of the conflict. When a conflict of interest occurs, Florida law requires that the borrower receive a copy of the following statement:

> *You are not required to purchase additional products or services from any person or entity suggested or recommended by (Broker/Lender/Correspondent Lender). However, the (Broker/Lender/Correspondent Lender) hereby reserves the right to approve the entity selected by the borrower, which approval may not be unreasonably withheld.*

Prohibited Practices

Under F.S. 494.0025, it is illegal to operate as a mortgage broker, mortgage brokerage business, mortgage lender, or correspondent lender without a current, active license issued by the DFS. The statute also specifically prohibits the use of any device, scheme, or artifice to defraud another person with regard to the sale, purchase, negotiation, promotion, advertisement, or **hypothecation**—defined as pledging real property as security for a loan without giving up possession of the property—of mortgage transactions. It is also illegal to obtain property by fraud, misrepresentation, or false promise.

Other F.S. 494 **prohibited practices** include falsifying, concealing, or covering up material facts or using false documents; failing to report that a mortgage lender or correspondent lender does not meet the net worth requirements within 48 hours of discovering that fact; and paying a fee or commission in a mortgage loan transaction to some person or organization other than a licensed mortgage brokerage business, lender, or correspondent lender, or someone legally exempt from licensure. Figure 3.1 summarizes the prohibited practices according to F.S. 494.

FIGURE 3.1 ■ Prohibited Practices under F.S. 494

1. To act as a mortgage broker, lender, or correspondent lender in this state without a current, active license issued by the office pursuant to ss. 494.006-494.0077
2. In any practice or transaction or course of business relating to the sale, purchase, negotiation, promotion, advertisement, or hypothecation of mortgage transactions, directly or indirectly:
   (a) To knowingly or willingly employ any device, scheme, or artifice to defraud;
   (b) To engage in any transaction, practice, or course of business that operates as a fraud upon any person in connection with the purchase or sale of any mortgage loan; or
   (c) To obtain property by fraud, willful misrepresentation of a future act, or false promise.
3. In any matter within the jurisdiction of the office, to knowingly and willfully falsify, conceal, or cover up by a trick, scheme, or device a material fact, make any false or fraudulent statement or representation, or make or use any false writing or document, knowing the same to contain any false or fraudulent statement or entry
4. To violate s. 655.922(2), subject to ss. 494.001-494.0077
5. To fail to report to the office the failure to meet the net worth requirements within 48 hours after the person's knowledge of such failure or within 48 hours after the person should have known of such failure
6. To pay a fee or commission in any mortgage loan transaction to any person or entity other than a mortgage brokerage business, mortgage lender, or correspondent mortgage lender, operating under an active license, or a person exempt from licensure under this chapter
7. To record a mortgage brokerage agreement or any other document, not rendered by a court of competent jurisdiction, which purports to enforce the terms of the mortgage brokerage agreement
8. To use the name or logo of a financial institution or its affiliates or subsidiaries when marketing or soliciting existing or prospective customers without the written consent of the financial institution and in a manner that would lead a reasonable person to believe that the material or solicitation originated from, was endorsed by, or is related to or the responsibility of the financial institution or its affiliates or subsidiaries

Prohibited Advertising

Licensees may not advertise that they can provide a loan applicant with unqualified access to credit without disclosing any factors that might limit the lender's willingness to extend credit. Typical limitations that might affect the application include the size of the down payment required, that a higher interest rate or points could be required, or that the lender may restrict the principal amount of the loan.

Licensees must also make certain that advertisements state that a particular rate for a loan may change or be unavailable at time of closing, and they must avoid advertising loans unless such loans are available to a reasonable number of qualified applicants. Advertising under a false name is also prohibited.

Mortgage brokers, mortgage brokerage businesses, lenders, and correspondent lenders are required to keep samples of their advertisements for a period of two years after the date of publication or broadcast of the advertisement.

Mortgage Fraud

F.S. 817.545 states the penalties for fraud related to mortgage lending. According to the statute, the term **mortgage lending process** means the process through which a person seeks or obtains a residential mortgage loan, including, but not limited to, the solicitation, application or origination, negotiation of terms, third-party provider services, underwriting, signing and closing, and funding of the loan. Some of the documents involved in the mortgage lending process include mortgages, deeds, surveys, inspection reports, Uniform Residential Loan Applications, or other loan applications; appraisal reports; HUD-1 settlement statements; W-2 forms, verifications of income and employment, credit reports, bank statements, tax returns, and payroll stubs; and any required disclosures.

A person has committed **mortgage fraud** if, with the intent to defraud, he or she knowingly

a. makes, uses, or facilitates any misstatement, misrepresentation, or omission during the mortgage lending process that will be relied on by a mortgage lender, borrower, or any other person or entity involved in the mortgage lending process;
b. receives any proceeds or any other funds in connection with the mortgage lending process that the person knew resulted from such misstatements, misrepresentations, or omissions; or
c. files or causes to be filed with the clerk of the circuit court for any county of this state a document related to the mortgage lending process that contains a misstatement, misrepresentation, or omission.

Mortgage fraud is a felony of the third degree.

KEY POINT REVIEW

- A *mortgage lender* makes, services, or sells a mortgage loan. A *correspondent lender* makes mortgage loans but cannot service the loan for more than four months after the loan was made or acquired.
- Licensure as a mortgage lender requires a net worth of $250,000; licensure as a correspondent mortgage lender requires a net worth of $25,000. These net worth amounts must be continuously maintained.
- The following institutions are exempt from licensure as a mortgage lender or correspondent lender: banks; bank holding companies; trust companies; savings associations; credit unions; insurance companies licensed in Florida; persons holding fiduciary responsibility and appointed by a court; a bank holding company subsidiary or wholly owned savings association approved by HUD, the VA, GNMA, Fannie Mae, or Freddie Mac; holders of purchase-money mortgages; lien holders; government agencies; consumer finance companies licensed before October 1, 1991; private investors; and persons who act as agents for government agencies servicing mortgage loans.
- A *principal representative* manages the business operations of a mortgage lender or correspondent lender and must hold a mortgage broker license but does not need experience in the mortgage industry.
- Licenses for lender and correspondent lender are renewed for two-year periods.
- Lenders and correspondent lenders must stop accepting loan applications immediately if their net worth falls below the required levels, and they have 48 hours to notify the DFS.
- Lenders and correspondent lenders must continuously maintain a surety bond of $10,000 issued by a company authorized to do business in Florida.
- Licensees who service mortgage loans must maintain a segregated set of records for accounts serviced by the licensee. An annual audit of the financial records of all loan servicing is required.
- All records relating to the mortgage business must be kept at a reasonable and convenient location in Florida and must be available for review three years from the date of original entry. If records are not held at the principal place of business, a letter from the DFS authorizing the alternative location must be kept on file.
- Lenders must make certain disclosures to loan applicants, including the person within the firm to whom the applicant can address questions.
- Lenders must promptly endorse all checks or negotiable instruments jointly payable to the lender and the insured.
- Disputes can be resolved using litigation or binding arbitration.
- The *lock-in agreement* is a promise by the lender that the mortgage loan will carry a specific rate. The lock-in agreement carries several required disclosures, and if borrowers rescind the agreement prior to being signed by the lender, the lender must refund the lock-in fee.
- The DFS can investigate any person suspected of violating the laws related to mortgage lending with or without a formal complaint. If the DFS believes a licensee has

violated or is about to violate the law, the DFS may ask the court for an injunction to stop the licensee from acting.

- A *conflict of interest* occurs when a licensee or a licensee's relative or a holding company is involved in providing additional products or services to the borrower, or the licensee is an officer in the firm that provides additional products or services.
- Advertising by licensees must disclose any factors that might affect the applicant's ability to qualify for a loan. Samples of advertising must be kept for two years.
- *Mortgage fraud* occurs when misstatements, misrepresentations, or omissions are relied on by anyone involved in the mortgage lending process; when a person receives any proceeds from such misstatements, misrepresentations, or omissions; or when a person files a mortgage document that contains misstatements, misrepresentations, or omissions.

REVIEW QUESTIONS

1. A company doing business as a correspondent lender
   a. has the same rights, responsibilities, and requirements as a mortgage lender.
   b. cannot service loans until the loans have been sold on the secondary market.
   c. can service loans for up to four months.
   d. is a subsidiary of a mortgage lender and works under the supervision of that lender.

2. Stephen wants to start a mortgage lending business. Stephen's business must have a net worth of at least
   a. $25,000.
   b. $250,000.
   c. $1 million.
   d. $7.5 million.

3. Cathy filed a complaint against her mortgage lender for overcharging her on a loan, but agreed to arbitrate the dispute. The results of Cathy's arbitration will be
   a. binding.
   b. negotiable.
   c. legally challengeable.
   d. not binding.

4. When a loan is closed, the lender must keep the records
   a. within the county where the transaction occurred.
   b. at the main office of the lending business.
   c. at the DFS.
   d. at the principal office or at a site approved by the DFS.

5. The person who accepts a position as a principal representative will
   a. manage the business operations of lenders.
   b. be exempt from licensure requirements while serving as the principal representative.
   c. have the legal right to keep all lock-in fees paid by borrowers even if loans cannot be sold on the secondary market.
   d. be required to avoid ownership of any percentage of the firm he or she works for.

6. The principal representative of Palm Tree Mortgage has just learned that the company's net worth has dropped below legal requirements. Palm Tree
   a. must stop taking loan applications.
   b. may continue to take applications if the company notifies the DFS immediately.
   c. is out of business.
   d. employees will have their licenses cancelled by the DFS automatically.

7. Lenders and correspondent lenders are required to keep surety bonds of
   a. $25,000.
   b. $250,000.
   c. $7.5 million.
   d. $10,000.

8. ABC mortgage lenders and XYZ correspondent lenders want to open separate mortgage brokerage businesses. ABC and XYZ
   a. are legally prohibited from acting as mortgage brokerage businesses.
   b. will have a special set of legal requirements if they open mortgage brokerage businesses.
   c. can act as mortgage brokerage businesses if they follow the mortgage brokerage business requirements.
   d. automatically acquire the right to open a mortgage brokerage business as part of licensure as a mortgage lender or correspondent lender.

9. Servicing loans for a period of six months can be done by a
   a. correspondent lender only.
   b. mortgage lender only.
   c. mortgage brokerage business only.
   d. lender or correspondent lender but not by a mortgage brokerage business.

10. The DFS suspects that mortgage broker Andrea Wilson may be guilty of illegal acts. The DFS can investigate Wilson
    a. only if there is a formal complaint against her.
    b. but it does not have the authority to investigate unlicensed individuals.
    c. without a formal complaint being filed.
    d. because she is a mortgage broker rather than a lender or correspondent lender.

11. A licensee who receives a subpoena duces tecum
    a. has violated the sections of F.S. 494 listing prohibited practices.
    b. is exempt from prosecution in exchange for his or her testimony.
    c. will be required to appear and produce all records regarding a transaction.
    d. will be tried in an appellate court.

12. According to F.S. 494, a licensee who has been found guilty of a pattern of misconduct has
    a. violated any law related to mortgage brokering or lending.
    b. violated F.S. 494 three times in one year.
    c. violated the mortgage lending law three times in a three-year period.
    d. a total of three violations within the licensee's renewal period.

13. The owner of Automatic Mortgages always refers borrowers to Semi-Automatic Appraisals, owned by his brother. This situation
    a. will result in an automatic cease and desist order if the DFS learns of the referral.
    b. will result in both owners having their business licenses revoked.
    c. is acceptable to the DFS so long as the owner of Semi-Automatic holds a license as well.
    d. requires a specific disclosure form to be provided to the borrower.

14. People's Mortgages, a licensed mortgage lender, discovered on Tuesday at 10 AM that it cannot meet the net worth requirements. When must this information be reported to the DFS?
    a. By the close of business Tuesday
    b. Within one week of the discovery
    c. By 10 AM Wednesday
    d. By 10 AM Thursday

15. An advertisement for a mortgage company states that mortgage rates may change at time of closing. Advertising that rates may differ at closing is considered
    a. an illegal practice.
    b. a legal act.
    c. unethical unless the rates actually do change.
    d. bait and switch advertising.

16. Which is NOT considered a relative under F.S. 494?
    a. Brother-in-law
    b. Daughter-in-law
    c. Cousin
    d. All are considered relatives.

17. Lender Larry told Mr. Bigelow which of his loan application fees were refundable, about how many days it would take to get a commitment, and whom to contact if he had questions about his application. The next day, Mr. Bigelow asked for his fee to be refunded. Larry
    a. is not required to refund the fee because he informed Mr. Bigelow of the conditions for a refund.
    b. must refund because borrowers are entitled to a refund under any circumstances.
    c. can appeal this matter to arbitration.
    d. must refund because the disclosure was verbal, not written.

18. A person who violates F.S. 494 will be charged with a felony of the first degree if the violation involved more than
    a. $50,000 and five victims.
    b. $100,000.
    c. $50,000 or five victims.
    d. $100,000 and five victims.

19. Mrs. Hogan has received a lock-in agreement from Odyssey Mortgages that is unsigned. Under F.S. 494, this agreement is
    a. legal and binding.
    b. illegal.
    c. not effective.
    d. assignable should Mrs. Hogan choose that option.

20. Veronica told a lender that Mr. Custer was expecting a large inheritance very soon and should have no trouble repaying a mortgage loan of $325,000. Later, Mr. Custer told Veronica he couldn't be sure he was going to receive the inheritance. Under Florida law
    a. Veronica is not responsible for her comment because Mr. Custer's inheritance will not be reflected in his loan application.
    b. if Mr. Custer does not include the possible inheritance on his loan application, he can be accused of committing an omission.
    c. Veronica may have committed mortgage fraud because she may have made a misrepresentation.
    d. Veronica should report Mr. Custer to the DFS.

21. Victor has been enjoined by the court from leaving the jurisdiction where he is being prosecuted for an illegal act. In order to do this, the court issued a
    a. subpoena.
    b. writ of habeas corpus.
    c. subpoena duces tecum.
    d. writ of ne exeat.

22. Mr. Seller sold his house to Mr. Buyer for $275,500 and agreed to hold a second mortgage for $135,000. Under F.S. 494, Mr. Seller is
    a. required to hold a mortgage lender's license because of the size of the loan.
    b. required to hold a mortgage lender's license because he is dealing in second mortgages.
    c. not required to hold a mortgage lender's license because he is dealing in second mortgages only.
    d. exempt from licensure.

23. The fee for renewing a correspondent lender license is
    a. $575.
    b. $475.
    c. $423.
    d. $325.

24. Under what circumstances may an unlicensed person employed by a lender or correspondent lender receive a commission in a mortgage loan transaction?
    a. If the unlicensed person is not a Florida resident
    b. If the unlicensed person has applied for licensure
    c. If the unlicensed person provides services that are necessary for all participants to bring the transaction to a successful conclusion
    d. Under no circumstances

25. The DFS has notified Superior Mortgage that the DFS wants to audit Superior's files. Superior's files must be ready for review within
    a. 24 hours.
    b. three business days.
    c. one week.
    d. seven business days.

26. In the 1970s, Lucille Larson served one year in prison for drug-related offenses. In 2008, she applied for licensure as a mortgage brokerage business. Lucille's application
    a. will probably be denied.
    b. may be granted on a temporary basis.
    c. will probably be approved.
    d. may be approved with certain restrictions.

CHAPTER 4

FEDERAL LAWS REGULATING MORTGAGE LENDING AND THE FLORIDA FAIR LENDING ACT

LEARNING OBJECTIVES

After finishing chapter 4, you should be able to understand and explain the

1. Real Estate Settlement Procedures Act;
2. Truth-in-Lending Act;
3. Fair Credit Reporting Act;
4. Equal Credit Opportunity Act;
5. Home Mortgage Disclosure Act;
6. Home Ownership and Equity Protection Act;
7. National Flood Insurance Act;
8. Homeowners Protection Act of 1998;
9. Fair and Accurate Credit Transactions Act;
10. USA Patriot Act; and
11. Florida Fair Lending Act.

KEY TERMS

adverse action
annual percentage rate (APR)
balloon payment
bridge loan
Equal Credit Opportunity Act (ECOA)
escrow
Fair and Accurate Credit Transactions Act (FACT Act)
Fair Credit Reporting Act (FCRA)
flood certification fee
Florida Fair Lending Act
high-cost home loan
Home Mortgage Disclosure Act (HMDA)
Home Ownership and Equity Protection Act (HOEPA)
Homeowners Protection Act of 1998
loan-to-value ratio (LTV)
National Flood Insurance Act (NFIA)
negative amortization
private mortgage insurance (PMI)
Real Estate Settlement Procedures Act (RESPA)
Regulation B
Regulation X
Regulation Z
right of rescission
subprime loans
triggering term
Truth-in-Lending Act
Uniform Settlement Statement (HUD-1)
USA Patriot Act

INTRODUCTION

For most people, buying or selling a home is the largest financial transaction they will make in their lifetime. In addition to the buyer and seller, others who have an interest in the financial aspects of a real estate transaction include real estate sales associates and brokers, mortgage brokers, bankers and lenders, closing agents, loan servicers, and local and state taxing authorities. Because of the large amount of money and number of individuals and organizations involved in a real estate transaction—as well as the complexity of the transaction—federal and state legislators have passed many different laws designed to protect all parties in buying, selling, and financing real property.

All mortgage professionals need to be familiar with the laws that govern mortgage transactions, a summary of which appears in Figure 4.1.

REAL ESTATE SETTLEMENT PROCEDURES ACT

The **Real Estate Settlement Procedures Act (RESPA)**, passed in 1974, requires that lenders inform buyers of any charges they will be expected to pay at closing. RESPA, which is also known as **Regulation X**, covers loans on residential property, including loans to purchase property or to refinance, as well as construction loans. RESPA is enforced by the Department of Housing and Urban Development (HUD) and applies to all federally related mortgage loans, which include loans made by banks, savings associations, the Federal Housing Administration (FHA), the Department of Veterans Affairs (VA), or loans intended to be sold on the secondary market. RESPA does not apply to commercial loans, loans on 25 or more acres, business loans, vacant land, private sources of funding, and bona fide secondary market transactions.

According to RESPA, lenders must provide borrowers with a *good faith estimate of closing costs* within three business days of receiving a loan application, not counting the date the application is signed. The lender makes the estimate based on current loan rates and past closings. Typical items on the good faith estimate include discount points, origination fee, taxes on the transaction, prepaid interest, recording fees, and other charges.

FIGURE 4.1 ■ Summary of Major Mortgage Legislation

Year	Act	Description
1968	Truth-in-Lending Act	Requires lenders to disclose the annual percentage rate (APR) and all costs associated with a loan
1968	Fair Credit Reporting Act	Regulates what credit reporting agencies can do with information about consumers
1968	National Flood Insurance Act	Created a government-subsidized insurance program for property in flood hazard areas
1974	Real Estate Settlement Procedures Act	Requires that lenders provide a good faith estimate (GFE) to inform buyers of charges they will be expected to pay at closing
1974	Equal Credit Opportunity Act	Requires that lenders extend credit to individuals fairly
1976	Home Mortgage Disclosure Act	Requires financial institutions to disclose how community housing credit needs are being met
1994	Homeownership and Equity Protection Act	Protects consumers from unfair lending practices on subprime loans
1998	Homeowners Protection Act	Allows homeowners to cancel private mortgage insurance when mortgage balance reaches 80 percent of property's original value
2002	Florida Fair Lending Act	Prohibits abusive lending practices
2003	Fair and Accurate Credit Transactions Act	Requires lenders to make disclosures about credit history to borrowers
2004	USA Patriot Act (Section 326)	Requires mortgage lenders to collect identifying information about loan applicants
2008	American Housing Rescue and Foreclosure Prevention Act of 2008	Offers a "rescue refinancing" package; tax credit for first time homebuyers; Fannie Mae/Freddie Mac reforms; and loan counseling

RESPA requires lenders to use the **Uniform Settlement Statement (HUD-1)** form at closing. The HUD-1 form (discussed in detail in chapter 9) discloses all the details associated with a particular transaction. The lender completes the HUD-1 form, and if the borrower so requests, the closing agent must provide the settlement statement for the borrower to review one business day before closing. However, if the transaction has no closing costs to the buyer or no actual closing costs were disclosed to the borrower at the time of application, use of the HUD-1 settlement statement is not required under RESPA. The lender must keep a copy of the HUD-1 form for two years unless the lender sells the loan or gives up servicing.

RESPA also prohibits kickbacks or fees, particularly in cases where the actual service was not performed. Lenders can, however, pay employees or their agents for services performed as part of a real estate or loan transaction such as title searches, title insurance, attorney real estate services, document preparation, surveys, credit reports, appraisals, and so forth. For example, it is legal for a lender to pay a mortgage broker a fee for his or her services. The lender must disclose any business relationship between the lender and any providers of settlement services unless the borrower is not paying any of the closing costs. Also, RESPA prohibits sellers from making the sale of the property conditional upon the buyer's use of a title company chosen by the seller.

RESPA also has rules regarding referrals between affiliated companies. Affiliated companies may have a *controlled business arrangement*, which Congress defined as an arrangement:

...in which (A) a person who is in a position to refer business incident to or a part of a real estate settlement service involving a federally related mortgage loan, or an associate of such person, has either an affiliate relationship with or a direct or beneficial ownership interest of more than 1 percent in a provider of settlement services; and (B) either of such persons directly or indirectly refers such business to that provider or affirmatively influences the selection of that provider.

Further, RESPA requires lenders to notify borrowers of escrow requirements. In the typical mortgage lending situation, the lender will hold a borrower's monthly tax and insurance payments in a special **escrow** account until due. In addition to requiring the lender to notify the borrower of escrow requirements at both the beginning and end of the tax year, RESPA also limits the amount a lender may hold in the escrow account to 12 months plus 2 months, or 14 months maximum. Disbursements from the account must be paid promptly, and when an escrow account has a surplus over $50, the lender must return the surplus to the borrower in a timely fashion.

Finally, lenders must also provide borrowers with a notice of *transfer of servicing disclosure* stating that their loan may be sold or transferred to another servicer. They are also required to provide loan applicants with a copy of the booklet *Settlement Costs and You* within three business days of receiving a loan application.

RESPA also mandates that a borrower be notified no fewer than 15 days prior to transfer, if loan servicing is being transferred, and that the new servicer notify the borrower within 60 days after the effective transfer date. Loan payments received by the previous servicer may not be considered late by the new servicer.

TRUTH-IN-LENDING ACT

In 1968, Congress passed legislation designed to help consumers understand credit costs before making purchases. Title I of the Consumer Credit Protection Act is the **Truth-in-Lending Act**. This act is implemented by Federal Reserve **Regulation Z**, which requires lenders to disclose to a borrower the annual percentage rate—which, if the loan has a finance charge, will be greater than the interest rate on the note—of all interest and finance charges within three business days of accepting a consumer's loan application. Regulation Z applies to consumer loans of $25,000 or less or any loan that is secured by residential property or a vacant lot; the law does not apply to business or agricultural loans. Although Regulation Z requires the lender to disclose loan terms, it does not regulate the interest rate charged by the lender. Under Regulation Z, every lender must also provide customers with a copy of the *Consumer Handbook on Adjustable-Rate Mortgages* (CHARM) or a suitable substitute to every borrower who applies for an adjustable-rate mortgage.

According to Regulation Z, lenders must inform applicants of any fees, service charges, discount points, or interest charges associated with a loan. In the case of a loan on a residence, the lender is required to disclose the **annual percentage rate (APR),** which is considered to be the true annual cost of borrowing funds. The APR may include interest, mortgage insurance premiums, loan origination fees, discount points, and other costs.

Lenders are not required to include fees for appraisals, titles, credit reports, surveys, and other closing expenses as part of the disclosure. Figure 4.2 is a Truth-in-Lending (TIL) disclosure statement.

FIGURE 4.2 ■ Truth-in-Lending Disclosure Statement

Federal Truth-In-Lending Disclosure Statement

Lender/Broker: Loan Number: Date Prepared:

Borrower(s): Property Address:

☐ Initial Disclosure estimated at time of application ☐ Final Disclosure based on contract terms

ANNUAL PERCENTAGE RATE	FINANCE CHARGE	Amount Financed	Total of Payments
The cost of your credit as a yearly rate.	The dollar amount the credit will cost you assuming the annual percentage rate does not change.	The amount of credit provided to you or on your behalf as of loan closing.	The amount you will have paid after you have made all payments as scheduled assuming the annual percentage rate does not change.
%	$	$	$

Your Payment Schedule Will Be:

Number of Payments	* Amount of Payments	Monthly Payments Are Due Beginning	Number of Payments	* Amount of Payments	Monthly Payments Are Due Beginning

* Includes mortgage insurance premiums, excludes taxes, hazard insurance and flood insurance.

☐ **Demand Feature:** This loan transaction has a demand feature.

☐ **Required Deposit:** The annual percentage rate does not take into account your required deposit.

☐ **Variable Rate Feature:** Your loan contains a Variable Rate Feature. Disclosures about the Variable Rate Feature have been provided to you separately.

Security Interest: You are giving security interest in:

☐ the goods or property being purchased. ☐ real property you already own.

Filing or Recording Fees: $

Late Charge: If a payment is more than days late, you will be charged $ / %

Prepayment: If you pay off your loan early, you

☐ may ☐ will not have to pay a penalty.

☐ may ☐ will not be entitled to a refund of part of the finance charge.

Insurance: Credit life insurance and credit disability insurance are not required to obtain credit, and will not be provided unless you sign and agree to pay the additional cost.

Type	Premium	Signature	
Credit Life		I want credit life insurance.	Signature:
Credit Disability		I want credit disability insurance.	Signature:
Credit Life and Disability		I want credit life and disability insurance.	Signature:

This loan transaction requires the following insurance:

☐ Hazard Insurance ☐ Flood Insurance ☐ Credit Insurance ☐ Credit Life Insurance ☐ MMI ☐ PMI

Borrower(s) may obtain hazard and flood insurance through any person of his/her choice, provided said carrier meets the requirements of the Lender. If Borrower desires Property Insurance to be obtained through the Lender's designated agency, the cost will be set forth in a separate insurance statement furnished by the Lender.

☐ If you purchase insurance from creditor, you will pay $ for a one-year term.

Assumption: Someone buying your house:

☐ may ☐ may, subject to conditions, ☐ may not assume the remainder of your loan on the original terms.

See your contract documents for additional information regarding nonpayment, default, right to accelerate the maturity of the obligation, prepayment rebates and penalties, and the Lender's policy regarding assumption of the obligation.

☐ All dates and numerical disclosures except late payment disclosures are estimates. means an estimate.

"The undersigned hereby acknowledge receiving and reading a completed copy of this disclosure along with copies of the documents provided. The delivery and signing of this disclosure does not constitute an obligation on the part of the lender to make, or the Borrower(s) to accept, the loan as identified."

Read, acknowledged and accepted this day of . By:

Borrower Date Co-borrower Date

REGZ – TIL 07/05 ~ Encompass™ from Ellie Mae ~ www.elliemae.com

Source: Form provided by Ellie Mae, Inc.

When an advertisement for a loan offers specific financial information known as a **triggering term**—such as loan interest rate, down payment, number of payments, payment amount, or finance charge—Regulation Z requires the advertisement to disclose all seven of the following:

1. Purchase price
2. Amount financed
3. Down payment
4. Monthly payment
5. Terms of repayment
6. Annual percentage rate
7. Deferred payment price

When ads offer general, rather than specific, information, such as "nothing down" or "credit available on-site," however, Regulation Z is not triggered and the lender need not disclose details of the loan in the advertisement.

The Truth-in-Lending Act also offers consumers the **right of rescission**, which means the consumer has three business days from closing to loan funding to cancel a loan transaction. This right does not apply to a mortgage for the purchase of residential property, trust deed loans, or purchase money mortgages, but it can be applied to construction loans, second mortgages, home equity lines of credit, and other types of financing on owner-occupied residential properties only.

When the annual percentage rate on a loan covered by the Truth-in-Lending Act changes by 0.125 percent or more, a new TIL disclosure must be issued no later than the closing. If anything other than the APR changes, a new TIL statement does not need to be reissued.

Violation of Regulation Z can result in heavy fines—$10,000 per day of noncompliance and up to $10,000 for a deceptive practice. The Truth-in-Lending Act is enforced by the Federal Trade Commission (FTC).

FAIR CREDIT REPORTING ACT

As part of the loan application process, lenders require potential borrowers to supply a significant amount of personal information regarding their current income and financial history. When a buyer applies for a mortgage loan, either the mortgage broker or lender will contact a credit bureau and request a credit report on the buyer. Lenders consider credit history to be a critical part of evaluating a borrower's creditworthiness.

The **Fair Credit Reporting Act (FCRA)** of 1968 regulates what credit reporting agencies may do with information about individuals. The FCRA also specifies what kind of information can be maintained in an individual's credit file. For example, bankruptcies that are over ten years old cannot be disclosed on the credit report, nor can negative financial information that is more than seven years old unless it relates to a loan of $150,000 or more. The FCRA requires that lenders make certain the information they maintain is accurate and also gives consumers the right to correct errors on their credit report. Finally, credit reports cannot be obtained without the written permission of the borrower.

When a lender denies a loan on the basis of an applicant's credit history—a practice known as **adverse action**—the FCRA requires the lender to notify the applicant of the denial and to provide the name, address, and telephone number of the credit reporting agency that provided the lender with information. If requested, the credit agency must provide the applicant with a free copy of his or her credit report. Under the FCRA, an individual may challenge the contents of the report or provide additional clarifying information.

The Federal Trade Commission (FTC) has responsibility for enforcing the FCRA.

EQUAL CREDIT OPPORTUNITY ACT

The **Equal Credit Opportunity Act (ECOA**, also known as **Regulation B**) was passed in 1974 with the intention of making certain that firms that extend credit to consumers do so fairly. Under the provisions of the ECOA, lenders may not discriminate based on any of the following:

- Race
- Color
- Religion
- National origin
- Sex
- Marital status
- Age
- Public assistance income
- Exercised rights under the Consumer Credit Protection Act

The ECOA also constrains lenders from asking certain questions related to family and marital status. Specifically, lenders cannot ask about family planning or if an applicant receives alimony or child support unless the applicant wants the lender to consider this income in evaluating creditworthiness. Furthermore, under the ECOA, lenders cannot require applicants to disclose their race, national origin, or sex unless the applicants choose to do so. However, the person who takes the loan application on behalf of the lender is required to note the race and sex of the applicant based on the interviewer's observation. This information is not used in evaluating creditworthiness, but only as part of the federal government's monitoring process.

Although some areas of the country prohibit discrimination based on disability status or sexual orientation, the ECOA does not specifically address these issues. Nonetheless, the provisions of the ECOA apply not only to applications, but to all aspects of the mortgage lending transaction, including advertising, underwriting, providing credit information, and record keeping. ECOA also gives consumers the right to a copy of their appraisal report if paid for and requested.

Finally, when a lender rejects an application, the ECOA requires the lender or mortgage broker to notify the applicant within 30 days of the reason for the rejection and within 90 days if the broker has not heard back from the borrower once the lender submits a counteroffer.

HOME MORTGAGE DISCLOSURE ACT

In 1976, Congress passed the **Home Mortgage Disclosure Act (HMDA)**, which allows regulators to determine if the housing needs of the community are being met by lenders. Under the HMDA, lenders must provide their supervisory body with information on loans made and purchased, as well as the race, gender, and income of applicants, and the geographic areas where the lenders made loans.

In 1989, Congress passed the Financial Institutions Reform, Recovery, and Enforcement Act, known as FIRREA. The act created the Office of Thrift Supervision to regulate federal savings associations, as well as the Federal Housing Finance Board to oversee 12 regional Federal Housing Finance Boards. Under the FIRREA, the provisions of the HMDA, which initially governed transactions by government agencies, were extended to independent—that is, nongovernmental—lenders.

HOME OWNERSHIP AND EQUITY PROTECTION ACT

The **Home Ownership and Equity Protection Act (HOEPA)** was passed by Congress in 1994 to protect consumers from unfair lending practices on subprime loans. In most cases, **subprime loans** involve higher risk to the lender because of the applicant's problems with mortgage credit, consumer credit, foreclosure, or other credit-related issues. Because of the perceived risk in making a subprime loan, lenders typically charge additional percentage points above their interest rate on lower-risk loans.

The HOEPA applies only to refinancing and closed-end home equity loans, and not to first mortgages on residences. Under the provisions of this act, when a lender's fees are greater than $400 (indexed annually) or 8 percent of the loan amount, or an interest rate is 10 percent higher than a rate based on a Treasury security, the HOEPA requires the lender to make certain disclosures to the borrower. It also places certain restrictions on loans that require a **balloon payment**—that is, a lump sum payment—in less than five years, as well as loans where the monthly payment is insufficient to cover the monthly interest owed, a practice known as **negative amortization.**

NATIONAL FLOOD INSURANCE ACT

In 1968, Congress passed the **National Flood Insurance Act (NFIA,** or NFIP for National Flood Insurance Plan), which created an insurance program through which homebuyers could purchase insurance from the federal government against damage from floods in communities that participate in the National Flood Insurance Program through enforcement of flood plain management ordinances. Flood hazard areas are defined by having a 1 percent probability of a flood in any given year or by the likelihood of a flood every 100 years. Flood zones are identified by the Federal Emergency Management Agency (FEMA).

The lender has responsibility for determining if a property lies within a flood hazard area. If the property is within the hazard area, lenders usually require borrowers to acquire special flood insurance before they will approve an application for a mortgage loan. According to Fannie Mae, the minimum amount of insurance for residential properties is the lowest of

- 100 percent of the replacement cost of the building;
- the maximum insurance available under the NFIP ($250,000 on the dwelling and $100,000 on the contents); or
- the unpaid principal balance of the mortgage.

Assessing if a property lies in a flood zone usually requires a **flood certification fee,** which can be paid as part of the closing costs on a transaction.

HOMEOWNERS PROTECTION ACT OF 1998

When a buyer's down payment on a property is less than 20 percent of the total purchase price, conventional lenders typically rely on **private mortgage insurance (PMI)** to protect against losses in case a borrower defaults on the loan. PMI insures the portion of a mortgage loan that exceeds 80 percent of a property's value and is required by most lenders.

Under the provisions of the **Homeowners Protection Act of 1998,** homeowners can cancel their PMI policy when the mortgage balance reaches 80 percent of the property's original value if payments are current. The law also requires lenders to cancel PMI automatically when the mortgage balance is reduced to 78 percent or less of the original value of the property.

To determine if PMI is no longer needed, lenders calculate the **loan-to-value ratio (LTV)** on the insured property. To find this ratio, the balance of the loan is divided by either the sale price or appraised value of the property at the time of purchase. Under this law, calculation of the LTV does not consider appreciation of a property's value when determining whether an owner must continue to pay PMI.

EXAMPLE: A buyer wants to purchase a home at $225,000 with a down payment of $40,000. What is the loan-to-value ratio?

Loan-to-value ratio, or LTV, is determined by dividing the loan amount ($225,000 purchase price ÷ $40,000 down payment = $185,000 loan amount) by the total purchase price. This results in an LTV of 82 percent ($185,000 ÷ $225,000 = 0.82), with the down payment accounting for 18 percent of the purchase price. Because the down payment is less than 20 percent of the purchase price, the lender will ask the buyer to buy mortgage insurance.

If, over time, the buyer makes sufficient payments so that the equity in the home reaches 20 percent and the loan balance is $148,000, the buyer can request that the mortgage insurance be canceled. If the LTV reaches 78 percent—$124,800—under the terms of the Homeowners Protection Act, the lender must automatically cancel the mortgage insurance.

Loan-to-value ratios are discussed more fully in chapter 11.

FAIR AND ACCURATE CREDIT TRANSACTIONS ACT (FACT ACT)

In 2003, Congress passed the **Fair and Accurate Credit Transactions Act,** which requires mortgage lenders to make certain disclosures regarding a borrower's credit history.

Under the FACT Act, lenders must disclose to the borrower his or her credit score, along with the range of scores possible, as well as any areas of their credit history that adversely affect their overall credit score. Lenders must also provide the name, address, and telephone number of the credit reporting agency that provided the credit report.

The FACT Act also gives consumers the right to their credit report free of charge every year in order to check for inaccuracies or unauthorized activity that might indicate identity theft. In addition, the act requires that the lender provide borrowers with the "National Credit Score Disclosure/Notice to the Home Loan Applicant."

USA PATRIOT ACT

As of January 1, 2004, Section 326 of the **USA Patriot Act** requires mortgage lenders to collect certain information from borrowers. This information includes name, date of birth, and address. In addition, applicants for mortgage loans must provide a taxpayer identification number or alien identification card that includes a photograph. Finally, borrowers must now disclose their ethnicity.

FLORIDA FAIR LENDING ACT

The **Florida Fair Lending Act** was passed in 2002 as a response to incidents of abusive mortgage lending. One of the most common forms of abusive lending is making loans that are equity-based rather than income-based. This occurs when a lender counts on the equity in a home to repay a loan rather than the loan being paid by the borrower's income. In these cases, a lender encourages a borrower to refinance, which generates points and fees that provide immediate income to the mortgage broker or loan originator. When homeowners refinance with high points and additional fees, they lose some of the equity in their home, and they can eventually be at risk for foreclosure. Violation of RESPA or the federal Truth-in-Lending Act is also a violation of the Florida Fair Lending Act.

Some of the important terms used in the Florida Fair Lending Act are defined on the following page.

Prohibited Acts

The Florida Fair Lending Act was passed by the Florida legislature to prevent certain practices in the mortgage lending industry. Some of the acts prohibited by the Florida Fair Lending Act include the following:

- **Prepayment penalties:** A high-cost home loan may not require a borrower to pay a prepayment penalty for paying all or part of the loan before the date payment is due except under certain conditions.
- **Default interest rate:** A high-cost home loan may not provide for a higher interest rate after default on the loan unless the higher rate is part of a variable rate loan.
- **Balloon payments:** A high-cost home loan that has a term of less than ten years cannot contain terms under which the total amount of the regular periodic payments would not fully pay the outstanding principal balance. This prohibition does not apply if the borrower has seasonal income or the loan is a bridge loan.
- **Negative amortization:** A high-cost home loan may not contain terms under which the amount of the outstanding principal will increase at any time over the course of the loan because payments do not cover the full amount of interest due.

THE FLORIDA FAIR LENDING ACT

	Definitions
affiliate	Any company that controls, is controlled by, or is in common control with another company as set forth in 12 U.S.C. ss. 1841 et seq. and the regulations adopted thereunder
annual percentage rate	The annual percentage rate for the loan calculated according to the provisions of 15 U.S.C.s, 1606 and the regulations adopted thereunder by the Federal Reserve Board
borrower	Any natural person obligated to repay a loan, including, but not limited to, a coborrower, cosigner, or guarantor
bridge loan	A loan with a maturity of less than 18 months that requires only the payment of interest until such time as the entire unpaid balance is due and payable and collateralized by the present home for the purpose of buying a new home. Bridge loans are secured by a currently owned property and are used to buy a new property. Applicants for a bridge loan must demonstrate they can meet all financial obligations on both properties.
department	The Department of Financial Services
high-cost home loan	A home loan as defined in 15 U.S.C. s. 1602 (aa) and regulations adopted thereunder—that is, a loan with an interest rate that is more than 10 percentage points above the yield on Treasury securities or points and fees that exceed the greater of 8 percent of the loan amount or $400
lender	Any person who makes a high-cost home loan or acts as a mortgage broker or lender, finance company, or retail installment seller with respect to a high-cost home loan, but shall not include any entity chartered by the United States Congress when engaging in secondary market mortgage transactions as an assignee or otherwise

- **Prepaid payments:** A high-cost home loan may not include terms under which more than two periodic payments required under the loan are consolidated and paid in advance from the loan proceeds to the borrower.
- **Extending credit without regard to the borrower's ability to pay:** Lenders may not extend loans based on a borrower's collateral without also considering the borrower's ability to repay the loan.
- **Payments by the lender to a home contractor:** Lenders may not make loan payments to a contractor directly.
- **Due-on-demand clause:** A high-cost home loan may not contain a provision that permits the lender to call or accelerate indebtedness of the borrower unless the borrower has failed to abide by the terms of the loan or committed fraud.

- **Refinancing within an 18-month period:** A lender cannot refinance any high-cost home loan to the same borrower within the first 18 months of the loan unless the refinancing has a reasonable benefit to the borrower.
- **Open-ended loans:** Open-ended loans that circumvent the provisions of the Florida Fair Lending Act are prohibited.
- **Recommendation of default:** A lender cannot recommend or encourage a borrower to default on an existing loan in connection with the closing of a high-cost home loan that refinances all or any portion of such existing loan or debt.
- **Prohibited door-to-door loans:** High-cost home loans cannot be made without a prearranged appointment between the lender and borrower.
- **Late payment fees:** Late payment fees can only be charged under the following conditions:
    - The fee is less than 5 percent of the amount of payment past due.
    - The payment is past due for 15 days or more.
    - The late payment fee cannot be charged more than once with respect to a single late payment.
- **Modification or deferral fees:** A lender may not charge a borrower any fees or other charges to modify, renew, extend, or amend a high-cost home loan or to defer any payment due under terms of the loan on a minimum of one modification, renewal, extension, or deferral per each 12 months of the length of the loan.

Disclosures. The Florida Fair Lending Act requires lenders who make high-cost home loans to make certain disclosures to the borrower. The first disclosure is a Notice to the Borrower that should be similar in wording to the following:

> *If you obtain this high-cost home loan, the lender will have a mortgage on your home. You could lose your home and any money you have put into it if you do not meet your obligations under the loan.*
>
> *Mortgage loan rates and closing costs and fees vary based on many factors, including your particular credit and financial circumstances, your employment history, the loan-to-value requested, and the type of property that will secure your loan. The loan rate and fees could also vary based on which lender or broker you select. As a borrower, you should shop around and compare loan rates and fees.*
>
> *You should also consider consulting a qualified independent credit counselor or other experienced financial advisor regarding the rates, fees, and provisions of this mortgage loan before you proceed. You should contact the United States Department of Housing and Urban Development for a list of credit counselors available in your area.*
>
> *You are not required to complete this agreement merely because you have received these disclosures or have signed a loan application.*
>
> *Borrowing for the purpose of debt consolidation can be an appropriate financial management tool. However, if you continue to incur significant new credit card charges or other debts after this high-cost home loan is closed and then experience financial difficulties, you could lose your home and any equity you have in it if you do not meet your mortgage loan obligations.*
>
> *Remember that property taxes and homeowners' insurance are your responsibility. Not all lenders provide escrow services for these payments. You should ask your lender about these services.*
>
> *Also, your payments on existing debts contribute to your credit rating. You should not accept any advice to ignore your regular payments to your existing creditors.*

A second disclosure concerns the annual percentage rate. In the case of a fixed-rate mortgage, the lender must disclose the annual percentage rate and the amount of the regular monthly payment. In the case of any other credit transaction, the lender must disclose the annual percentage rate; the amount of the regular monthly payment and the amount of any balloon payment permitted under this section; that the interest rate and monthly payment may increase; and the amount of the maximum monthly payment based on the maximum interest rate allowed pursuant to law.

Finally, all high-cost home loans must contain a notice about the Florida Fair Lending Act:

> *Notice:*
>
> *This is a mortgage subject to the provisions of the Florida Fair Lending Act. Purchasers and assignees of this mortgage could be liable for all claims and defenses with respect to the mortgage that the borrower could assert against the creditor.*

Enforcement. Violation of the Florida Fair Lending Act will result in the lender forfeiting the entire interest charged or contracted to be charged in the high-cost home loan. However, if a lender acting in good faith inadvertently overcharges a borrower and corrects the situation within 60 days, this will not count as a violation. The Department of Financial Services regulates the Florida Fair Lending Act.

KEY POINT REVIEW

- The *Real Estate Settlement Procedures Act (RESPA)* requires that a good faith estimate of closing costs be supplied to borrowers within three business days of receiving a loan application.
- Lenders must return *escrow* balances to borrowers when the surplus in the escrow account after disbursements is over $50. The maximum number of months escrow can be held is 14.
- The purpose of the *Truth-in-Lending Act* is to help consumers understand the true cost of credit before committing to a loan.
- *Regulation Z* requires lenders to disclose the annual percentage rate of all interest and finance charges within three business days of accepting a borrower's loan application. The *annual percentage rate* includes interest, mortgage brokerage fees, discount points, and other costs in obtaining credit.
- A *triggering term* in an advertisement requires the disclosure of specific financial information about the loan.
- The *right of rescission* offers consumers the right to cancel a loan transaction within three business days of the credit contract being signed by all parties *and* delivery of the right to rescind notice. This right does not apply to a new mortgage for the purchase of a primary residence.
- The *Fair Credit Reporting Act* regulates what lenders may do with credit information.
- The *Equal Credit Opportunity Act* (ECOA; also known as Regulation B) prohibits discrimination based on the following: race, color, religion, national origin, sex, marital status, age, public assistance income, and exercise of rights under the Consumer Credit Protection Act.
- Although loan applicants are not required to disclose their race, national origin, or sex if they choose not to do so, for federal monitoring purposes only, the person taking the loan application is required to note the race and sex of the applicant based on observation.
- Lenders cannot ask about income from alimony or child support unless the income will be used in qualifying for a loan.
- The *Home Mortgage Disclosure Act (HMDA)* requires lenders to collect and report demographic information on borrowers to determine if a community's financing needs are being met.
- Flood areas are defined as having at least a 1 percent probability of a flood in any given year. The lender has ultimate responsibility for determining if a property lies within a flood hazard area.
- *Private mortgage insurance* insures the portion of a mortgage loan that exceeds 80 percent of a property's value on conventional loans. Lenders are required to cancel private mortgage insurance automatically when the mortgage balance reaches 78 percent of the original value of the property.
- The *loan-to-value ratio (LTV)* on a property is determined by dividing the amount of the loan by the value of the property at the time of purchase.

- The *Fair and Accurate Credit Transactions Act* requires lenders to disclose to borrowers their credit score and identify areas of the credit history that adversely affected their credit score.
- The *USA Patriot Act* requires borrowers to disclose their name, date of birth, address, and ethnicity.
- *High-cost home loans* cannot have the following: prepayment penalties; a higher default interest rate; a balloon payment if the term is less than ten years; negative amortization; or a due-on-demand clause. Lenders cannot make payments directly to a home contractor or refinance a high-cost home loan to the same borrower within the first 18 months of the loan unless the refinancing benefits the borrower.

REVIEW QUESTIONS

1. In Florida, a licensee can be found guilty of abusive lending if the
   a. lender requires a down payment of 20 percent or more.
   b. mortgage broker charges a fee to accept a loan application.
   c. mortgage broker makes a profit on selling a loan to an investor.
   d. lender looks only to the equity in a home to repay a mortgage.

2. An ad for homes in a subdivision promises financing at 5.75 percent. The advertiser is required to state
   a. the length of the repayment period.
   b. the down payment.
   c. the purchase price.
   d. all of the above.

3. Jack has a high-cost home loan and wants to refinance at an interest rate only slightly lower than his current rate. According to Florida law, his current lender can refinance
   a. at any time.
   b. in 6 months.
   c. in 12 months.
   d. in 18 months.

4. At Southern Style Mortgage Company, all new employees are reminded that the three-business-day right of rescission does *NOT* apply to
   a. new mortgages on the purchase of primary residences.
   b. construction loans.
   c. second mortgages.
   d. home equity loans.

5. Susan submitted a loan application Friday afternoon at 4 PM. She should expect to receive a good faith estimate of closing costs
   a. 24 hours prior to closing on the property.
   b. at the time she applied for the loan.
   c. within three business days after the lender receives the application.
   d. only if she requests such information.

6. Louis Casey, Jr., received an adverse action notice regarding his loan application because of too many late payments on his credit report. Louis has never missed any of his payments, so the credit report the loan company received must concern the credit history of his father, Louis Casey, Sr. Louis Casey, Jr., has the legal right to correct information on his credit report through
   a. RESPA.
   b. HOEPA.
   c. FCRA.
   d. ECOA.

7. According to the Florida Fair Lending Act, late payment fees charged to borrowers who miss their monthly loan payment
   a. must be 5 percent or less of the past due payment.
   b. must be for payments 15 or more days late.
   c. cannot be charged more than once on a single payment.
   d. All of the above

8. Susie would like to cancel her private mortgage insurance. She can do this
   a. if the loan balance exceeds 80 percent of the value of the property.
   b. if the loan balance is 75 percent of the original loan and the lender agrees.
   c. if the loan balance is 78 percent of the original loan.
   d. unless she signed an Agreement of Noncancellation at the closing.

9. According to Regulation Z, lenders are required to
   a. provide the closing statement to the buyer one business day prior to closing.
   b. disclose the annual percentage rate.
   c. ensure that all individuals have equal access to credit.
   d. make credit reports available at no charge annually.

10. John's lender tells him he qualifies for a subprime loan. This means that John
    a. will probably pay a higher interest rate.
    b. will probably pay a lower interest rate.
    c. qualifies for financing on a large project such as a subdivision.
    d. qualifies for a loan that is not regulated by federal statute.

11. Janet bought a home from Mark. Louis did the appraisal and Gloria financed the transaction. Ultimate responsibility for determining if the property lies in a flood hazard area lies with
    a. Janet.
    b. Mark.
    c. Louis.
    d. Gloria.

12. Ajax Loan Servicers collects taxes and insurance payments for lenders. According to RESPA, Ajax must return escrowed funds to the borrower when the surplus in the escrow account exceeds
    a. $50.
    b. $100.
    c. $250.
    d. $500.

13. The Fair Credit Reporting Act
    a. requires that all persons receive equal access to credit.
    b. states what information must be provided to borrowers.
    c. requires that companies maintain accurate credit records on borrowers.
    d. prohibits questions about race, sex, and religion on loan applications.

14. An investor is looking at buying agricultural property that lies in a flood hazard area. This means that the property
    a. has been flooded five times in the past 100 years.
    b. has a 1 percent probability of a flood in any given year.
    c. has a 5 percent probability of a flood in any given year.
    d. has been designated as likely to flood by local, state, and federal officials.

15. The Home Ownership and Equity Protection Act protects consumers on what kind of loans and refinances?
    a. Residential first mortgages
    b. Business mortgages
    c. Subprime loans
    d. Consumer credit loans

16. When the mortgage broker explained the various loan options to Mr. Borrower, he mentioned one loan that had the possibility of negative amortization. This means that with regard to that particular loan
    a. the interest payments could actually go down over the life of the loan.
    b. the monthly payment might be insufficient to cover the interest owed.
    c. the mortgage would not be amortized but require a lump-sum payment at the end of the term.
    d. the lender will forgo interest payments in the first years of the loan.

17. Sharon has learned there is some negative information on her credit report that is more than seven years old. This information
    a. probably concerns coborrowers.
    b. must be related to a loan of $150,000 or more.
    c. could concern repeated late car payments.
    d. could be any of the above.

18. Under the Florida Fair Lending Act, lenders cannot make a home loan
    a. requiring a higher interest rate if the borrower defaults.
    b. that adjusts to higher rates every year.
    c. with balloon payments for a borrower with seasonal income.
    d. that charges late fees on each late payment.

19. A citizen of Argentina is applying for a loan to purchase a three-bedroom home in Palm Beach. As part of the application, the applicant will be required to disclose his ethnicity. This disclosure is required by
    a. RESPA.
    b. the Truth-in-Lending Act.
    c. the Patriot Act.
    d. the National Homeownership Equity Act.

20. The FACT Act gives consumers the right to a free credit report once a year so that the consumer can
    a. check for unauthorized activity.
    b. submit the credit report as part of the loan application package.
    c. refinance credit balances with a higher interest rate.
    d. remove any negative information about the consumer's credit history.

21. Sky High Mortgages regularly violates the Florida Fair Lending Act by overcharging borrowers on high interest loans. If the DFS discovers what Sky High is doing, the penalty for Sky High will be
    a. license cancellation.
    b. suspension of license for 30 days.
    c. forfeiture of interest collected.
    d. a fine of $1,000 per incident of overcharging.

22. Tom is selling Marie his condo at New Smyrna Beach for $235,000. Marie is making a down payment of $40,000, assuming a mortgage of $130,000, and getting a new mortgage for the balance. Tom has chosen Centurion Title to handle the closing. This situation is
    a. legal if Tom is paying for the title insurance.
    b. legal if Marie is paying all closing costs.
    c. illegal because it is an assumption that will require a second closing.
    d. illegal in any case.

23. Under what circumstances can the lender of a high-cost home loan invoke the due-on-demand clause?
    a. If the equity in the borrower's house has fallen below 10 percent
    b. If the borrower fails to abide by the terms of the high-cost home loan
    c. If the borrower accelerates payments so as to minimize the interest paid to the lender
    d. Under no circumstances

24. Jocelyn plans to buy a town house in Tampa for $219,000. She is considering making a down payment of $55,000 and financing the balance with a mortgage with a 6.5 percent interest rate. The loan-to-value ratio on this transaction will be
    a. 25 percent.
    b. 65 percent.
    c. 75 percent.
    d. 80 percent.

25. Under what circumstances will Jocelyn need PMI?
    a. If her mortgage loan amount equals 85 percent of the value of the transaction
    b. If her mortgage loan amount equals 75 percent of the value of the transaction
    c. If her mortgage loan amount equals 80 percent of the value of the transaction
    d. A mortgage lender has the right to ask for PMI on any transaction as a requirement for funding the loan.

26. Mr. Larson hasn't sold his house valued at $210,000, but he made an offer on another property valued at $375,000 and asked his bank about a bridge loan. The bank
    a. is unlikely to consider Mr. Larson's request because of RESPA requirements.
    b. will be in violation of the Florida Fair Lending Act if it makes a loan to Mr. Larson.
    c. is legally required to grant Mr. Larson's request if he has a good credit history.
    d. may consider Mr. Larson's request if he is able to make payments on both properties.

CHAPTER 5

REAL ESTATE OWNERSHIP

LEARNING OBJECTIVES

After finishing chapter 5, you should be able to

1. identify the elements of a real estate contract;
2. distinguish between lien theory states and title theory states;
3. understand deeds of trust; and
4. explain the different forms of real estate ownership.

KEY TERMS

competence of parties
consideration
contract
deed of trust
deficiency judgment
enforceable contract
estate for years
fee simple
freehold estates
joint tenancy
leasehold estates
legal form
legal purpose
lien theory
life estate
marketability of title
mutual assent
novation
right of redemption
right of survivorship
statute of frauds
subject to the mortgage
tenancy at sufferance
tenancy at will
tenancy by the entireties
tenancy in common
title
title search
title theory

INTRODUCTION

The process of finding a mortgage lender usually begins with a real estate transaction. A buyer and a seller agree on terms under which the seller will transfer his or her ownership in real property to the buyer. Under the terms of most real estate contracts, the buyer has a specified number of days to find a lender willing to finance purchase of the property. Chapter 5 looks at the aspects of real estate ownership that affect the mortgage lending process.

ELEMENTS OF A REAL ESTATE CONTRACT

A **contract** is an agreement to perform some action, and it is the basis of the relationship between both the buyer and seller of real property, as well as between a borrower and a mortgage lender, and a mortgage broker and a loan applicant.

An **enforceable contract** must meet certain legal requirements. These requirements vary from state to state, but all states require a legal real estate contract to contain certain elements, including competence of parties, mutual assent, consideration, legality of purpose, and legal form.

Competence of Parties

All parties agreeing to a contract must have *competence* to do so. **Competence of parties** means that each party must be of legal age and not suffering from any mental handicap that would impair his or her ability to make a valid contract. In other words, the parties to the contract must not be insane or underage. In some cases, being under the influence of alcohol or drugs when a contract is signed may render a party incompetent. Contracts in which one or more of the parties is not competent can be voided.

Mutual Assent

The willingness of all parties to enter into a contract is called **mutual assent,** or meeting of the minds. Mutual assent occurs through *offer and acceptance*, which refers to one party making an offer and the other party accepting that offer. As soon as one party communicates his or her acceptance of an offer, the contract is formed.

Contracts that are made under duress, menace, or undue influence are not legal. *Unconscionable contracts* are grossly unfair to one party and may be unenforceable. When an informed party creates a contract that takes advantage of another party's lack of information (such as selling a property "as is" to first-time homebuyers), the court may rule the contract unconscionable, void the contract, or strike out the section of the contract it considers unconscionable.

Legal Purpose

Contracts that do not have a **legal purpose** are not enforceable. A contract to pay a commission to an unlicensed individual for brokering a mortgage loan is illegal in Florida and would not be enforceable.

Consideration

Consideration consists of an obligation made between parties to a contract. *Good consideration* refers to a promise that cannot be measured in money. Love and affection is an example of good consideration. *Valuable consideration*, in contrast, is consideration that can be measured in monetary terms. A buyer agrees to pay a seller a certain amount of money, for example, and in return, the seller agrees to transfer title of a property to the buyer.

Legal Form

Finally, contracts for real property must have **legal form.** All states have enacted a **statute of frauds,** which requires that real estate contracts be in writing and signed to be enforceable. Sometimes oral contracts are enforceable, but written contracts usually have legal precedence over oral contracts if there are conflicts between an oral and a written contract.

To be legal, a real estate contract must have the signatures of the buyer and the seller. The requirements of a legal real estate contract can be remembered by the acronym COLIC:

C Competence of parties
O Offer and acceptance (mutual assent)
L Legality of purpose
I In writing and signed (legal form)
C Consideration

CONTRACT FOR SALE AND PURCHASE OF REAL PROPERTY

When a buyer and seller agree on terms regarding transfer of ownership in a property, they both sign a contract that describes the conditions for the sale. The typical contract for sale and purchase contains paragraphs regarding the purchase price, deadlines for offer and acceptance, the closing date, and many other matters related to the transaction.

Figure 5.1 illustrates the Contract for Sale and Purchase jointly developed by the Florida Association of REALTORS® and the Florida Bar and used in most residential real estate transactions in Florida.

One of the most important parts of the contract identifies the manner in which the transaction will be financed. The buyer checks a box in Section IV to indicate which of four methods he or she plans to use:

1. Cash payment without financing
2. New financing
3. Assumption of an existing mortgage
4. Purchase money note and mortgage to seller

When the buyer *assumes* a mortgage, he or she takes responsibility for an already existing loan. The seller or original mortgagor is also held responsible for repayment of the loan in the event the buyer or new mortgagor defaults. The sales contract must state the interest rate, term, assumption fees, and other aspects of the mortgage being assumed. **Novation,** which refers to substituting a new person for the original mortgagor on an existing loan, is an additional optional step when assuming a loan. When novation takes place, the seller or original mortgagor is relieved of his or her obligation to repay the loan and only the new mortgagor is held responsible.

Another form of assumption is buying **subject to the mortgage,** in which the buyer takes title, but the note remains the sole obligation of the seller. The buyer may make payments to the lender, but the buyer has no legal obligation for repaying the loan. Should the buyer default, the seller will be responsible for making the mortgage payments on a subject to the mortgage transaction.

FIGURE 5.1 ■ Contract for Sale and Purchase

THIS FORM HAS BEEN APPROVED BY THE FLORIDA ASSOCIATION OF REALTORS® AND THE FLORIDA BAR

Contract For Sale And Purchase

FLORIDA ASSOCIATION OF REALTORS® AND THE FLORIDA BAR

PARTIES: ______________________________ ("Seller"), and ______________________________ ("Buyer"), hereby agree that Seller shall sell and Buyer shall buy the following described Real Property and Personal Property (collectively "Property") pursuant to the terms and conditions of this Contract for Sale and Purchase and any riders and addenda ("Contract"):

I. **DESCRIPTION:**

(a) Legal description of the Real Property located in ______________ County, Florida: ______________

(b) Street address, city, zip, of the Property: ______________

(c) Personal Property includes existing range(s), refrigerator(s), dishwasher(s), ceiling fan(s), light fixture(s), and window treatment(s) unless specifically excluded below.

Other items included are: ______________

Items of Personal Property (and leased items, if any) excluded are: ______________

II. **PURCHASE PRICE** (U.S. currency): . . . . $______

PAYMENT:

(a) Deposit held in escrow by ______________ ("Escrow Agent") in the amount of (checks subject to clearance) $______

Escrow Agent's address: ______________ Phone: ______________

(b) Additional escrow deposit to be made to Escrow Agent within _____ days after Effective Date in the amount of. . . . . $______

(c) Financing in the amount of ("Loan Amount") see Paragraph IV below . . . . $______

(d) Other . . . . $______

(e) Balance to close by cash, wire transfer or LOCALLY DRAWN cashier's or official bank check(s), subject to adjustments or prorations . . . . $______

III. **TIME FOR ACCEPTANCE OF OFFER AND COUNTEROFFERS; EFFECTIVE DATE:**

(a) If this offer is not executed by and delivered to all parties OR FACT OF EXECUTION communicated in writing between the parties on or before ______________, the deposit(s) will, at Buyer's option, be returned and this offer withdrawn. **Unless otherwise stated, the time for acceptance of any counteroffers shall be 2 days from the date the counteroffer is delivered.**

(b) The date of Contract ("Effective Date") will be the date when the last one of the Buyer and Seller has signed or initialed this offer or the final counteroffer. If such date is not otherwise set forth in this Contract, then the "Effective Date" shall be the date determined above for acceptance of this offer or, if applicable, the final counteroffer.

IV. **FINANCING:**

❑ (a) This is a cash transaction with no contingencies for financing;

❑ (b) This Contract is contingent on Buyer obtaining written loan commitment which confirms underwriting loan approval for a loan to purchase the Property ("Loan Approval") within _____ days (if blank, then 30 days) after Effective Date ("Loan Approval Date") for (CHECK ONLY ONE): ❑ a fixed; ❑ an adjustable; or ❑ a fixed or adjustable rate loan, in the Loan Amount (See Paragraph II.(c)) at an initial interest rate not to exceed ______%, and for a term of ______ years. Buyer will make application within _____ days (if blank, then 5 days) after Effective Date.

BUYER: Buyer shall use reasonable diligence to: obtain Loan Approval; **notify Seller in writing of receipt of Loan Approval by Loan Approval Date**; satisfy terms of the Loan Approval; and close the loan. Loan Approval which requires a condition related to the sale of other property shall not be deemed Loan Approval for purposes of this subparagraph. Buyer shall pay all loan expenses. Buyer authorizes the mortgage broker(s) and lender(s) to disclose information regarding the conditions, status, and progress of loan application and Loan Approval to Seller, Seller's attorney, real estate licensee(s), and Closing Agent.

SELLER: If Buyer does not deliver to Seller written notice of Loan Approval by Loan Approval Date, Seller may thereafter cancel this Contract by delivering written notice ("Seller's Cancellation Notice") to Buyer, but not later than seven (7) days prior to Closing. Seller's Cancellation Notice shall notify Buyer that Buyer has three (3) days to deliver to Seller written notice waiving this Financing contingency, or the Contract shall be cancelled.

DEPOSIT(S) (for purposes of this Financing Paragraph IV(b) only): If Buyer has used reasonable diligence but does not obtain Loan Approval by Loan Approval Date, and thereafter either party elects to cancel this Contract, the deposit(s) shall be returned to Buyer. If Buyer obtains Loan Approval or waives this Financing contingency, and thereafter the Contract does not close, then the deposit(s) shall be paid to Seller; provided however, if the failure to close is due to: (i) Seller's failure or refusal to close or Seller otherwise fails to meet the terms of the Contract, or (ii) Buyer's lender fails to receive and approve an appraisal of the Property in an amount sufficient to meet the terms of the Loan Approval, then the deposit(s) shall be returned to Buyer.

❑ (c) Assumption of existing mortgage (see rider for terms); or

❑ (d) Purchase money note and mortgage to Seller (see Standards B and K and riders; addenda; or special clauses for terms).

V. **TITLE EVIDENCE:** At least ____ days (if blank, then 5 days) before Closing a title insurance commitment with legible copies of instruments listed as exceptions attached thereto ("Title Commitment") and, after Closing, an owner's policy of title insurance (see Standard A for terms) shall be obtained by:

(CHECK ONLY ONE): ❑ (1) Seller, at Seller's expense and delivered to Buyer or Buyer's attorney; or
❑ (2) Buyer at Buyer's expense.

(CHECK HERE): ❑ If an abstract of title is to be furnished instead of title insurance, and attach rider for terms.

VI. **CLOSING DATE:** This transaction shall be closed and the closing documents delivered on ______________ ("Closing"), unless modified by other provisions of this Contract. In the event of extreme weather or other conditions or events constituting "force majeure", Closing will be extended a reasonable time until: (i) restoration of utilities and other services essential to Closing, and (ii) availability of Hazard, Wind, Flood, or Homeowners' insurance. If such conditions continue more than _____ days (if blank, then 14 days) beyond Closing Date, then either party may cancel this Contract.

FAR/BAR-8 Rev. 9/07 **Page 1 of 4**

Source: ©2007 Florida Association of REALTORS®. Reprinted with permission.

FIGURE 5.1 ■ Contract for Sale and Purchase (Continued)

VII. RESTRICTIONS; EASEMENTS; LIMITATIONS: Seller shall convey marketable title subject to: comprehensive land use plans, zoning, restrictions, prohibitions and other requirements imposed by governmental authority; restrictions and matters appearing on the plat or otherwise common to the subdivision; outstanding oil, gas and mineral rights of record without right of entry; unplatted public utility easements of record (located contiguous to real property lines and not more than 10 feet in width as to the rear or front lines and 7 1/2 feet in width as to the side lines); taxes for year of Closing and subsequent years; and assumed mortgages and purchase money mortgages, if any (if additional items, see addendum); provided, that there exists at Closing no violation of the foregoing and none prevent use of the Property for ____________________ purpose(s).

VIII. OCCUPANCY: Seller shall deliver occupancy of Property to Buyer at time of Closing unless otherwise stated herein. If Property is intended to be rented or occupied beyond Closing, the fact and terms thereof and the tenant(s) or occupants shall be disclosed pursuant to Standard F. If occupancy is to be delivered before Closing, Buyer assumes all risks of loss to Property from date of occupancy, shall be responsible and liable for maintenance from that date, and shall be deemed to have accepted Property in its existing condition as of time of taking occupancy.

IX. TYPEWRITTEN OR HANDWRITTEN PROVISIONS: Typewritten or handwritten provisions, riders and addenda shall control all printed provisions of this Contract in conflict with them.

X. ASSIGNABILITY: (CHECK ONLY ONE): Buyer ❑ may assign and thereby be released from any further liability under this Contract; ❑ may assign but not be released from liability under this Contract; or ❑ may not assign this Contract.

XI. DISCLOSURES:

(a) The Property may be subject to unpaid special assessment lien(s) imposed by a public body ("public body" does not include a Condominium or Homeowners' Association). Such lien(s), if any, whether certified, confirmed and ratified, pending, or payable in installments, as of Closing, shall be paid as follows: **❑ by Seller at closing ❑ by Buyer (if left blank, then Seller at Closing).** If the amount of any assessment to be paid by Seller has not been finally determined as of Closing, Seller shall be charged at Closing an amount equal to the last estimate or assessment for the improvement by the public body.

(b) Radon is a naturally occurring radioactive gas that when accumulated in a building in sufficient quantities may present health risks to persons who are exposed to it over time. Levels of radon that exceed federal and state guidelines have been found in buildings in Florida. Additional information regarding radon or radon testing may be obtained from your County Public Health unit.

(c) Mold is naturally occurring and may cause health risks or damage to property. If Buyer is concerned or desires additional information regarding mold, Buyer should contact an appropriate professional.

(d) Buyer acknowledges receipt of the Florida Energy-Efficiency Rating Information Brochure required by Section 553.996, F.S.

(e) If the Real Property includes pre-1978 residential housing then a lead-based paint rider is mandatory.

(f) If Seller is a "foreign person" as defined by the Foreign Investment in Real Property Tax Act, the parties shall comply with that Act.

(g) **BUYER SHOULD NOT EXECUTE THIS CONTRACT UNTIL BUYER HAS RECEIVED AND READ THE HOMEOWNERS' ASSOCIATION/COMMUNITY DISCLOSURE.**

(h) PROPERTY TAX DISCLOSURE SUMMARY: BUYER SHOULD NOT RELY ON THE SELLER'S CURRENT PROPERTY TAXES AS THE AMOUNT OF PROPERTY TAXES THAT THE BUYER MAY BE OBLIGATED TO PAY IN THE YEAR SUBSEQUENT TO PURCHASE. A CHANGE OF OWNERSHIP OR PROPERTY IMPROVEMENTS TRIGGERS REASSESSMENTS OF THE PROPERTY THAT COULD RESULT IN HIGHER PROPERTY TAXES. IF YOU HAVE ANY QUESTIONS CONCERNING VALUATION, CONTACT THE COUNTY PROPERTY APPRAISER'S OFFICE FOR INFORMATION.

XII. MAXIMUM REPAIR COSTS: Seller shall not be responsible for payments in excess of:

(a) $____________ for treatment and repair under Standard D (if blank, then 1.5% of the Purchase Price).

(b) $____________ for repair and replacement under Standard N not caused by Wood Destroying Organisms (if blank, then 1.5% of the Purchase Price).

XIII. HOME WARRANTY: ❑ Seller ❑ Buyer ❑ N/A will pay for a home warranty plan issued by ____________ at a cost not to exceed $____________.

XIV. RIDERS; ADDENDA; SPECIAL CLAUSES: CHECK those riders which are applicable AND are attached to and made part of this Contract:
❑ CONDOMINIUM ❑ VA/FHA ❑ HOMEOWNERS' ASSN. ❑ LEAD-BASED PAINT ❑ COASTAL CONSTRUCTION CONTROL LINE
❑ INSULATION ❑ "AS IS" ❑ EVIDENCE OF TITLE (SOUTH FLORIDA CONTRACTS) ❑ Other Comprehensive Rider Provisions ❑ Addenda
Special Clause(s): ____________________

____

____

____

XV. STANDARDS FOR REAL ESTATE TRANSACTIONS ("Standards"): Buyer and Seller acknowledge receipt of a copy of Standards A through Y on the reverse side or attached, which are incorporated as part of this Contract.

THIS IS INTENDED TO BE A LEGALLY BINDING CONTRACT. IF NOT FULLY UNDERSTOOD, SEEK THE ADVICE OF AN ATTORNEY PRIOR TO SIGNING.

THIS FORM HAS BEEN APPROVED BY THE FLORIDA ASSOCIATION OF REALTORS® AND THE FLORIDA BAR.

Approval does not constitute an opinion that any of the terms and conditions in this Contract should be accepted by the parties in a particular transaction. Terms and conditions should be negotiated based upon the respective interests, objectives and bargaining positions of all interested persons.

AN ASTERISK(*) FOLLOWING A LINE NUMBER IN THE MARGIN INDICATES THE LINE CONTAINS A BLANK TO BE COMPLETED.

____________	________	____________	________
(BUYER)	(DATE)	(SELLER)	(DATE)
____________	________	____________	________
(BUYER)	(DATE)	(SELLER)	(DATE)

Buyers' address for purposes of notice ____________ Sellers' address for purposes of notice ____________

____________ ____________

____________ Phone ____________ Phone

BROKERS: The brokers (including cooperating brokers, if any) named below are the only brokers entitled to compensation in connection with this Contract:

Name: ____________ ____________

Cooperating Brokers, if any **Listing Broker**

FIGURE 5.1 ■ Contract for Sale and Purchase (Continued)

STANDARDS FOR REAL ESTATE TRANSACTIONS

A. TITLE INSURANCE: The Title Commitment shall be issued by a Florida licensed title insurer agreeing to issue Buyer, upon recording of the deed to Buyer, an owner's policy of title insurance in the amount of the purchase price, insuring Buyer's marketable title to the Real Property, subject only to matters contained in Paragraph VII and those to be discharged by Seller at or before Closing. Marketable title shall be determined according to applicable Title Standards adopted by authority of The Florida Bar and in accordance with law. Buyer shall have 5 days from date of receiving the Title Commitment to examine it, and if title is found defective, notify Seller in writing specifying defect(s) which render title unmarketable. Seller shall have 30 days from receipt of notice to remove the defects, failing which Buyer shall, within 5 days after expiration of the 30 day period, deliver written notice to Seller either: (1) extending the time for a reasonable period not to exceed 120 days within which Seller shall use diligent effort to remove the defects; or (2) requesting a refund of deposit(s) paid which shall be returned to Buyer. If Buyer fails to so notify Seller, Buyer shall be deemed to have accepted the title as it then is. Seller shall, if title is found unmarketable, use diligent effort to correct defect(s) within the time provided. If, after diligent effort, Seller is unable to timely correct the defects, Buyer shall either waive the defects, or receive a refund of deposit(s), thereby releasing Buyer and Seller from all further obligations under this Contract. If Seller is to provide the Title Commitment and it is delivered to Buyer less than 5 days prior to Closing, Buyer may extend Closing so that Buyer shall have up to 5 days from date of receipt to examine same in accordance with this Standard.

B. PURCHASE MONEY MORTGAGE; SECURITY AGREEMENT TO SELLER: A purchase money mortgage and mortgage note to Seller shall provide for a 30 day grace period in the event of default if a first mortgage and a 15 day grace period if a second or lesser mortgage; shall provide for right of prepayment in whole or in part without penalty; shall permit acceleration in event of transfer of the Real Property; shall require all prior liens and encumbrances to be kept in good standing; shall forbid modifications of, or future advances under, prior mortgage(s); shall require Buyer to maintain policies of insurance containing a standard mortgagee clause covering all improvements located on the Real Property against fire and all perils included within the term "extended coverage endorsements" and such other risks and perils as Seller may reasonably require, in an amount equal to their highest insurable value; and the mortgage, note and security agreement shall be otherwise in form and content required by Seller, but Seller may only require clauses and coverage customarily found in mortgages, mortgage notes and security agreements generally utilized by savings and loan institutions or state or national banks located in the county wherein the Real Property is located. All Personal Property and leases being conveyed or assigned will, at Seller's option, be subject to the lien of a security agreement evidenced by recorded or filed financing statements or certificates of title. If a balloon mortgage, the final payment will exceed the periodic payments thereon.

C. SURVEY: Buyer, at Buyer's expense, within time allowed to deliver evidence of title and to examine same, may have the Real Property surveyed and certified by a registered Florida surveyor. If the survey discloses encroachments on the Real Property or that improvements located thereon encroach on setback lines, easements, lands of others or violate any restrictions, Contract covenants or applicable governmental regulations, the same shall constitute a title defect.

D. WOOD DESTROYING ORGANISMS: "Wood Destroying Organisms" (WDO) shall be deemed to include all wood destroying organisms required to be reported under the Florida Structural Pest Control Act, as amended. Buyer, at Buyer's expense, may have the Property inspected by a Florida Certified Pest Control Operator ("Operator") within 20 days after the Effective Date to determine if there is any visible active WDO infestation or visible damage from WDO infestation, excluding fences. If either or both are found, Buyer may within said 20 days (1) have cost of treatment of active infestation estimated by the Operator; (2) have all damage inspected and cost of repair estimated by an appropriately licensed contractor; and (3) report such cost(s) to Seller in writing. Seller shall cause the treatment and repair of all WDO damage to be made and pay the costs thereof up to the amount provided in Paragraph XII(a). If estimated costs exceed that amount, Buyer shall have the option of canceling this Contract by giving written notice to Seller within 20 days after the Effective Date, or Buyer may elect to proceed with the transaction and receive a credit at Closing equal to the amount provided in Paragraph XII(a). If Buyer's lender requires an updated WDO report, then Buyer shall, at Buyer's expense, have the opportunity to have the Property re-inspected for WDO infestation and have the cost of active infestation or new damage estimated and reported to Seller in writing at least 10 days prior to Closing, and thereafter, Seller shall cause such treatment and repair to be made and pay the cost thereof; provided, Seller's total obligation for treatment and repair costs required under both the first and second inspection shall not exceed the amount provided in Paragraph XII (a).

E. INGRESS AND EGRESS: Seller warrants and represents that there is ingress and egress to the Real Property sufficient for its intended use as described in Paragraph VII hereof and title to the Real Property is insurable in accordance with Standard A without exception for lack of legal right of access.

F. LEASES: Seller shall, at least 10 days before Closing, furnish to Buyer copies of all written leases and estoppel letters from each tenant specifying the nature and duration of the tenant's occupancy, rental rates, advanced rent and security deposits paid by tenant. If Seller is unable to obtain such letter from each tenant, the same information shall be furnished by Seller to Buyer within that time period in the form of a Seller's affidavit, and Buyer may thereafter contact tenant to confirm such information. If the terms of the leases differ materially from Seller's representations, Buyer may terminate this Contract by delivering written notice to Seller at least 5 days prior to Closing. Seller shall, at Closing, deliver and assign all original leases to Buyer.

G. LIENS: Seller shall furnish to Buyer at time of Closing an affidavit attesting to the absence, unless otherwise provided for herein, of any financing statement, claims of lien or potential lienors known to Seller and further attesting that there have been no improvements or repairs to the Real Property for 90 days immediately preceding date of Closing. If the Real Property has been improved or repaired within that time, Seller shall deliver releases or waivers of construction liens executed by all general contractors, subcontractors, suppliers and materialmen in addition to Seller's lien affidavit setting forth the names of all such general contractors, subcontractors, suppliers and materialmen, further affirming that all charges for improvements or repairs which could serve as a basis for a construction lien or a claim for damages have been paid or will be paid at the Closing of this Contract.

H. PLACE OF CLOSING: Closing shall be held in the county wherein the Real Property is located at the office of the attorney or other closing agent ("Closing Agent") designated by the party paying for title insurance, or, if no title insurance, designated by Seller.

I. TIME: Calendar days shall be used in computing time periods except periods of less than six (6) days, in which event Saturdays, Sundays and state or national legal holidays shall be excluded. Any time periods provided for herein which shall end on a Saturday, Sunday, or a legal holiday shall extend to 5:00 p.m. of the next business day. **Time is of the essence in this Contract.**

J. CLOSING DOCUMENTS: Seller shall furnish the deed, bill of sale, certificate of title, construction lien affidavit, owner's possession affidavit, assignments of leases, tenant and mortgagee estoppel letters and corrective instruments. Buyer shall furnish mortgage, mortgage note, security agreement and financing statements.

K. EXPENSES: Documentary stamps on the deed and recording of corrective instruments shall be paid by Seller. All costs of Buyer's loan (whether obtained from Seller or third party), including, but not limited to, documentary stamps and intangible tax on the purchase money mortgage and any mortgage assumed, mortgagee title insurance commitment with related fees, and recording of purchase money mortgage to Seller, deed and financing statements shall be paid by Buyer. Unless otherwise provided by law or rider to this Contract, charges for related closing services, title search, and closing fees (including preparation of closing statement), shall be paid by the party responsible for furnishing the title evidence in accordance with Paragraph V.

L. PRORATIONS; CREDITS: Taxes, assessments, rent, interest, insurance and other expenses of the Property shall be prorated through the day before Closing. Buyer shall have the option of taking over existing policies of insurance, if assumable, in which event premiums shall be prorated. Cash at Closing shall be increased or decreased as may be required by prorations to be made through day prior to Closing, or occupancy, if occupancy occurs before Closing. Advance rent and security deposits will be credited to Buyer. Escrow deposits held by mortgagee will be credited to Seller. Taxes shall be prorated based on the current year's tax with due allowance made for maximum allowable discount, homestead and other exemptions. If Closing occurs at a date when the current year's millage is not fixed and current year's assessment is available, taxes will be prorated based upon such assessment and prior year's millage. If current year's assessment is not available, then taxes will be prorated on prior year's tax. If there are completed improvements on the Real Property by January 1st of year of Closing, which improvements were not in existence on January 1st of prior year, then taxes shall be prorated based upon prior year's millage and at an equitable assessment to be agreed upon between the parties; failing which, request shall be made to the County Property Appraiser for an informal assessment taking into account available exemptions. A tax proration based on an estimate shall, at request of either party, be readjusted upon receipt of current year's tax bill.

M. (RESERVED - purposely left blank)

N. INSPECTION AND REPAIR: Seller warrants that the ceiling, roof (including the fascia and soffits), and exterior and interior walls, and foundation of the Property do not have any visible evidence of leaks, water damage, or structural damage and that dockage, seawalls, septic tank, pool, all appliances, mechanical items,

FIGURE 5.1 ■ Contract for Sale and Purchase (Continued)

STANDARDS FOR REAL ESTATE TRANSACTIONS (CONTINUED)

heating, cooling, electrical, plumbing systems, and machinery are in Working Condition. The foregoing warranty shall be limited to the items specified unless otherwise provided in an addendum. Buyer may inspect, or, at Buyer's expense, have a firm or individual specializing in home inspections and holding an occupational license for such purpose (if required), or by an appropriately licensed Florida contractor, make inspections of, those items within 20 days after the Effective Date. Buyer shall, prior to Buyer's occupancy but not more than 20 days after Effective Date, report in writing to Seller such items that do not meet the above standards as to defects. Unless Buyer timely reports such defects, Buyer shall be deemed to have waived Seller's warranties as to defects not reported. If repairs or replacements are required to comply with this Standard, Seller shall cause them to be made and shall pay up to the amount provided in Paragraph XII (b). Seller is not required to make repairs or replacements of a Cosmetic Condition unless caused by a defect Seller is responsible to repair or replace. If the cost for such repair or replacement exceeds the amount provided in Paragraph XII (b), Buyer or Seller may elect to pay such excess, failing which either party may cancel this Contract. If Seller is unable to correct the defects prior to Closing, the cost thereof shall be paid into escrow at Closing. For purposes of this Contract: (1) "Working Condition" means operating in the manner in which the item was designed to operate; (2) "Cosmetic Condition" means aesthetic imperfections that do not affect the Working Condition of the item, including, but not limited to: pitted marcite or other pool finishes; missing or torn screens; fogged windows; tears, worn spots, or discoloration of floor coverings, wallpaper, or window treatments; nail holes, scratches, dents, scrapes, chips or caulking in ceilings, walls, flooring, fixtures, or mirrors; and minor cracks in floors, tiles, windows, driveways, sidewalks, or pool decks; and (3) cracked roof tiles, curling or worn shingles, or limited roof life shall not be considered defects Seller must repair or replace, so long as there is no evidence of actual leaks or leakage or structural damage, but missing tiles will be Seller's responsibility to replace or repair.

O. RISK OF LOSS: If, after the Effective Date, the Property is damaged by fire or other casualty ("Casualty Loss") before Closing and cost of restoration (which shall include the cost of pruning or removing damaged trees) does not exceed 1.5% of the Purchase Price, cost of restoration shall be an obligation of Seller and Closing shall proceed pursuant to the terms of this Contract and if restoration is not completed as of Closing, restoration costs will be escrowed at Closing. If the cost of restoration exceeds 1.5% of the Purchase Price, Buyer shall either take the Property as is, together with the 1.5% or receive a refund of deposit(s) thereby releasing Buyer and Seller from all further obligations under this Contract. Seller's sole obligation with respect to tree damage by casualty or other natural occurrence shall be the cost of pruning or removal.

P. CLOSING PROCEDURE: The deed shall be recorded upon clearance of funds. If the title agent insures adverse matters pursuant to Section 627.7841, F.S., as amended, the escrow and closing procedure required by this Standard shall be waived. Unless waived as set forth above the following closing procedures shall apply: (1) all closing proceeds shall be held in escrow by the Closing Agent for a period of not more than 5 days after Closing; (2) if Seller's title is rendered unmarketable, through no fault of Buyer, Buyer shall, within the 5 day period, notify Seller in writing of the defect and Seller shall have 30 days from date of receipt of such notification to cure the defect; (3) if Seller fails to timely cure the defect, all deposits and closing funds shall, upon written demand by Buyer and within 5 days after demand, be returned to Buyer and, simultaneously with such repayment, Buyer shall return the Personal Property, vacate the Real Property and reconvey the Property to Seller by special warranty deed and bill of sale; and (4) if Buyer fails to make timely demand for refund, Buyer shall take title as is, waiving all rights against Seller as to any intervening defect except as may be available to Buyer by virtue of warranties contained in the deed or bill of sale.

Q. ESCROW: Any Closing Agent or escrow agent (collectively "Agent") receiving funds or equivalent is authorized and agrees by acceptance of them to deposit them promptly, hold same in escrow and, subject to clearance, disburse them in accordance with terms and conditions of this Contract. Failure of funds to clear shall not excuse Buyer's performance. If in doubt as to Agent's duties or liabilities under the provisions of this Contract, Agent may, at Agent's option, continue to hold the subject matter of the escrow until the parties hereto agree to its disbursement or until a judgment of a court of competent jurisdiction shall determine the rights of the parties, or Agent may deposit same with the clerk of the circuit court having jurisdiction of the dispute. An attorney who represents a party and also acts as Agent may represent such party in such action. Upon notifying all parties concerned of such action, all liability on the part of Agent shall fully terminate, except to the extent of accounting for any items previously delivered out of escrow. If a licensed real estate broker, Agent will comply with provisions of Chapter 475, F.S., as amended. Any suit between Buyer and Seller wherein Agent is made a party because of acting as Agent hereunder, or in any suit wherein Agent interpleads the subject matter of the escrow, Agent shall recover reasonable attorney's fees and costs incurred with these amounts to be paid from and out of the escrowed funds or equivalent and charged and awarded as court costs in favor of the prevailing party. The Agent shall not be liable to any party or person for misdelivery to Buyer or Seller of items subject to the escrow, unless such misdelivery is due to willful breach of the provisions of this Contract or gross negligence of Agent.

R. ATTORNEY'S FEES; COSTS: In any litigation, including breach, enforcement or interpretation, arising out of this Contract, the prevailing party in such litigation, which, for purposes of this Standard, shall include Seller, Buyer and any brokers acting in agency or nonagency relationships authorized by Chapter 475, F.S., as amended, shall be entitled to recover from the non-prevailing party reasonable attorney's fees, costs and expenses.

S. FAILURE OF PERFORMANCE: If Buyer fails to perform this Contract within the time specified, including payment of all deposits, the deposit(s) paid by Buyer and deposit(s) agreed to be paid, may be recovered and retained by and for the account of Seller as agreed upon liquidated damages, consideration for the execution of this Contract and in full settlement of any claims; whereupon, Buyer and Seller shall be relieved of all obligations under this Contract; or Seller, at Seller's option, may proceed in equity to enforce Seller's rights under this Contract. If for any reason other than failure of Seller to make Seller's title marketable after diligent effort, Seller fails, neglects or refuses to perform this Contract, Buyer may seek specific performance or elect to receive the return of Buyer's deposit(s) without thereby waiving any action for damages resulting from Seller's breach.

T. CONTRACT NOT RECORDABLE; PERSONS BOUND; NOTICE; COPIES: Neither this Contract nor any notice of it shall be recorded in any public records. This Contract shall bind and inure to the benefit of the parties and their successors in interest. Whenever the context permits, singular shall include plural and one gender shall include all. Notice and delivery given by or to the attorney or broker representing any party shall be as effective as if given by or to that party. All notices must be in writing and may be made by mail, personal delivery or electronic media. A legible facsimile or electronic (including "pdf") copy of this Contract and any signatures hereon shall be considered for all purposes as an original.

U. CONVEYANCE: Seller shall convey marketable title to the Real Property by statutory warranty, trustee's, personal representative's, or guardian's deed, as appropriate to the status of Seller, subject only to matters contained in Paragraph VII and those otherwise accepted by Buyer. Personal Property shall, at the request of Buyer, be transferred by an absolute bill of sale with warranty of title, subject only to such matters as may be otherwise provided for herein.

V. OTHER AGREEMENTS: No prior or present agreements or representations shall be binding upon Buyer or Seller unless included in this Contract. No modification to or change in this Contract shall be valid or binding upon the parties unless in writing and executed by the parties intended to be bound by it.

W. SELLER DISCLOSURE: There are no facts known to Seller materially affecting the value of the Property which are not readily observable by Buyer or which have not been disclosed to Buyer.

X. PROPERTY MAINTENANCE; PROPERTY ACCESS; REPAIR STANDARDS; ASSIGNMENT OF CONTRACTS AND WARRANTIES: Seller shall maintain the Property, including, but not limited to lawn, shrubbery, and pool in the condition existing as of Effective Date, ordinary wear and tear and Casualty Loss excepted. Seller shall, upon reasonable notice, provide utilities service and access to the Property for appraisal and inspections, including a walk-through prior to Closing, to confirm that all items of Personal Property are on the Real Property and, subject to the foregoing, that all required repairs and replacements have been made, and that the Property has been maintained as required by this Standard. All repairs and replacements shall be completed in a good and workmanlike manner, in accordance with all requirements of law, and shall consist of materials or items of quality, value, capacity and performance comparable to, or better than, that existing as of the Effective Date. Seller will assign all assignable repair and treatment contracts and warranties to Buyer at Closing.

Y. 1031 EXCHANGE: If either Seller or Buyer wish to enter into a like-kind exchange (either simultaneous with Closing or deferred) with respect to the Property under Section 1031 of the Internal Revenue Code ("Exchange"), the other party shall cooperate in all reasonable respects to effectuate the Exchange, including the execution of documents; provided (1) the cooperating party shall incur no liability or expense related to the Exchange and (2) the Closing shall not be contingent upon, nor extended or delayed by, such Exchange.

FAR/BAR-8 Rev. 9/07 © 2007 Florida Association of Realtors® and The Florida Bar All Rights Reserved **Page 4 of 4**

Another important concept is the *effective date* of the sales contract. The effective date is defined as the date when the last party to the transaction signs the contract. In cases where the buyer plans to apply for new financing, the contract typically limits the number of days from the effective date that a buyer has to obtain a loan commitment from a lender, as well as the number of days the buyer has to submit an application for a loan. The contract also states the amount, terms, and interest rate of the new financing that the buyer is willing to accept. When the buyer plans to use seller financing, the sales contract will specify the terms of the mortgage that will be held by the seller, such as a requirement that the buyer obtain hazard insurance coverage equal to at least the value of the property. The contract will also specify the rights of both the buyer and seller in case the buyer defaults on the mortgage. If the buyer is unable to find financing, however, the contract becomes voidable.

Another key part of the sales contract is the requirement that the seller provide evidence of the **marketability of title**—that is, that the seller has indisputable ownership of the property and can convey title for consideration. Documenting the marketability of title begins with a **title search,** which is an examination of public documents to determine the property's legal owner. Evidence of marketability can be provided by either an attorney's opinion of title or acquiring title insurance. The buyer usually has a specified number of days to examine the title to see if it has any defects or reasons to question who owns the property.

LIEN THEORY AND TITLE THEORY

At the time of sale, ownership of real property typically transfers from the seller to either the buyer or the lender. The **title** to the property being purchased—which is a legal concept signifying ownership—is conveyed by a deed. Who holds the title—the buyer or the mortgage company—is an important distinction, and ownership of title depends on whether the property being purchased is located in a lien theory state or a title theory state.

As defined in chapter 1, a mortgage is the pledge of real property as security for the repayment of a debt. In a **lien theory** state—which is the case in Florida and the majority of states—the person who buys the property with money borrowed from a lender takes title to the property while repaying the loan. The buyer signs a mortgage that gives the lender a lien on the property allowing the lender to start the legal process to take back title if the buyer defaults on the note.

In a **title theory** state, on the other hand, at closing the lender receives title to a property through a mortgage deed. A disinterested third party, someone other than the borrower or lender, holds title until the mortgage loan is paid. If the borrower defaults on the mortgage, the lender keeps title. Georgia is a title theory state and uses a deed of trust as a security instrument.

Both lien and title theory states require a note that is held by the lender.

DEEDS OF TRUST

In some cases, lenders rely on deeds of trust rather than mortgages. Like a mortgage, a **deed of trust** comes with a promissory note. The deed of trust appoints a *trustee*, a third party who holds title to a property on behalf of the lender. The lender holds the note.

The deed of trust details the steps the trustee may take to claim the property should the borrower default on the loan. In such cases, the court proceedings necessary for a foreclosure may not be necessary for the trustee to force the sale of the property to satisfy the note.

One advantage of a deed of trust to the lender is that the borrower has no **right of redemption.** This right allows a borrower to reclaim a property by paying all indebtedness before the property is sold in foreclosure. Because the holder of a deed of trust is not bound by the right of redemption, the trustee can go ahead and force the sale of the property once the borrower has defaulted.

An advantage for the borrower is that deeds of trust do not allow a **deficiency judgment,** which is a judgment against a borrower when a foreclosure sale fails to produce enough funds to pay the mortgage in full. Under the terms of a deed of trust, if the sale of the property nets an amount less than the outstanding balance of the mortgage, the lender cannot sue the borrower to make up the difference.

FORMS OF REAL ESTATE OWNERSHIP

Ownership of real estate can be for an indefinite period of time, or it can be for a limited period. *Freehold estates* are held indefinitely; *leasehold estates* are time-limited.

Freehold Estates

There are two kinds of **freehold estates. Fee simple** is the most desirable form of property ownership. An individual who has fee simple ownership of real property can hold the property indefinitely or dispose of the property however he or she chooses. The owner of a fee simple estate can also pass on the property to his or her heirs.

A **life estate,** on the other hand, refers to property that a person owns during his or her lifetime, but that reverts to the original owner or a predetermined party known as a *remainderman* when the life estate holder dies. If the life estate reverts to the original grantor, an estate in reversion is created; if it goes to a remainderman, the estate is a remainder estate. The holder of a life estate must maintain the value of the property during his or her period of ownership.

Joint Ownership of Real Estate

When individuals own freehold property together, in Florida the form of ownership is likely to be tenancy by the entireties, tenancy in common, or joint tenancy.

Tenancy by the entireties refers to ownership between a legally married husband and wife where both have separate, 100 percent interests in the estate. When one partner in the marriage dies, the surviving spouse automatically has complete ownership because that person already holds 100 percent interest. Ownership of the property passes directly to the surviving spouse; no partner in a tenancy by the entireties can will his or her part of the property to someone other than a spouse. This is known as the *right of survivorship*.

In addition, creditors cannot lay claim to the property for repayment of a debt unless the debt is in the name of both the husband and the wife. In terms of title to a property, the deed need not have the names of both the husband and the wife for a tenancy by the entireties to exist.

A tenancy by the entireties can be ended by divorce. When this happens, the relationship between the co-owners—that is, the husband and wife—becomes a tenancy in common.

Tenancy in common refers to a relationship in which any number of people can be owners of a property. These co-owners can have acquired their interest in the property at different times, and they can hold different percentages of ownership. Although each person has separate legal title, ownership is in the *entire* property, not just a particular part. Ownership in a tenancy in common property can be passed on to heirs, who then become tenants in common with the other partners in the property.

In contrast with the tenancy by the entireties property, a tenancy in common property can be attached by creditors for repayment of an individual's debts. The claim would be against only that part of the property owned by the debtor and not against the entire property.

Joint tenancy refers to the situation where owners have undivided possession, but equal interest in real property. All partners acquired the property at the same time, and all their names are on the title. Joint tenancy differs from tenancy in common, however, in that it comes with **right of survivorship,** which means that when a member of the joint tenancy dies, his or her share is divided among the surviving co-owners and does not go to the deceased tenant's heirs.

The forms of co-ownership found in Florida are summarized in the following box.

FORMS OF CO-OWNERSHIP

Tenancy by the Entireties	Joint Tenancy	Tenancy in Common
Right of survivorship	Right of survivorship	No right of survivorship (heritable estate)
Equal interest	Equal interest	Equal or unequal shares
No unilateral disposition	No unilateral disposition	Owners can sell their shares at any time
Husband and wife	Any number of people	Any number of people

Leasehold (Nonfreehold) Estates

In contrast with freehold estates, **leasehold estates** have a definite period of duration, and they do not allow ownership to be passed on to others. Types of leasehold estates include an estate for years, tenancy at will, and tenancy at sufferance.

An **estate for years** conveys tenancy of a property for a specified period of time—weeks, months, years, and so forth—in writing, usually in the form of a lease. The tenant assumes possession and control of the property, but the owner usually does not convey title to the tenant.

Tenancy at will refers to a situation where an individual has tenancy for an unspecified period with the permission of the owner, who retains title. There is no specific termination date.

Finally, **tenancy at sufferance** occurs when a tenant who has had lawful possession of a property continues to occupy that property after the period of legal possession has ended. The tenant does not have permission from the owner to occupy the property.

KEY POINT REVIEW

- A *contract* is a promise to perform some action. To be *enforceable*, a contract must have been made by competent parties, have mutual assent, have legal purpose, be in writing and signed, and offer consideration.
- The *statute of frauds* requires that real estate contracts be in writing and signed to be enforceable.
- Evidence of the *marketability of title* is provided through an attorney's opinion of title or title insurance.
- In a *lien theory* state, such as Florida, the person who buys the property takes title and offers a mortgage as security to the lender; in a *title theory* state such as Georgia, a lender or third party holds title until the mortgage is paid in full.
- A *deed of trust* is issued when a trustee holds title to a property on behalf of a lender. A deed of trust has no *right of redemption*.
- A *deficiency judgment* is a judgment against a borrower's other assets when a foreclosure sale of the mortgaged property fails to produce enough funds to pay the mortgage in full.
- *Fee simple* is the most complete type of property ownership.
- A *life estate* is owned by an individual for the duration of his or her lifetime. Life estate holders do not have the right to convey the property without the permission of the *remainderman* or party to whom the property will revert.
- *Tenancy by the entireties* refers to ownership between a husband and wife and comes with right of survivorship.
- *Tenancy in common* refers to a relationship where any number of people can own a property, have acquired their ownership at different times, and hold different percentages of ownership. Tenancy in common has the right of inheritability, not the right of survivorship.
- *Joint tenancy* refers to situations where owners have undivided possession but equal interest in a property. Joint tenancy comes with right of survivorship.
- An *estate for years* conveys tenancy for a specified period but without title. *Tenancy at will* refers to tenancy for an unspecified period with the permission of the person who holds title. *Tenancy at sufferance* refers to possession of a property beyond the period when the right to possession has expired and is held by the tenant without the permission of the owner.

REVIEW QUESTIONS

1. Luis offered to buy Amanda's house and made an earnest money deposit of $3,500. Amanda asked for 24 hours to think about the offer, then told her friends she planned to accept. At that point
   a. no contract was formed because nothing had been legally recorded.
   b. no contract was formed because Amanda did not communicate her acceptance of an offer to Luis.
   c. a contract was formed when Luis offered the $3,500 consideration.
   d. a contract was formed when Amanda publicly stated her intention to accept Luis's offer.

2. Mr. Morgan bought a shopping center in 2001 and in 2003 sold a 30 percent interest to his uncle. What kind of ownership do Mr. Morgan and his uncle have?
   a. Tenancy by the entireties
   b. Tenancy in common
   c. Joint tenancy
   d. Leasehold

3. Karen and her sisters own ten acres of agricultural property as a tenancy in common. Karen lost a lawsuit related to a business deal and owes her creditors $78,000. With regard to her interest in the agricultural property
   a. the creditors may attach Karen's share of the property for payment of the debt.
   b. the property cannot be attached by the creditor.
   c. Karen's share of the property can be attached if her sisters agree.
   d. all shares in the property can be attached.

4. To be legal, a real estate contract must have the
   a. signature of the buyer only.
   b. signature of the seller only.
   c. signatures of both the buyer and seller.
   d. signatures of the buyer, seller, and a witness.

5. When a marriage ends in divorce, with regard to jointly owned property, the husband and wife become
   a. joint tenants.
   b. tenants in common.
   c. tenants by the entireties.
   d. either joint tenants or tenants in common.

6. The right of redemption
   a. does not apply in a deed of trust situation.
   b. must be exercised before a property can be sold in foreclosure.
   c. can be applied in title theory states only.
   d. can be applied in lien theory states only.

7. Cynthia lives in a lien theory state. When she sells her house
   a. the buyer will take title to the property.
   b. the lender will take title to the property.
   c. a third party will take title to the property.
   d. the court will hold title until the buyer pays the mortgage.

8. A legal contract has all of the following EXCEPT
   a. mutual assent.
   b. consideration.
   c. notarization.
   d. legal purpose.

9. Mrs. Alvarez wants to buy a property that offers the most comprehensive type of property ownership. The type of ownership Mrs. Alvarez is looking for is
   a. fee simple.
   b. life estate.
   c. leasehold estate.
   d. estate for years.

10. A lawsuit brought on the basis of the statute of frauds most likely concerns
    a. a fraudulent real estate transaction where a seller failed to disclose defects.
    b. any kind of fraudulent transaction involving real estate.
    c. the requirement that real estate contracts be in writing to be enforceable.
    d. fraud unrelated to a real estate transaction.

11. Mr. Han has a tenancy at will interest in a property. This means that
    a. he has tenancy of a property for a specified period.
    b. he is a tenant keeping possession of a property after his legal period of possession has ended.
    c. a seller has accepted his offer on a property but Mr. Han cannot take possession of the property because the transaction has not closed.
    d. Mr. Han has possession of a property for an unspecified period with the permission of the owner.

12. Mr. Dunn sold an older, two-bedroom house "as is" to Lucy Hill, a first-time homebuyer, who agreed to all terms Mr. Dunn proposed. Mr. Dunn may have violated which element of a legal contract?
    a. Competence of parties
    b. Mutual assent
    c. Legal purpose
    d. Legal form

13. A buyer and a seller have come to an agreement on the sale of a property that will involve novation. Most likely this means that
    a. the buyer must be approved for a new mortgage.
    b. the buyer will assume an existing mortgage and be solely responsible for its repayment.
    c. the buyer will apply for a new mortgage.
    d. the seller will hold a second mortgage.

14. At the closing, the document that will actually convey title to a property is the
   a. deed.
   b. mortgage.
   c. promissory note.
   d. contract for sale and purchase.

15. A homeowner defaulted on a mortgage and his house was sold at auction. After the auction, the mortgage company decided to seek a deficiency judgment
   a. to make up the difference between the sales price and the down payment.
   b. to force the seller to deliver title at the closing.
   c. because problems with the borrower's application caused the default.
   d. to try and make up the difference between the sales price of the property and the mortgage balance.

16. Paul and Betty have a tenancy by the entireties form of ownership on the deed. If Paul and Betty default, the lender
   a. can lay claim to their property for repayment of the mortgage loan.
   b. cannot lay claim if either Paul and Betty are still living.
   c. can lay claim to the property only if Paul and Betty's other debts have been satisfied.
   d. cannot lay claim to the property if it is their primary residence.

17. If a buyer wants assurance regarding the marketability of title, the buyer should look to the
   a. survey.
   b. sales contract.
   c. promissory note.
   d. title insurance.

18. A 12-year-old girl inherited a property from her grandmother. Mr. Albright would like to buy that property but is likely to have difficulty because
   a. a 12-year-old cannot own property in her own name.
   b. there would be questions about the competence of the girl.
   c. it is illegal for an adult to make an offer to a minor regarding real estate.
   d. Mr. Albright would have to demonstrate to the court that he plans to use the property for a legal purpose.

19. Eva bought her condo in Tallahassee for $215,000. She made a down payment of $72,000 and took title to the property. However, the seller is responsible for making payments to the mortgage company. This arrangement is called
   a. a deferred payment mortgage.
   b. novation.
   c. buying subject to the mortgage.
   d. a deed of trust mortgage.

20. In which type of estate is a mortgage company LEAST likely to be involved?
   a. Tenancy at will
   b. Fee simple
   c. Life estate
   d. Freehold

C H A P T E R

6

MORTGAGE DOCUMENTS

LEARNING OBJECTIVES

After finishing chapter 6, you should be able to

1. understand the different kinds of deeds;
2. explain the importance of the promissory note;
3. know the clauses in a mortgage contract;
4. understand amortization and the monthly mortgage payment table;
5. explain the difference between fixed-rate and adjustable-rate mortgages;
6. know the differences between a contract for deed and a purchase-money mortgage;
7. recognize the different kinds of mortgages;
8. know the three kinds of mortgage loans;
9. understand the purpose of Alt-A loans, subprime loans, and private money; and
10. understand the procedures for dealing with default and foreclosure.

KEY TERMS

acceleration clause
adjustable-rate mortgages (ARMs)
adjustment cap
alienation clause
Alt-A programs
amortization
bargain and sale deed
biweekly mortgage
buydown mortgage
cash-out refinance mortgage
Certificate of Reasonable Value (CRV)
contract for deed
deed
deed-in-lieu of foreclosure
default
defeasance
deficiency judgment
due-on-sale clause
exculpatory clause
fixed-rate mortgages
forbearance
foreclosure
general warranty deed
graduated payment mortgages
grantee
grantor
growing equity mortgage (GEM)
index
junior mortgage
limited cash-out refinance mortgage
margin
marketable title
mortgage contract
nonassumption clause
open-end clause
package mortgage
partial-release clause
PITI
prepayment penalty clause
prepayment privilege clause
private money
private mortgage insurance (PMI)
promissory note
purchase-money mortgage
quitclaim deed
reverse mortgage
right of redemption
satisfaction of mortgage
shared appreciation mortgage
special warranty deed
subordination
subprime loans
term mortgage
upfront mortgage insurance premium (UFMIP)
voluntary lien
wraparound mortgage

INTRODUCTION

In the typical real estate closing, three documents are essential: the deed to the property, the mortgage, and the promissory note. The deed transfers ownership of a property, the promissory note is a promise to repay the debt associated with the purchase of a property, and the mortgage pledges the property as collateral for repayment of the debt.

This chapter looks at these important documents, special features of mortgage contracts, and the different types of mortgage loans. A standard Fannie Mae/Freddie Mac single-family mortgage document appears in the Appendix.

THE DEED

A **deed** is an instrument of conveyance that transfers ownership or property rights from one party to another. The deed conveys the title to a property. The party giving title is known as the **grantor;** the **grantee** is the party who receives title. For a deed to be valid, it must be signed by a competent grantor and witnessed by two people. Furthermore, for title to be transferred, the deed must be delivered and voluntarily accepted.

A property is said to have **marketable title** when it has no financial encumbrances against it. An easement (discussed in chapter 9), in which someone has the right to use another person's property, is a physical encumbrance; a lien is a financial encumbrance. Most properties require clear title before ownership can be transferred.

Although deeds used in real estate transactions vary depending on where a property is located, there are four basic types. The type of deed is important because different deeds offer lenders different levels of assurance that there are no problems concerning title to the property. This assurance is critical to the lender because the lender relies on the property as security for the loan. Lenders are unlikely to loan money in situations where someone other than the mortgagor may have a claim on the property.

A **quitclaim deed** allows a grantor to relinquish all rights in a property without providing any warranty regarding the title. Quitclaim deeds are used to clear any questions about ownership. The grantor agrees only to surrender his or her rights in the property without making any promises regarding the rights of other parties who may have a claim. Using a quitclaim deed, the grantor does not have to hold title or have the right to convey the property—the grantor of a quitclaim deed is simply giving whatever rights he or she may hold in the property to the grantee.

A **bargain and sale deed** transfers title but allows only limited warranty regarding the title. The grantor acknowledges that he or she holds title to the property, but makes no warranties against possible claims by others. With a **special warranty deed,** the grantor promises that he or she has done nothing to create a cloud on the title. That is, the grantor promises only that the property was not encumbered during the time the grantor held title.

Finally, a **general warranty deed** represents the highest level of security in terms of title by promising the buyer protection against future claims on the property. A general warranty deed provides the following unique covenants:

- *Covenant of seisin*, in which the grantor warrants that he or she owns the property and has the right to convey it
- *Covenant against encumbrances*, in which the grantor assures the grantee that the property has no liens or encumbrances
- *Covenant of quiet enjoyment*, in which the grantor warrants that the title being given to the grantee will withstand challenges in court
- *Covenant of further assurance*, in which the grantor guarantees to deliver any documents necessary to uphold the title
- *Covenant of warranty forever*, in which the grantor promises to make good any losses should there be a problem with the title

When the type of deed to be used in a real estate transaction is not specified, Florida law requires use of the general warranty deed.

THE PROMISSORY NOTE

The **promissory note** is the borrower's personal promise to repay the debt associated with the financing of real property. The note states the amount to be repaid, the interest rate, and the period during which the debt will be repaid. The note lists only the amount of the principal and interest payment; escrowed items, such as taxes, insurance, and the annual percentage rate, are not included as part of the note.

The first payment on the note is due on the first of the month following a full month after closing. The note also states that if the borrower fails to make the required payment by the 15th of the month, he or she will be charged a late charge amounting to 4 percent of the principal and interest for a Federal Housing Administration (FHA) loan and 5 percent of the principal and interest on a conventional loan.

Individuals who sign the promissory note are not required to have their names on the deed. For example, parents of a young couple may cosign (guarantee) the couple's mortgage loan. The parents would sign the note, but they would not be required to sign the mortgage unless their names were on the deed. However, lenders require all persons whose names appear on the deed—and thus having a legal interest in the property—to sign the mortgage. If the mortgage has a guarantor or cosigner, that person may not have an ownership interest in the property, but he or she will have joint and several liability for repayment of the note along with the owner of the property.

All mortgages require an accompanying promissory note. Notes do not require witnesses, nor are they usually recorded. Figure 6.1 illustrates a promissory note.

THE MORTGAGE CONTRACT

The **mortgage contract** spells out the terms and conditions by which a borrower pledges real property as security for a loan. The mortgage is security for the promissory note, and it stays with the property until the loan is paid. In Florida, the note must be secured when dealing with real property.

As you may recall from chapter 1, the borrower offers a mortgage on the property to the lender and is known as the *mortgagor;* the lender is the *mortgagee.* The mortgagor promises to repay the mortgagee the money loaned to buy or refinance the property, pay all real estate taxes, maintain the property in good condition, and acquire sufficient hazard insurance to protect the lender's interests if the property is damaged.

The Fannie Mae/Freddie Mac mortgage contract used in the majority of real estate transactions (Form 3010) is a 16-page document (see Appendix). The first part of the contract identifies the borrower and the lender and defines terms such as borrower, lender, escrow items, mortgage insurance, successor in interest of borrower, and so forth.

The second part of the contract describes in legal terms the property to be pledged. In the third section, titled *Uniform Covenants*, the borrower agrees to pay the principal and interest on the promissory note as well as any prepayment charges (defined below) or late charges. The borrower also agrees to pay escrow items such as taxes and assessments, leasehold payments if any, hazard insurance premiums, mortgage insurance premiums, and community association dues, fees, and assessments, if applicable.

The next section, which makes up the rest of the mortgage contract, covers other topics, such as property and mortgage insurance; protection of the lender's interest in the property; liabilities; transfer of the property; the right of the lender to sell the promissory note and to accelerate the payments if the borrower defaults on the loan; and the assurance that the lender will release the borrower from the pledge of his or her property upon payment of all monies owed to the lender.

A mortgage is a **voluntary lien,** which is a claim against a property made with the owner's consent. To be valid, the borrower must sign the note promising repayment of the loan. Mortgages are recorded in the county where the property is located, and the date and time of their recording establishes their priority in terms of repayment. That is, in the event of default, liens similar in nature that are recorded first must be paid before other liens on the property can be paid. The maximum term for a first or second mortgage from Fannie Mae may not exceed 40 years beyond the date of the first payment.

FIGURE 6.1 ■ Promissory Note

NOTE

______________________, ________   ______________________, ____________
[Date]   [City]   [State]

____
[Property Address]

1. BORROWER'S PROMISE TO PAY

In return for a loan that I have received, I promise to pay U.S. $________________ (this amount is called "Principal"), plus interest, to the order of the Lender. The Lender is ____ ____. I will make all payments under this Note in the form of cash, check or money order.

I understand that the Lender may transfer this Note. The Lender or anyone who takes this Note by transfer and who is entitled to receive payments under this Note is called the "Note Holder."

2. INTEREST

Interest will be charged on unpaid principal until the full amount of Principal has been paid. I will pay interest at a yearly rate of ____________%.

The interest rate required by this Section 2 is the rate I will pay both before and after any default described in Section 6(B) of this Note.

3. PAYMENTS

(A) Time and Place of Payments

I will pay principal and interest by making a payment every month.

I will make my monthly payment on the ________ day of each month beginning on ______________, _____. I will make these payments every month until I have paid all of the principal and interest and any other charges described below that I may owe under this Note. Each monthly payment will be applied as of its scheduled due date and will be applied to interest before Principal. If, on ________________________, 20____, I still owe amounts under this Note, I will pay those amounts in full on that date, which is called the "Maturity Date."

I will make my monthly payments at ____ ________________________ or at a different place if required by the Note Holder.

(B) Amount of Monthly Payments

My monthly payment will be in the amount of U.S. $________________________.

4. BORROWER'S RIGHT TO PREPAY

I have the right to make payments of Principal at any time before they are due. A payment of Principal only is known as a "Prepayment." When I make a Prepayment, I will tell the Note Holder in writing that I am doing so. I may not designate a payment as a Prepayment if I have not made all the monthly payments due under the Note.

I may make a full Prepayment or partial Prepayments without paying a Prepayment charge. The Note Holder will use my Prepayments to reduce the amount of Principal that I owe under this Note. However, the Note Holder may apply my Prepayment to the accrued and unpaid interest on the Prepayment amount, before applying my Prepayment to reduce the Principal amount of the Note. If I make a partial Prepayment, there will be no changes in the due date or in the amount of my monthly payment unless the Note Holder agrees in writing to those changes.

5. LOAN CHARGES

If a law, which applies to this loan and which sets maximum loan charges, is finally interpreted so that the interest or other loan charges collected or to be collected in connection with this loan exceed the permitted limits, then: (a) any such loan charge shall be reduced by the amount necessary to reduce the charge to the permitted limit; and (b) any sums already collected from me which exceeded permitted limits will be refunded to me. The Note Holder may choose to make this refund by reducing the Principal I owe under this Note or by making a direct payment to me. If a refund reduces Principal, the reduction will be treated as a partial Prepayment.

MULTISTATE FIXED RATE NOTE—Single Family—**Fannie Mae/Freddie Mac** UNIFORM INSTRUMENT   **Form 3200 1/01** *(page 1 of 3 pages)*

FIGURE 6.1 ■ Promissory Note (Continued)

6. BORROWER'S FAILURE TO PAY AS REQUIRED

(A) Late Charge for Overdue Payments

If the Note Holder has not received the full amount of any monthly payment by the end of ___________ calendar days after the date it is due, I will pay a late charge to the Note Holder. The amount of the charge will be _____% of my overdue payment of principal and interest. I will pay this late charge promptly but only once on each late payment.

(B) Default

If I do not pay the full amount of each monthly payment on the date it is due, I will be in default.

(C) Notice of Default

If I am in default, the Note Holder may send me a written notice telling me that if I do not pay the overdue amount by a certain date, the Note Holder may require me to pay immediately the full amount of Principal which has not been paid and all the interest that I owe on that amount. That date must be at least 30 days after the date on which the notice is mailed to me or delivered by other means.

(D) No Waiver By Note Holder

Even if, at a time when I am in default, the Note Holder does not require me to pay immediately in full as described above, the Note Holder will still have the right to do so if I am in default at a later time.

(E) Payment of Note Holder's Costs and Expenses

If the Note Holder has required me to pay immediately in full as described above, the Note Holder will have the right to be paid back by me for all of its costs and expenses in enforcing this Note to the extent not prohibited by applicable law. Those expenses include, for example, reasonable attorneys' fees.

7. GIVING OF NOTICES

Unless applicable law requires a different method, any notice that must be given to me under this Note will be given by delivering it or by mailing it by first class mail to me at the Property Address above or at a different address if I give the Note Holder a notice of my different address.

Any notice that must be given to the Note Holder under this Note will be given by delivering it or by mailing it by first class mail to the Note Holder at the address stated in Section 3(A) above or at a different address if I am given a notice of that different address.

8. OBLIGATIONS OF PERSONS UNDER THIS NOTE

If more than one person signs this Note, each person is fully and personally obligated to keep all of the promises made in this Note, including the promise to pay the full amount owed. Any person who is a guarantor, surety or endorser of this Note is also obligated to do these things. Any person who takes over these obligations, including the obligations of a guarantor, surety or endorser of this Note, is also obligated to keep all of the promises made in this Note. The Note Holder may enforce its rights under this Note against each person individually or against all of us together. This means that any one of us may be required to pay all of the amounts owed under this Note.

9. WAIVERS

I and any other person who has obligations under this Note waive the rights of Presentment and Notice of Dishonor. "Presentment" means the right to require the Note Holder to demand payment of amounts due. "Notice of Dishonor" means the right to require the Note Holder to give notice to other persons that amounts due have not been paid.

10. UNIFORM SECURED NOTE

This Note is a uniform instrument with limited variations in some jurisdictions. In addition to the protections given to the Note Holder under this Note, a Mortgage, Deed of Trust, or Security Deed (the "Security Instrument"), dated the same date as this Note, protects the Note Holder from possible losses which might result if I do not keep the promises which I make in this Note. That Security Instrument describes how and under what conditions I may be required to make immediate payment in full of all amounts I owe under this Note. Some of those conditions are described as follows:

> If all or any part of the Property or any Interest in the Property is sold or transferred (or if Borrower is not a natural person and a beneficial interest in Borrower is sold or transferred) without Lender's prior written consent, Lender may require immediate payment in full of all sums secured by this Security Instrument. However, this option shall not be exercised by Lender if such exercise is prohibited by Applicable Law.

MULTISTATE FIXED RATE NOTE—Single Family—**Fannie Mae/Freddie Mac UNIFORM INSTRUMENT** **Form 3200 1/01** *(page 2 of 3 pages)*

FIGURE 6.1 ■ Promissory Note (Continued)

If Lender exercises this option, Lender shall give Borrower notice of acceleration. The notice shall provide a period of not less than 30 days from the date the notice is given in accordance with Section 15 within which Borrower must pay all sums secured by this Security Instrument. If Borrower fails to pay these sums prior to the expiration of this period, Lender may invoke any remedies permitted by this Security Instrument without further notice or demand on Borrower.

WITNESS THE HAND(S) AND SEAL(S) OF THE UNDERSIGNED.

______________________________(Seal)
- Borrower

______________________________(Seal)
- Borrower

______________________________(Seal)
- Borrower

[Sign Original Only]

According to Fannie Mae guidelines, a coborrower does not need to take title to a property that is being financed. That is, the coborrower's name does not have to appear on the deed. However, if the income of the coborrower is used to qualify for the loan, the coborrower must sign the note. Along the same lines, if a married applicant purchases a property without involving his or her spouse in either the purchase or ownership of the property, Fannie Mae requires the nonpurchasing spouse to sign the mortgage as well. In this way, the spouse, who may have a legal claim to the property, will give up all rights to claim the property as his or her homestead and make foreclosure easier.

Clauses in a Mortgage Contract

As stated earlier, the mortgage pledges a piece of property as security for a loan and gives the lender the right to foreclose the property if the borrower fails to repay the loan. In addition to the standard clauses in a mortgage contract described above, mortgages can have other clauses that affect the way the loan is repaid. Some of these optional clauses are explained below.

Prepayment privilege clause. Sometimes borrowers want to pay off their mortgage in shorter periods of time than those specified in the mortgage in order to save on interest payments. The prepayment clause defines the conditions under which the borrower can do this. The **prepayment privilege clause** has the opposite effect of the *prepayment penalty clause*.

Prepayment penalty clause. When a borrower pays off a mortgage earlier than scheduled, the lender loses the interest that would have been paid over a longer period of time. A **prepayment penalty clause** notifies the borrower that prepaying the mortgage will result in certain monetary penalties. If a mortgage has a prepayment privilege clause, however, it is unlikely there will be a penalty for early payment. VA and FHA loans—discussed later in this chapter—may not have a prepayment penalty. If other loans are silent with regard to penalty, in Florida there is no prepayment penalty. If the contract indicates a penalty, however, both parties must agree to the prepayment penalty in writing.

Open-end clause. The repayment schedule for most mortgages requires payments over time until the borrower has repaid a specific loan amount. When a mortgage has an **open-end clause,** however, the borrower can re-borrow any principal already repaid. If, for example, a borrower has an open-end mortgage for $100,000 and has paid back $20,000, the borrower can borrow against the $20,000 without applying for a new loan as long as the total amount borrowed does not exceed the original loan amount. With most open-end mortgages, however, the lender reserves the right to adjust the interest rate at the time of the new borrowing.

Due-on-sale clause. In most cases, when a property is sold, the existing loan becomes due immediately. The **due-on-sale clause** ensures the lender that as soon as a borrower sells a property with a mortgage, proceeds from that sale will be used to pay off the balance of the mortgage—the borrower cannot simply transfer the mortgage to the new owner of the property. The due-on-sale clause prevents another party from assuming a mortgage without the permission of the lender, and for this reason, it is also known as an **alienation clause** or **nonassumption clause**.

Exculpatory clause. The **exculpatory clause** releases a borrower from personal responsibility for repaying a loan. This means that if the borrower defaults on mortgage payments, the lender does not have the legal right to recover damages from the borrower through a deficiency judgment for any losses related to the loan on the property.

Partial-release clause. Sometimes a developer acquires a mortgage on a property that he or she plans to subdivide and then sell off as individual lots. Under the due-on-sale clause of most mortgages, the sale of a property requires payment of the mortgage in full. With a **partial-release clause,** however, a developer can sell subdivided parcels of a mortgaged property and have them released from the mortgage by paying off a portion of the loan. In a sense, the partial-release clause negates the due-on-sale clause. This clause can also require that attorney legal and filing fees, loan interest, and penalties also be paid immediately.

Acceleration clause. When multiple mortgage payments are past due or other serious violations of the mortgage contract occur, the borrower is declared in default and the lender is likely to invoke the **acceleration clause.** This clause requires that the entire remaining balance on the loan be paid in full. The acceleration clause also allows lenders to charge any legal or administrative fees to the defaulted borrower.

Subordination clause. In terms of mortgages, **subordination** refers to making one mortgage inferior to another. For example, a buyer may acquire a mortgage to buy a property and then, later, apply for a home equity loan using that same property as security for the home equity loan. The home equity loan will be *subordinate* to the first mortgage. This means that should the borrower default or the house be sold, the first mortgage must be paid in full before the lender who made the home equity loan is paid.

Right of redemption clause. Right of redemption—also known as *equitable right of redemption*—refers to a borrower's legal right to stop foreclosure by paying all past due principal and interest owed to the lender, as well as any penalties and fees incurred by the lender during the process of foreclosing. Payment stops the foreclosure, but in Florida, the right of redemption must be exercised before the foreclosure action is concluded. Once the foreclosure is completed, it negates the lender's acceleration privileges.

Defeasance clause. The term **defeasance** has more than one meaning. The defeasance clause ends the mortgage after all payments have been made. Defeasance is also used to prevent the lender—that is, defeat an attempt by the lender—from taking title to the property as long as all conditions required of the borrower are being met. Title is transferred back to the mortgagor.

AMORTIZATION

Amortization refers to the payment of a loan and its interest over a specified period of time. Most mortgage loans have an amortization period of 30 years or 15 years. When the mortgage loan has a fixed interest rate, the amount of the monthly payment stays the same throughout the length of the repayment period. Adjustable-rate mortgages (ARMs), on the other hand, adjust monthly payment amounts to reflect changes in interest rates. Fixed-rate mortgages and ARMs are discussed in the next section of this chapter.

When the loan amount, interest rate, and period of repayment are known, then the monthly repayment amount can be calculated. Part of each payment goes toward the principal and part goes toward the interest. In the first years of a mortgage loan, almost all of the monthly payment goes toward paying interest. In later years, most of the payment goes toward repaying the principal.

A typical mortgage payment includes principal, interest, taxes, and insurance, which is referred to as **PITI.** Along with the principal and interest, known as the "PI" part of a mortgage payment, a portion of most monthly mortgage payments goes toward paying annual property taxes, hazard insurance, and, in some cases, mortgage insurance premiums. The parts of the mortgage payment for taxes and insurance are known as the "TI." Tax and insurance payments are held in the borrower's escrow account by the company servicing the mortgage loan. The servicing company then pays taxes and insurance premiums when they come due at different times during the year. Figure 6.2 illustrates a typical PITI breakdown of payments on a $225,000 loan with a term of 30 years.

Calculation of principal and interest are discussed in more detail in chapter 11.

According to Fannie Mae guidelines, mortgage documents must contain a provision for escrowing taxes and insurance payments. This requirement can be waived, however, by the lender. If the borrower fails to make tax and insurance payments on time, Fannie Mae may require the lender to collect the funds to be escrowed so that the property insurance stays in force and taxing agencies do not put a lien on the property.

FIXED-RATE AND ADJUSTABLE-RATE MORTGAGES

Interest rates on mortgage loans are either fixed or adjustable. Under the terms of **fixed-rate mortgages,** borrowers repay a fixed amount each month for the term of the loan. As Figure 6.2 illustrates, the amount of this payment applied toward repaying the loan principal is quite small in the first years of the mortgage, with most of the payment going toward the interest on the loan. Over time, however, the loan amount decreases, lowering the amount of interest owed. As this happens, a larger part of the monthly payment goes toward repaying the principal.

In a fixed-rate mortgage, the amount of the payment applied toward the principal and the amount applied toward the interest vary with each payment—the amount of interest

FIGURE 6.2 ■ PITI Example

If John acquires a fixed-rate mortgage for $225,000 with a term of 30 years and an interest rate of 7 percent, his $1,496.93 monthly payment will be divided between principal and interest (the PI) in the first five months as follows:

	Principal	Interest	Loan Balance
First month	$184.43	$1,312.50	$224,815.57
Second month	$185.51	$1,311.42	$224,630.06
Third month	$186.57	$1,310.34	$224,443.47
Fourth month	$187.68	$1,309.25	$224,255.80
Fifth month	$188.77	$1,308.16	$224,067.03

If property taxes of $1,600 and an annual hazard insurance premium of $800 are included in the monthly payment (the TI), the PITI would be as follows:

$$\text{Monthly TI payment} = \frac{\text{Property taxes} + \text{Annual insurance premium}}{12 \text{ months}}$$

$$= (\$1{,}600 + \$800) \div 12 = \$200$$

This would result in a PITI payment for John of $1,496.93 + $200, or **$1,696.93.**

paid gets smaller and the amount paid on the principal gets larger each month. But neither the interest rate nor the total monthly payment amount changes over the term of the loan. Fannie Mae also requires that amortized fixed-rate mortgages with a balloon payment include a provision that the balloon payment will not come due during the first seven years of the mortgage loan.

Adjustable-rate mortgages (ARMs), in contrast, allow lenders to adjust the interest rate charge on a loan to reflect economic conditions. Borrowers often prefer ARMs because ARMs typically have lower interest rates than traditional fixed-rate mortgages. Lenders also like ARMs because being able to change the interest rate protects the lender from losing money when interest rates go higher. Most ARMs adjust once per year.

ARMs have certain characteristics not found in fixed-rate mortgages. For example, ARMs base their interest rates on an **index,** which is some general economic measure of the cost of borrowing funds. Legally, the index that a lender uses to set an interest rate must be beyond the control of the lender and verifiable by the borrower. Typical indexes used by lenders include the one-year Treasury bill, the general cost of funds index such as the 11th District of the Federal Home Loan Bank Cost of Funds Index, or the London Interbank Offering Rate (LIBOR).

The **margin** is the amount, expressed as a percentage rate, that the lender charges above the index. The margin covers the expenses of the lender as well as the lender's profit on the loan. Although an index is likely to change during the life of a loan, lenders are not allowed to change their margin during that period. The formula for the interest rate on an adjustable-rate mortgage is

Interest rate = Index + Margin

Most adjustable loans also have an **adjustment cap,** which sets the maximum amount a loan's interest rate can increase. In the typical ARM, the annual adjustment cannot exceed 2 percent, and the total adjustment over the life of the loan cannot exceed 6 percent. If the adjusted payment does not cover the interest due on the principal, however, negative amortization can occur.

The Truth-in-Lending Act requires certain mandatory disclosures for adjustable-rate mortgages.

CONTRACT FOR DEED AND PURCHASE-MONEY MORTGAGE

A contract for deed—also known as an agreement for deed—and a purchase-money mortgage are two types of owner financing.

Sometimes a buyer and seller agree to an arrangement whereby the buyer takes possession of a property but the seller retains title until a certain amount of the purchase price has been paid. This arrangement, known as a **contract for deed** or an *installment sale,* allows a buyer to acquire a property with little cash investment. When the buyer has paid the agreed amount, the seller then transfers title to the buyer.

In some cases, the buyer makes a down payment and the seller finances the rest of the loan. When the buyer has paid the amount agreed upon, he or she can then assume the existing mortgage or obtain new financing. The advantage of this arrangement for the buyer is that a property can be acquired with little cash up front. The advantage for the seller is that he or she retains title and typically charges a higher rate of interest on the outstanding balance of the loan.

Sometimes a buyer will ask a seller to "take back" a mortgage. In a typical residential transaction, this means that the buyer will obtain or assume a loan to buy the property but will ask the seller to hold a second mortgage for the amount of the down payment. This arrangement is one example of a **purchase-money mortgage.**

Title to the property passes to the buyer, and the seller holds a second mortgage. In these cases, the portion of the purchase-money mortgage held by the seller is subordinate to the larger first mortgage and is called a **junior mortgage.**

Other Types of Mortgages

Although most mortgages are amortized over 30 years and feature either a fixed or adjustable interest rate, lenders have developed several variations of the standard mortgage for use in special situations. These variations are described below.

Buydown. A **buydown mortgage** is typically used when a seller, such as a builder, pays the lender an upfront fee in order to lower the interest rate on the mortgage loan. In many cases, this enables the borrower to qualify for a larger loan at the same time that it allows the seller to maintain the original asking price for the property.

Reverse. A **reverse mortgage** allows homeowners age 62 and over to borrow the equity they have built up in their property without ever having to make a payment on the loan. The lender allows an amount to be borrowed based on the homeowner's equity and life expectancy. Within a certain period after the owner vacates the home, the loan must be paid off. Reverse mortgages are government-insured and closely regulated.

Term. Some mortgages require payment of interest only during the term of the mortgage. When this term ends, the original amount of the mortgage is due to the lender. A **term mortgage** often covers periods shorter than the typical 30 years. Term mortgages are non-amortized loans.

Package. In some cases, a mortgage covers both real and personal property. When a borrower acquires an office building that includes furniture and equipment, for example, he or she may apply for a package mortgage. A **package mortgage** covers the value of the furniture in addition to the value of the property.

Biweekly. In recent years, **biweekly mortgages** have become popular with some borrowers. The main advantage of the biweekly mortgage is that it allows a borrower to build up equity in a property more quickly. Individuals with a biweekly mortgage typically make half the normal payment every two weeks. Because there are 52 weeks in a year, borrowers make 26 half payments rather than 12 full payments. This amounts to the equivalent of an extra monthly payment each year. The additional payments allow the borrower to pay off a 30-year mortgage in a shorter period of time. Payments on biweekly mortgages must be drafted directly from the borrower's bank account. The example below illustrates the advantages of a biweekly mortgage.

EXAMPLE: Earlier we gave the example of John acquiring a 30-year mortgage for $225,000 with an interest rate of 7 percent. The terms of the mortgage would require John to make 360 payments of $1,496.93.

If John had chosen a biweekly mortgage, however, he would be making 26 payments per year rather than 12. Each payment would be $748.47 (half of $1,496.93). His mortgage would be paid in 23 years rather than 30. Total interest payments on the 30-year mortgage would be $313,895.02; on the biweekly mortgage they would be $233,907.14—a savings of $79,987.88.

Graduated payment. Graduated payment mortgages, also known as **growing equity mortgages (GEMs),** allow borrowers to start at a lower payment in the first years of a loan. Over time, the amount of payment increases until it reaches a specified amount, then stays at that level until the mortgage is paid in full. A buydown mortgage (discussed above) starts with a series of graduated payments.

Shared appreciation. In a **shared appreciation mortgage,** a lender charges the borrower an interest rate that is below market value in exchange for a share of the appreciation of the property when the owner sells.

Cash-out refinance and limited cash-out refinance. The **cash-out refinance mortgage** allows the borrower to pay off existing loans, include the closing costs of the refinanced loan, and take out the remaining equity in the property. The **limited cash-out refinance mortgage** allows the borrower to pay off existing loans, cover the closing costs of the refinanced loan, and take out the lower of $2,000 or 2 percent of the loan amount in cash.

Wraparound. A **wraparound mortgage** is created when a seller or other party agrees to pay the mortgage on a property while, at the same time, lending money to the buyer at a higher rate of interest. In this way, the seller collects higher payments from the mortgage with the buyer that the seller uses to make lower payments on the seller's original mortgage. Wraparound mortgages are used when either the buyer wants to use as little cash as possible to purchase a property or if an existing mortgage has a prepayment penalty clause. However, wraparound mortgages are not allowed when a mortgage has a due-on-sale clause.

SATISFACTION OF MORTGAGE

When a mortgage has been paid in full, Florida statutes require the lender or investor holding the loan to provide the borrower with a document known as a **satisfaction of mortgage** within 60 days. This document must also be recorded in the public records within 60 days. The mortgage lien is then canceled.

TYPES OF MORTGAGE LOANS

Although mortgage loans can come from a variety of sources, including commercial banks, savings banks, credit unions, and insurance companies, historically, most mortgage loans were one of three types: FHA, VA, or conventional. In recent years, however, lenders have developed some alternatives to traditional financing.

FHA Loans

The National Housing Act of 1934 created the Federal Housing Administration, an agency of the federal government that assists lenders in investing in the housing industry. Interestingly, FHA loans are not made by the FHA. Rather, the FHA fully *insures* loans made by approved private lenders. Interest rates for these loans are set by the lender based on supply and demand. The maximum allowable term for an FHA loan is 30 years.

FHA loans require the borrower to use his or her own funds to pay at least 3 percent of the selling price on a property. The maximum loan amount FHA will finance varies, depending on housing costs in different parts of the country. Certain closing costs may also be included as part of an FHA loan. FHA minimum loan limits in 2008 ranged from $271,050 for designated standard-cost areas to $729,750 for designated high-cost areas.

FHA also requires borrowers to pay an **upfront mortgage insurance premium (UFMIP),** which is 1.5 percent of the loan on a 30-year mortgage. Mortgage insurance protects the lender against default on the part of the borrower. Borrowers often finance the upfront mortgage insurance premium as part of the loan amount and pay the annual mortgage insurance premiums through the monthly PITI payment. As you may recall, the Homeowners Protection Act requires that when the balance on a mortgage loan reaches 78 percent of the value of the property, MIP is automatically cancelled. However, with FHA loans, the borrower must also pay MIP for at least five years. Even though the UFMIP is cancelled, the mortgage insurance continues for the life of the loan.

VA Loans

As discussed in Chapter 1, VA loans were established at the end of World War II to help veterans buy houses. The advantage of the VA loan to the lender is that it *guarantees* the lender partial payment of any loan made to a veteran should the veteran default on the loan. VA loans are available to active duty service personnel and surviving spouses as well as veterans, and they can be used to improve, refinance, or purchase owner-occupied real property as long as it is a first mortgage on a one- to four-family dwelling. The maximum term allowable on a VA loan is 30 years.

Veterans or other eligible parties who wish to participate in the VA program must first provide a copy of form DD-214—a proof of discharge—before they can obtain a Certificate of Eligibility from the Department of Veterans Affairs. A VA appraiser determines the value of the property the person wants to buy, then issues a **Certificate of Reasonable Value (CRV),** which is an appraisal used to determine the maximum amount the VA will guarantee. The VA will require that the value of the property be at least equal to the amount the buyer is asking to borrow. Also, the guarantee issued by the VA to the lender will be based on the loan amount, and not the actual value of the property. Lenders can lend up to a minimum of four times the amount of the certificate of eligibility used by the VA. The VA guarantees the first 25 percent of the loan. Under VA regulations, there is a maximum guarantee, but no maximum loan amount.

VA loans offer certain advantages over FHA loans. VA loans do not require mortgage insurance premiums, nor do they require a down payment from the buyer. Nonveterans can also assume VA loans provided the certificate of eligibility remains attached to the loan. However, closing costs such as discount points, the credit report fee, and state taxes cannot be financed as part of the loan amount unless the loan is a refinance rather than a purchase. VA loans also require a one-time funding fee paid by the borrowers, which can be added to the loan balance and amortized over the life of the loan.

Conventional Loans

Conventional loans are made by institutional lenders without either the insurance associated with an FHA loan or the guarantees associated with a VA loan. Because these loans carry more risk, conventional lenders typically require higher down payments from borrowers—usually 20 percent—before they will approve a loan application. When the loan-to-value ratio (LTV) is greater than 80 percent, lenders will often require **private mortgage insurance (PMI),** which protects the lender against loss due to default on the part of the borrower. PMI is paid as part of the monthly PITI. As you may recall, once PMI is paid down or cancelled, there is no insurance on the remaining loan balance. For PMI contracts issued after January 1, 2007, PMI premiums are tax deductible for new homeowners with an adjusted gross income of $100,000 or less.

FHA and conventional loans can be used for purchase of investment property and do not require the borrower to live in the property being purchased. VA loans, on the other hand, can only be used for a borrower's principal place of residence.

Alt-A Programs, Subprime Loans, and Private Money

Sometimes buyers do not qualify for FHA, VA, or conventional loans because of factors in their background, such as a poor credit history or poorly documented sources of income. These borrowers may apply for an Alt-A loan, a subprime loan, or use private money to finance a purchase.

Alt-A programs typically allow the borrower to provide less documentation regarding qualifying factors. These loans offer greater flexibility to borrowers who may have no regular income or assets, and who would not qualify for FHA, VA, or conventional loans. **Subprime loans** are typically used by borrowers who have experienced credit problems in the past. Subprime loans usually carry a higher interest rate than other loans. They can be used for purchases or refinancing, and they come with either a fixed or adjustable interest rate. Finally, **private money** refers to loans from noninstitutional investors.

DEFAULT CONDITIONS AND FORECLOSURES

Default occurs when a borrower fails to comply with the terms of an agreement, such as missing payments on his or her mortgage loan. When default occurs, the lender has several options, including initiating a lawsuit, foreclosure, forbearance, and deed-in-lieu of foreclosure.

Initiating a Lawsuit

When a borrower fails to make payments on a mortgage, the lender can initiate a lawsuit based on the promissory note. If the lender wins the suit, he or she can use the judgment against any property owned by the borrower. The lender could allow the homeowner to keep the property pledged as security for the mortgage loan and attempt to collect from another asset owned by the borrower.

Foreclosure

Another strategy a lender may use against a borrower in default is to foreclose on the mortgaged property. In this case, the lender exercises the acceleration clause of the mortgage, which requires that the balance of the mortgage be paid in full. If the borrower fails to pay, the lender then files a lawsuit asking the court to require the property to be sold. Proceeds from the sale are used to repay the lender.

If the sale of the foreclosed property results in a price greater than the amount owed to the lender, the extra proceeds go to the homeowner. If the proceeds are less than the balance due on the note, the lender can ask for a **deficiency judgment,** which allows the lender to go after other assets of the borrower to obtain sufficient funds to cover the balance.

When a property is sold at **foreclosure,** the disbursement of funds must follow a specific order. The first priority is any government liens, such as taxes, followed by the expenses in managing the sale. Special assessments are paid next, followed by federal estate taxes. Only after all of these are paid does the lender get paid.

Forbearance

Sometimes a lender has reason to believe that a borrower who is in default will be able to pay at a later date. **Forbearance** is the practice of refraining from foreclosing in the expectation that mortgage payments will be made in the future.

Deed-in-Lieu of Foreclosure

Deed-in-lieu of foreclosure refers to a situation where a homeowner surrenders the deed to his or her home to a lender rather than go through the foreclosure process. This process is sometimes referred to as a "friendly foreclosure."

KEY POINT REVIEW

- The *deed* transfers ownership rights associated with a property from one party to another. The party who gives title is the *grantor;* the receiving party is the *grantee*. A valid deed must be signed by a competent grantor, witnessed by two people, delivered, and voluntarily accepted.
- A *quitclaim deed* offers the fewest guarantees to grantees; a *general warranty deed* offers the most guarantees.
- The date and time a mortgage is recorded establishes its legal priority in terms of repayment.
- *Subordination* refers to making one mortgage inferior to another in terms of priority.
- A *contract for deed* allows a buyer to take possession of a property with the seller retaining title until a certain amount of the purchase price has been paid.
- With a *purchase-money mortgage*, the seller typically finances the down payment on a property.
- *Amortization* refers to the systematic reduction of the loan's principal balance.
- The typical monthly mortgage payment covers principal, interest, and escrowed items such as taxes and insurance, referred to as *PITI*.
- Lenders base *adjustable-rate mortgage* rates on an *index* that is beyond their control and independently verifiable by the borrower. The *margin* covers the expenses of the lender as well as the lender's profit margin.
- The advantage of a *biweekly mortgage* is that it allows the borrower to make half the mortgage payments every two weeks or the equivalent of 13 full payments rather than 12, thereby lowering the interest costs and shortening the term.
- A *wraparound mortgage* is a secondary lien that wraps around the seller's first mortgage.
- The FHA insures loans and requires an upfront *mortgage insurance premium* to protect against default by the borrowers. VA loans are partially guaranteed by the Department of Veterans Affairs and do not require mortgage insurance. Conventional loans are made by institutional lenders without guarantees and usually require higher down payments and private mortgage insurance.
- *Alt-A programs*, *subprime loans*, and *private money* are sources of funding often used by borrowers who do not qualify for FHA, VA, or conforming conventional loans.
- The four remedies for *default* are: *lawsuit*, *foreclosure*, *forbearance*, and *deed-in-lieu of foreclosure*.
- The priorities for repayment in a foreclosure sale are government liens first, sales expenses second, special assessments third, estate taxes fourth, and finally, the balance on the mortgage.

REVIEW QUESTIONS

1. The mortgagee
   a. promises to repay the mortgagor.
   b. is usually the same as the seller of the property.
   c. promises to repay the grantee.
   d. accepts payments from the mortgagor.

2. Marian is buying a condo in Palm Beach for $335,000 with a conventional loan. The mortgage is for 30 years at 6.75 percent interest rate. To avoid mortgage insurance, Marian will likely need to make a down payment of
   a. $16,750.
   b. $33,500.
   c. $67,000.
   d. $83,750.

3. Veronica wants to buy a property using a contract for deed. This means that
   a. Veronica will pay the sales price in full.
   b. Veronica will not take title until she pays off the mortgage balance.
   c. the seller will finance part of the purchase price and hold the title.
   d. Veronica and several parties will buy the property together.

4. The priority of a mortgage in terms of lien position is determined by the
   a. size of the mortgage.
   b. lender who has granted the mortgage.
   c. date and time of recording.
   d. location of the property.

5. If a Florida mortgage has no provision for prepayment,
   a. the borrower can prepay the loan without penalty.
   b. the borrower can prepay only if the lender agrees.
   c. the borrower can prepay but with penalties.
   d. it is illegal because all Florida mortgages have a provision for prepayment.

6. One of the most important documents at the closing is the promissory note. This document
   a. lists the principal, interest, taxes, and insurance to be paid by the borrower each month.
   b. lists the principal and interest only because taxes and insurance may be escrowed.
   c. is not necessary if the deed and mortgage have been signed.
   d. promises the transfer of real property in case of default.

7. Because Jack was required to get a Certificate of Reasonable Value, Jack must be applying for a(n)
   a. VA loan.
   b. FHA loan.
   c. subprime loan.
   d. conventional loan.

8. A home on Elm Street has been sold at foreclosure. In terms of repayment, the first priority will be
   a. the mortgage loan.
   b. any special assessments.
   c. tax liens.
   d. sale expenses.

9. A deed
   a. is a promise to repay.
   b. transfers ownership rights.
   c. pledges property as security for a loan.
   d. commits the mortgage company to making a loan.

10. The maximum term for a mortgage that Fannie Mae will purchase is
    a. 15 years.
    b. 30 years.
    c. 40 years.
    d. none because there is no maximum term.

11. If the mortgage payment is late, the lender will assess a late fee based on
    a. the principal and interest only.
    b. the principal, interest, and taxes only.
    c. the principal, interest, taxes, and insurance.
    d. any of the above that the lender chooses to assess as part of the late charge.

12. Some buyers consider the contract for deed as advantageous because the
    a. buyer isn't required to take title.
    b. seller can charge a higher interest rate and pass the savings on to the buyer.
    c. contract for deed grants the buyer an exculpatory clause.
    d. buyer does not need to come up with much cash to take possession of the property.

13. Anthony had a loan of $100,000 on his condo. He repaid $25,000, then borrowed an additional $20,000 without refinancing the loan. Anthony must have a(n)
    a. due-on-sale mortgage.
    b. open-end mortgage.
    c. partial-release mortgage.
    d. exculpatory mortgage.

14. Two brothers buy a home together and arrange financing, but only one brother plans to live in the home. The brother who will NOT live in the property
    a. must take title and sign the note.
    b. may take title without signing a note.
    c. cannot take title to the property unless he will live there, too.
    d. need not take title to the property but must sign the note.

15. In which default situation is a borrower most likely to retain title to his or her property?
    a. Lawsuit
    b. Foreclosure
    c. Forbearance
    d. Deed-in-lieu of foreclosure

16. Mr. Homebuyer doesn't know whether to apply for a fixed-rate mortgage at 7.125 percent or go with an adjustable. With a fixed-rate mortgage, Mr. Homebuyer can be sure that the
    a. amount of interest paid will remain the same in each payment.
    b. amount of principal paid will remain the same in each payment.
    c. amount going to principal and interest will vary with each payment.
    d. rate of payment can be adjusted depending on his financial situation.

17. When Pablo acquired his beachfront property, the seller provided him with a bargain and sale deed that
    a. transfers title but makes no guarantees about others' claims on the property.
    b. protects Pablo against future claims on the property.
    c. relinquishes title without giving Pablo any warranties.
    d. transfers title but only for a specified period of time.

18. An index is
    a. the profit the lender makes.
    b. a general economic measure of the cost of borrowing funds.
    c. the percentage the lender charges above the margin.
    d. similar to the adjustment cap.

19. Amortization refers to the
    a. gradual increase of taxes on a property.
    b. period after the mortgage has been paid.
    c. period before the mortgage has been recorded.
    d. systematic payment of a loan's principal and interest over time.

20. Julie is buying a home for her elderly mother. To provide her mother the highest level of assurance regarding title, Julie should ask for a
    a. quitclaim deed.
    b. general warranty deed.
    c. special warranty deed.
    d. bargain and sale deed.

21. The kind of mortgage that allows elderly homeowners to receive money for the equity in their property is called
    a. buydown.
    b. reverse.
    c. term.
    d. package.

22. Bobbie Anne wants to buy a property using a purchase-money mortgage. In a typical purchase-money mortgage transaction
    a. Bobbie Anne will need to borrow additional money to buy the property.
    b. either FHA or VA will finance all of the mortgage.
    c. the transaction will be in cash, lowering fees for both Bobbie Anne and the seller.
    d. both Bobbie Anne and the seller will hold title to the property.

23. Many borrowers like ARMs because
    a. they are more profitable to both the borrower and the lender.
    b. they often have lower interest rates than fixed-rate mortgages.
    c. interest rates can be adjusted upward in order to take advantage of tax deductions.
    d. their mortgages are likely to be paid before the end of the term of the loan.

24. Mr. Warren is buying a large piece of land where he plans to build three houses that he will sell later. The deal is risky, so to protect himself from personal responsibility for repaying the lender if he defaults on the mortgage, Mr. Warren should ask for a(n)
    a. open-end clause.
    b. partial-release clause.
    c. exculpatory clause.
    d. prepayment clause.

25. Conventional mortgages require mortgage insurance on loans that are greater than what percentage of the value of a property?
    a. 85 percent
    b. 80 percent
    c. 95 percent
    d. 97 percent

26. The advantage of a VA loan from the lender's perspective is that the loan
    a. is insured.
    b. cannot be defaulted by the borrower.
    c. can be transferred to an FHA loan easily.
    d. is partially guaranteed.

27. A builder is offering homes on a golf course with mortgages that require interest payments only. What kind of mortgage is the builder offering?
    a. Graduated payment
    b. Reverse
    c. Term
    d. Open-end

28. Second City Mortgages has agreed that, in case of default, Mr. and Mrs. Carlisle can repay Second City after their mortgage with Major Mortgages is paid. This practice is known as
    a. an exclusionary mortgage with an exculpatory clause.
    b. a contract for deed.
    c. a due-on-sale mortgage.
    d. subordination.

29. Three years ago a finance company repossessed Mr. Long's car because he wasn't making payments. Now Mr. Long would like to buy a house. What type of loan is Mr. Long most likely to qualify for?
    a. FHA
    b. VA
    c. Alt-A
    d. Conventional

30. A buyer acquires a new home for $225,000. His UFMIP will most likely be
    a. $2,250.
    b. $3,375.
    c. $4,500.
    d. $5,625.

CHAPTER

7

THE LOAN APPLICATION PROCESS

LEARNING OBJECTIVES

After finishing chapter 7, you should be able to

1. understand the loan interview and application process;
2. understand the contents of the loan application;
3. explain the Verification of Deposit and Verification of Employment forms;
4. interpret a credit report;
5. know the requirements for reestablishing credit;
6. recognize the importance of the sales contract and mortgage payment history in the approval process;
7. know the requirements for self-employed applicants;
8. understand what documents are forwarded to underwriting; and
9. know the penalties for falsifying information on a loan application.

KEY TERMS

commission income
completion reserve
conditional approval
credit
credit score
debt-to-income ratio
Fair Isaac Corporation
FmHA loans
housing expense ratio (HER)
prequalifying
qualifying for a loan
representative credit score
Request for Verification of Deposit
Request for Verification of Employment
total obligations ratio (TOR)
Uniform Residential Loan Application
Uniform Underwriting and Transmittal Summary
Verification of Mortgage (VOM) form

INTRODUCTION

When a potential borrower applies to a potential lender for a mortgage loan, the borrower starts a complicated process called **qualifying for a loan,** in which the lender assesses the risk associated with loaning money to the applicant. The entire loan approval process is based on evaluating the loan applicant in three areas: the applicant's ability to repay a debt; his or her willingness to repay a debt; and the security the applicant offers for the debt. Sometimes borrowers will apply for a loan without having identified a property they plan to purchase. This process is known as **prequalifying** and it is used to determine the amount the borrower would be able to repay. Prequalifying can result in **conditional approval,** which is a statement by the lender of the amount of the loan the lender would offer the borrower as well as an interest rate ceiling.

During the loan approval process, the lender asks the applicant for extensive information about both the applicant and the property the applicant wants to use as collateral for the loan. The lender will want to know about the applicant's income, assets, credit history, employment, housing expenses, and liabilities. In addition to this personal information, the lender will require an appraisal of the value of the property and, in most cases, an inspection to see if the property has been damaged by termites or other pests.

According to federal guidelines, the maximum age for applications, credit reports, verifications, and all loan documents is 120 days from the signing of the note and mortgage, and 180 days if the loan is for new construction.

The following text box summarizes the kinds of information a borrower may be asked to provide as part of a loan application.

THE LOAN APPLICATION

The loan application process usually begins with a meeting between the borrower and the mortgage broker, although applications can also be taken over the telephone, through the mail, or via the Internet. When the application process begins, the broker provides the applicant with an instructional letter that explains the process and gives directions on completing the application, what additional information and documents will be needed, and the fees associated with the application process.

Most lenders require applicants to use the **Uniform Residential Loan Application** (Fannie Mae Form 1003 or 1003[S]; Freddie Mac Form 65). Applicants complete this form themselves or with the assistance of a mortgage broker or loan originator who submits it to the lender. The original submission may be handwritten, but if the lender approves the loan, a typed version of the application will be used as part of the closing. The application also requires the borrower to attest to the accuracy of the information provided. Under the Real Estate Settlement Procedures Act (RESPA), false information on the application can result in imprisonment or a fine of up to $10,000. The revised form of the application includes signature lines for the applicant to indicate whether the application is for joint or individual credit.

The Uniform Residential Loan Application has ten sections (see Figure 7.1). Section I asks the type of mortgage for which the potential borrower is applying. In addition to FHA, VA, and conventional loans, the application also lists the categories of USDA/Rural Housing Service and Other. The loan application asks for the Social Security numbers of the borrower and any coborrower. However, Fannie Mae does not require that borrowers have a Social Security number.

LOAN APPLICATION INFORMATION

Property information

- Sale and Purchase Contract
- Legal description of property
- A multiple listing service sheet, if available

Borrower information

- Social Security number
- Home addresses for last two years
- Names and addresses of landlords for last two years
- Names and addresses of all employers for last two years

Asset information

- IRS W-2 forms
- Tax returns from the past two years with schedules
- Two most recent paycheck stubs
- Bank statements for the past three months
- Checking account numbers and locations
- Savings account numbers and locations
- Credit union account numbers and locations
- Mutual fund account numbers and locations
- IRA and 401(k) information
- Information on other income if used for qualifying, including child support, bonuses, overtime, Social Security or disability payments, pension income, or rental property income
- Copies of documents showing money owed to the borrower

Debt information

- Payment book or billing statement for all debts
- Documentation of current mortgages or home equity loans
- Documentation of car payments
- Information about student loans
- Divorce decree or separation agreement
- Clarification of divorced person's debts
- Information about payments automatically debited from accounts
- Copy of any bankruptcy proceedings
- Explanation of source for closing costs
- Explanation for any late payments, judgments, liens, bankruptcies, or foreclosures
- Copy of a Certificate of Resident Alien Status (green card), if applicable

Source: *All About Mortgages,* 3rd edition; New York: Kaplan Publishing.

FIGURE 7.1 ■ Uniform Residential Loan Application

Uniform Residential Loan Application

This application is designed to be completed by the applicant(s) with the Lender's assistance. Applicants should complete this form as "Borrower" or "Co-Borrower," as applicable. Co-Borrower information must also be provided (and the appropriate box checked) when ☐ the income or assets of a person other than the Borrower (including the Borrower's spouse) will be used as a basis for loan qualification or ☐ the income or assets of the Borrower's spouse or other person who has community property rights pursuant to state law will not be used as a basis for loan qualification, but his or her liabilities must be considered because the spouse or other person has community property rights pursuant to applicable law and Borrower resides in a community property state, the security property is located in a community property state, or the Borrower is relying on other property located in a community property state as a basis for repayment of the loan.

If this is an application for joint credit, Borrower and Co-Borrower each agree that we intend to apply for joint credit (sign below):

Borrower ____________________ Co-Borrower ____________________

I. TYPE OF MORTGAGE AND TERMS OF LOAN

Mortgage Applied for: ☐ VA ☐ FHA ☐ Conventional ☐ USDA/Rural Housing Service ☐ Other (explain):				Agency Case Number	Lender Case Number
Amount $	Interest Rate %	No. of Months	**Amortization Type:**	☐ Fixed Rate ☐ GPM	☐ Other (explain): ☐ ARM (type):

II. PROPERTY INFORMATION AND PURPOSE OF LOAN

Subject Property Address (street, city, state & ZIP)	No. of Units
Legal Description of Subject Property (attach description if necessary)	Year Built

Purpose of Loan ☐ Purchase ☐ Construction ☐ Other (explain): ☐ Refinance ☐ Construction-Permanent

Property will be: ☐ Primary Residence ☐ Secondary Residence ☐ Investment

Complete this line if construction or construction-permanent loan.

Year Lot Acquired	Original Cost	Amount Existing Liens	(a) Present Value of Lot	(b) Cost of Improvements	Total (a + b)
	$	$	$	$	$

Complete this line if this is a refinance loan.

Year Acquired	Original Cost	Amount Existing Liens	Purpose of Refinance	Describe Improvements ☐ made ☐ to be made
	$	$		Cost: $

Title will be held in what Name(s)	Manner in which Title will be held	Estate will be held in: ☐ Fee Simple ☐ Leasehold (show expiration date)
Source of Down Payment, Settlement Charges, and/or Subordinate Financing (explain)		

III. BORROWER INFORMATION

Borrower				Co-Borrower			
Borrower's Name (include Jr. or Sr. if applicable)				Co-Borrower's Name (include Jr. or Sr. if applicable)			
Social Security Number	Home Phone (incl. area code)	DOB (mm/dd/yyyy)	Yrs. School	Social Security Number	Home Phone (incl. area code)	DOB (mm/dd/yyyy)	Yrs. School
☐ Married ☐ Unmarried (include single, divorced, widowed) ☐ Separated		Dependents (not listed by Co-Borrower) no.	ages	☐ Married ☐ Unmarried (include single, divorced, widowed) ☐ Separated		Dependents (not listed by Borrower) no.	ages
Present Address (street, city, state, ZIP) ☐ Own ☐ Rent ___No. Yrs.				Present Address (street, city, state, ZIP) ☐ Own ☐ Rent ___No. Yrs.			
Mailing Address, if different from Present Address				Mailing Address, if different from Present Address			

If residing at present address for less than two years, complete the following:

Borrower	Co-Borrower
Former Address (street, city, state, ZIP) ☐ Own ☐ Rent ___No. Yrs.	Former Address (street, city, state, ZIP) ☐ Own ☐ Rent ___No. Yrs.

IV. EMPLOYMENT INFORMATION

Borrower			Co-Borrower		
Name & Address of Employer	☐ Self Employed	Yrs. on this job	Name & Address of Employer	☐ Self Employed	Yrs. on this job
		Yrs. employed in this line of work/profession			Yrs. employed in this line of work/profession
Position/Title/Type of Business	Business Phone (incl. area code)		Position/Title/Type of Business	Business Phone (incl. area code)	

If employed in current position for less than two years or if currently employed in more than one position, complete the following:

FIGURE 7.1 ■ Uniform Residential Loan Application (Continued)

IV. EMPLOYMENT INFORMATION (cont'd)

Borrower			Co-Borrower		
Name & Address of Employer	☐ Self Employed	Dates (from – to) Monthly Income $	Name & Address of Employer	☐ Self Employed	Dates (from – to) Monthly Income $
Position/Title/Type of Business	Business Phone (incl. area code)		Position/Title/Type of Business	Business Phone (incl. area code)	
Name & Address of Employer	☐ Self Employed	Dates (from – to) Monthly Income $	Name & Address of Employer	☐ Self Employed	Dates (from – to) Monthly Income $
Position/Title/Type of Business	Business Phone (incl. area code)		Position/Title/Type of Business	Business Phone (incl. area code)	

V. MONTHLY INCOME AND COMBINED HOUSING EXPENSE INFORMATION

Gross Monthly Income	Borrower	Co-Borrower	Total	Combined Monthly Housing Expense	Present	Proposed
Base Empl. Income*	$	$	$	Rent	$	
Overtime				First Mortgage (P&I)		$
Bonuses				Other Financing (P&I)		
Commissions				Hazard Insurance		
Dividends/Interest				Real Estate Taxes		
Net Rental Income				Mortgage Insurance		
Other (before completing, see the notice in "describe other income," below)				Homeowner Assn. Dues		
				Other:		
Total	$	$	$	**Total**	$	$

* **Self Employed Borrower(s) may be required to provide additional documentation such as tax returns and financial statements.**

Describe Other Income *Notice:* **Alimony, child support, or separate maintenance income need not be revealed if the Borrower (B) or Co-Borrower (C) does not choose to have it considered for repaying this loan.**

B/C		Monthly Amount
		$

VI. ASSETS AND LIABILITIES

This Statement and any applicable supporting schedules may be completed jointly by both married and unmarried Co-Borrowers if their assets and liabilities are sufficiently joined so that the Statement can be meaningfully and fairly presented on a combined basis; otherwise, separate Statements and Schedules are required. If the Co-Borrower section was completed about a non-applicant spouse or other person, this Statement and supporting schedules must be completed about that spouse or other person also.

Completed ☐ Jointly ☐ Not Jointly

ASSETS Description	Cash or Market Value
Cash deposit toward purchase held by:	$

Liabilities and Pledged Assets. List the creditor's name, address, and account number for all outstanding debts, including automobile loans, revolving charge accounts, real estate loans, alimony, child support, stock pledges, etc. Use continuation sheet, if necessary. Indicate by (*) those liabilities, which will be satisfied upon sale of real estate owned or upon refinancing of the subject property.

List checking and savings accounts below		LIABILITIES	Monthly Payment & Months Left to Pay	Unpaid Balance
Name and address of Bank, S&L, or Credit Union		Name and address of Company	$ Payment/Months	$
Acct. no.	$	Acct. no.		
Name and address of Bank, S&L, or Credit Union		Name and address of Company	$ Payment/Months	$
Acct. no.	$	Acct. no.		
Name and address of Bank, S&L, or Credit Union		Name and address of Company	$ Payment/Months	$
Acct. no.	$	Acct. no.		

Freddie Mac Form 65 7/05 Page 2 of 5 Fannie Mae Form 1003 7/05

FIGURE 7.1 ■ Uniform Residential Loan Application (Continued)

VI. ASSETS AND LIABILITIES (cont'd)

Name and address of Bank, S&L, or Credit Union		Name and address of Company	$ Payment/Months	$
Acct. no.	$	Acct. no.		
Stocks & Bonds (Company name/ number & description)	$	Name and address of Company	$ Payment/Months	$
		Acct. no.		
Life insurance net cash value Face amount: $	$	Name and address of Company	$ Payment/Months	$
Subtotal Liquid Assets	$			
Real estate owned (enter market value from schedule of real estate owned)	$			
Vested interest in retirement fund	$			
Net worth of business(es) owned (attach financial statement)	$	Acct. no.		
Automobiles owned (make and year)	$	Alimony/Child Support/Separate Maintenance Payments Owed to:	$	
Other Assets (itemize)	$	Job-Related Expense (child care, union dues, etc.)	$	
		Total Monthly Payments	$	
Total Assets a.	$	Net Worth (a minus b) ► $	**Total Liabilities b.**	$

Schedule of Real Estate Owned (If additional properties are owned, use continuation sheet.)

Property Address (enter S if sold, PS if pending sale or R if rental being held for income) ▼		Type of Property	Present Market Value	Amount of Mortgages & Liens	Gross Rental Income	Mortgage Payments	Insurance, Maintenance, Taxes & Misc.	Net Rental Income
			$	$	$	$	$	$
		Totals	$	$	$	$	$	$

List any additional names under which credit has previously been received and indicate appropriate creditor name(s) and account number(s):

Alternate Name	Creditor Name	Account Number

VII. DETAILS OF TRANSACTION

a.	Purchase price	$
b.	Alterations, improvements, repairs	
c.	Land (if acquired separately)	
d.	Refinance (incl. debts to be paid off)	
e.	Estimated prepaid items	
f.	Estimated closing costs	
g.	PMI, MIP, Funding Fee	
h.	Discount (if Borrower will pay)	
i.	Total costs (add items a through h)	

VIII. DECLARATIONS

If you answer "Yes" to any questions a through i, please use continuation sheet for explanation.	**Borrower** Yes	No	**Co-Borrower** Yes	No
a. Are there any outstanding judgments against you?	☐	☐	☐	☐
b. Have you been declared bankrupt within the past 7 years?	☐	☐	☐	☐
c. Have you had property foreclosed upon or given title or deed in lieu thereof in the last 7 years?	☐	☐	☐	☐
d. Are you a party to a lawsuit?	☐	☐	☐	☐
e. Have you directly or indirectly been obligated on any loan which resulted in foreclosure, transfer of title in lieu of foreclosure, or judgment? (This would include such loans as home mortgage loans, SBA loans, home improvement loans, educational loans, manufactured (mobile) home loans, any mortgage, financial obligation, bond, or loan guarantee. If "Yes," provide details, including date, name, and address of Lender, FHA or VA case number, if any, and reasons for the action.)	☐	☐	☐	☐

Freddie Mac Form 65 7/05 Page 3 of 5 Fannie Mae Form 1003 7/05

FIGURE 7.1 ■ Uniform Residential Loan Application (Continued)

VII. DETAILS OF TRANSACTION	
j. Subordinate financing	
k. Borrower's closing costs paid by Seller	
l. Other Credits (explain)	
m. Loan amount (exclude PMI, MIP, Funding Fee financed)	
n. PMI, MIP, Funding Fee financed	
o. Loan amount (add m & n)	
p. Cash from/to Borrower (subtract j, k, l & o from i)	

VIII. DECLARATIONS	Borrower Yes	Borrower No	Co-Borrower Yes	Co-Borrower No
If you answer "Yes" to any questions a through i, please use continuation sheet for explanation.				
f. Are you presently delinquent or in default on any Federal debt or any other loan, mortgage, financial obligation, bond, or loan guarantee? If "Yes," give details as described in the preceding question.	☐	☐	☐	☐
g. Are you obligated to pay alimony, child support, or separate maintenance?	☐	☐	☐	☐
h. Is any part of the down payment borrowed?	☐	☐	☐	☐
i. Are you a co-maker or endorser on a note?	☐	☐	☐	☐
j. Are you a U.S. citizen?	☐	☐	☐	☐
k. Are you a permanent resident alien?	☐	☐	☐	☐
l. **Do you intend to occupy the property as your primary residence?** If "Yes," complete question m below.	☐	☐	☐	☐
m. Have you had an ownership interest in a property in the last three years?	☐	☐	☐	☐
(1) What type of property did you own—principal residence (PR), second home (SH), or investment property (IP)?	______		______	
(2) How did you hold title to the home—solely by yourself (S), jointly with your spouse (SP), or jointly with another person (O)?	______		______	

IX. ACKNOWLEDGEMENT AND AGREEMENT

Each of the undersigned specifically represents to Lender and to Lender's actual or potential agents, brokers, processors, attorneys, insurers, servicers, successors and assigns and agrees and acknowledges that: (1) the information provided in this application is true and correct as of the date set forth opposite my signature and that any intentional or negligent misrepresentation of this information contained in this application may result in civil liability, including monetary damages, to any person who may suffer any loss due to reliance upon any misrepresentation that I have made on this application, and/or in criminal penalties including, but not limited to, fine or imprisonment or both under the provisions of Title 18, United States Code, Sec. 1001, et seq.; (2) the loan requested pursuant to this application (the "Loan") will be secured by a mortgage or deed of trust on the property described in this application; (3) the property will not be used for any illegal or prohibited purpose or use; (4) all statements made in this application are made for the purpose of obtaining a residential mortgage loan; (5) the property will be occupied as indicated in this application; (6) the Lender, its servicers, successors or assigns may retain the original and/or an electronic record of this application, whether or not the Loan is approved; (7) the Lender and its agents, brokers, insurers, servicers, successors, and assigns may continuously rely on the information contained in the application, and I am obligated to amend and/or supplement the information provided in this application if any of the material facts that I have represented herein should change prior to closing of the Loan; (8) in the event that my payments on the Loan become delinquent, the Lender, its servicers, successors or assigns may, in addition to any other rights and remedies that it may have relating to such delinquency, report my name and account information to one or more consumer reporting agencies; (9) ownership of the Loan and/or administration of the Loan account may be transferred with such notice as may be required by law; (10) neither Lender nor its agents, brokers, insurers, servicers, successors or assigns has made any representation or warranty, express or implied, to me regarding the property or the condition or value of the property; and (11) my transmission of this application as an "electronic record" containing my "electronic signature," as those terms are defined in applicable federal and/or state laws (excluding audio and video recordings), or my facsimile transmission of this application containing a facsimile of my signature, shall be as effective, enforceable and valid as if a paper version of this application were delivered containing my original written signature.

Acknowledgement. Each of the undersigned hereby acknowledges that any owner of the Loan, its servicers, successors and assigns, may verify or reverify any information contained in this application or obtain any information or data relating to the Loan, for any legitimate business purpose through any source, including a source named in this application or a consumer reporting agency.

Borrower's Signature	Date	Co-Borrower's Signature	Date
X		X	

X. INFORMATION FOR GOVERNMENT MONITORING PURPOSES

The following information is requested by the Federal Government for certain types of loans related to a dwelling in order to monitor the lender's compliance with equal credit opportunity, fair housing and home mortgage disclosure laws. You are not required to furnish this information, but are encouraged to do so. The law provides that a lender may not discriminate either on the basis of this information, or on whether you choose to furnish it. If you furnish the information, please provide both ethnicity and race. For race, you may check more than one designation. If you do not furnish ethnicity, race, or sex, under Federal regulations, this lender is required to note the information on the basis of visual observation and surname if you have made this application in person. If you do not wish to furnish the information, please check the box below. (Lender must review the above material to assure that the disclosures satisfy all requirements to which the lender is subject under applicable state law for the particular type of loan applied for.)

BORROWER ☐ I do not wish to furnish this information	**CO-BORROWER** ☐ I do not wish to furnish this information
Ethnicity: ☐ Hispanic or Latino ☐ Not Hispanic or Latino	**Ethnicity:** ☐ Hispanic or Latino ☐ Not Hispanic or Latino
Race: ☐ American Indian or Alaska Native ☐ Asian ☐ Black or African American ☐ Native Hawaiian or Other Pacific Islander ☐ White	**Race:** ☐ American Indian or Alaska Native ☐ Asian ☐ Black or African American ☐ Native Hawaiian or Other Pacific Islander ☐ White
Sex: ☐ Female ☐ Male	**Sex:** ☐ Female ☐ Male

To be Completed by Interviewer	Interviewer's Name (print or type)	Name and Address of Interviewer's Employer
This application was taken by: ☐ Face-to-face interview ☐ Mail ☐ Telephone ☐ Internet	Interviewer's Signature — Date	
	Interviewer's Phone Number (incl. area code)	

FIGURE 7.1 ■ Uniform Residential Loan Application (Continued)

CONTINUATION SHEET/RESIDENTIAL LOAN APPLICATION		
Use this continuation sheet if you need more space to complete the Residential Loan Application. Mark **B** f or Borrower or **C** for Co-Borrower.	Borrower:	Agency Case Number:
	Co-Borrower:	Lender Case Number:

I/We fully understand that it is a Federal crime punishable by fine or imprisonment, or both, to knowingly make any false statements concerning any of the above facts as applicable under the provisions of Title 18, United States Code, Section 1001, et seq.

Borrower's Signature	Date	Co-Borrower's Signature	Date
X		**X**	

FmHA loans—for Farmer's Home Administration—are made through the Rural Housing Service of the Department of Agriculture to individuals who are ineligible for most other kinds of loans. FmHA loans are made on real estate in rural areas, usually with a population of less than 20,000. The Farmer's Home Administration is discussed further in chapter 10.

The "Other" category on the loan application refers to special loan programs available to applicants who fit special categories.

VERIFICATION OF DEPOSIT

In some cases, loan applicants provide lenders with copies of their most recent bank statements as evidence of the financial assets listed on the loan application. More commonly, however, lenders ask the applicant's bank or financial institution to verify these assets by completing the **Request for Verification of Deposit** form (Fannie Mae Form 1006). The lender completes the first part of this form, identifies specifically what is to be verified—for example, checking, savings, money market, or stock brokerage accounts—then forwards the form to the applicant's financial institution. The purpose of this form (shown in Figure 7.2) is to verify that the applicant has sufficient cash for the down payment and any closing costs associated with the purchase as well as adequate reserves after closing. If the property is an investment property, Fannie Mae requires the borrower to have six months of principal, interest, taxes, and insurance (PITI) reserves, but if it is an owner-occupied or second home, usually no reserves are required.

The financial institution completes the bottom of the form, which requests information about the applicant's accounts, current balances, and average balances. The form also asks about any outstanding loans, their balances, monthly or quarterly payments, and number of late payments.

Some of the types of income that can be used to qualify for a loan include overtime, bonuses, income from a part-time or seasonal job, retirement or disability benefits, Social Security, military income, and 75 percent of gross rents generated by income property owned by the borrower.

In many cases, a loan applicant plans to use proceeds from the sale of his or her current home to help pay for the property being purchased. If the sale has already closed, the proceeds will be sourced with a copy of the Housing and Urban Development Settlement Statement (HUD-1) and an updated bank statement or verification of deposit (VOD). On the other hand, if the sale has not closed, the lender needs verification of the proceeds the borrower expects to receive. Loan applicants need to submit the contract for the sale of their property along with an analysis of costs associated with the sale and expected gains.

VERIFICATION OF EMPLOYMENT

Because an applicant's income is a key factor in determining risk associated with a loan, lenders ask employers to verify the applicant's employment history. Most lenders require that this information come directly from the employer to the lender and not through the applicant. Although some lenders may accept verbal verification of employment or an employee's most recent pay stub for the past 30 days as proof of employment, lenders usually acquire this information through the verification of employment form. For salaried

FIGURE 7.2 ■ Request for Verification of Deposit Form

FannieMae

Request for Verification of Deposit

Privacy Act Notice: This information is to be used by the agency collecting it or its assignees in determining whether you qualify as a prospective mortgagor under its program. It will not be disclosed outside the agency except as required and permitted by law. You do not have to provide this information, but if you do not your application for approval as a prospective mortgagor or borrower may be delayed or rejected. The information requested in this form is authorized by Title 38, USC, Chapter 37 (If VA); by 12 USC, Section 1701 et.seq. (If HUD/FHA); by 42 USC, Section 1452b (if HUD/CPD); and Title 42 USC, 1471 et.seq. or 7 USC, 1921 et.seq. (If USDA/FmHA).

Instructions: Lender — Complete Items 1 through 8. Have applicant(s) complete Item 9. Forward directly to depository named in Item 1.
Depository — Please complete Items 10 through 18 and return DIRECTLY to lender named in Item 2.
The form is to be transmitted directly to the lender and is not to be transmitted through the applicant(s) or any other party.

Part I — Request

1. To (Name and address of depository)	2. From (Name and address of lender)

I certify that this verification has been sent directly to the bank or depository and has not passed through the hands of the applicant or any other party.

3. Signature of lender	4. Title	5. Date	6. Lender's No. (Optional)

7. Information To Be Verified

Type of Account	Account in Name of	Account Number	Balance
			$
			$
			$

To Depository: I/We have applied for a mortgage loan and stated in my financial statement that the balance on deposit with you is as shown above. You are authorized to verify this information and to supply the lender identified above with the information requested in Items 10 through 13. Your response is solely a matter of courtesy for which no responsibility is attached to your institution or any of your officers.

8. Name and Address of Applicant(s)	9. Signature of Applicant(s)

To Be Completed by Depository

Part II — Verification of Depository

10. Deposit Accounts of Applicant(s)

Type of Account	Account Number	Current Balance	Average Balance For Previous Two Months	Date Opened
		$	$	
		$	$	
		$	$	

11. Loans Outstanding To Applicant(s)

Loan Number	Date of Loan	Original Amount	Current Balance	Installments (Monthly/Quarterly)		Secured By	Number of Late Payments
		$	$	$	per		
		$	$	$	per		
		$	$	$	per		

12. Please include any additional information which may be of assistance in determination of credit worthiness. (Please include information on loans paid-in-full in Item 11 above.)

13. If the name(s) on the account(s) differ from those listed in Item 7, please supply the name(s) on the account(s) as reflected by your records.

Part III — Authorized Signature - Federal statutes provide severe penalties for any fraud, intentional misrepresentation, or criminal connivance or conspiracy purposed to influence the issuance of any guaranty or insurance by the VA Secretary, the U.S.D.A., FmHA/FHA Commissioner, or the HUD/CPD Assistant Secretary.

14. Signature of Depository Representative	15. Title (Please print or type)	16. Date
17. Please print or type name signed in item 14	18. Phone No.	

Fannie Mae
Form 1006 July 96

employees, most lenders require a statement showing current year-to-date earnings, the most recent 30-day payroll period, and the past two years of W-2 earnings forms.

The **Request for Verification of Employment** (VOE) form (Fannie Mae Form 1005) asks the applicant's employer to provide information about the applicant's gross earnings, overtime or bonus pay, and the likelihood of a pay increase (see Figure 7.3). In addition, the form asks about the probability that the applicant will continue to be employed at that company or organization. In recent years, lenders have put more emphasis on the *stability of income*—that is, that the income will continue into the foreseeable future—rather than focusing solely on the applicant's current income. From the lender's perspective, how long a person has worked at a particular job is not as important as the prospect of that person being employed with at least the same level of income in the future. In general, lenders evaluate income using the rule of "look back two years, forward three." That is, they want to see the stability of the income over the past two years and be reasonably assured that it will continue for the next three.

If the potential borrower lists on the application a company where he or she no longer works, the lender asks the former employer to verify when the applicant was hired, his or her salary at termination, and the employee's reason for leaving. In cases where the applicant is not working or has no employment history at all, lenders will require a satisfactory explanation for any absences in excess of 30 days.

Both the VOD and VOE must be signed by the loan applicant before they can be processed. The borrower is not allowed to deliver the VOD or VOE to his or her employer or banking institution.

Commission Income

Because **commission income** can vary from year to year, lenders average the past two years of income to qualify the borrower. If commission income represents 25 percent or more of the borrower's total annual income, the borrower must submit federal income tax forms for the past two years along with information about his or her current employment and earnings. For commission income to be counted as stable, recurring income, the income must be documented as having been received for at least the past year.

Other Income

Fannie Mae will also consider other types of income, including disability payments or child support payments with a remaining term of at least three years and unemployment benefits that are documented, have been received for the past two years, and are likely to continue. If the borrower can document that an automobile allowance has been received for the past two years, this can also count as income.

Federal Income Tax Returns

Lenders require applicants to submit Internal Revenue Service (IRS) returns along with W-2 forms for the two or three years preceding the loan application. With some lenders, federal income tax returns, along with pay stubs from a current job, can substitute for a VOE form. When submitting tax returns to a lender, borrowers must submit the complete return, and not just the front pages.

FIGURE 7.3 ■ Request for Verification of Employment Form

FannieMae

Request for Verification of Employment

Privacy Act Notice: This information is to be used by the agency collecting it or its assignees in determining whether you qualify as a prospective mortgagor under its program. It will not be disclosed outside the agency except as required and permitted by law. You do not have to provide this information, but if you do not your application for approval as a prospective mortgagor or borrower may be delayed or rejected. The information requested in this form is authorized by Title 38, USC, Chapter 37 (if VA); by 12 USC, Section 1701 et. seq. (if HUD/FHA); by 42 USC, Section 1452b (if HUD/CPD); and Title 42 USC, 1471 et. seq., or 7 USC, 1921 et. seq. (if USDA/FmHA).

Instructions: **Lender** — Complete items 1 through 7. Have applicant complete item 8. Forward directly to employer named in item 1.
Employer — Please complete either Part II or Part III as applicable. Complete Part IV and return directly to lender named in item 2.
The form is to be transmitted directly to the lender and is not to be transmitted through the applicant or any other party.

Part I — Request

1. To (Name and address of employer)	2. From (Name and address of lender)

I certify that this verification has been sent directly to the employer and has not passed through the hands of the applicant or any other interested party.

3. Signature of Lender	4. Title	5. Date	6. Lender's Number (Optional)

I have applied for a mortgage loan and stated that I am now or was formerly employed by you. My signature below authorizes verification of this information.

7. Name and Address of Applicant (include employee or badge number)	8. Signature of Applicant

Part II — Verification of Present Employment

9. Applicant's Date of Employment	10. Present Position	11. Probability of Continued Employment

12A. Current **Gross** Base Pay (Enter Amount and Check Period)

$ ________ ☐ Annual ☐ Hourly ☐ Monthly ☐ Other (Specify) ☐ Weekly

12B. **Gross** Earnings

Type	Year To Date	Past Year	Past Year
Base Pay	Thru ______ $	$	$
Overtime	$	$	$
Commissions	$	$	$
Bonus	$	$	$
Total	$ 0.00	$ 0.00	$ 0.00

13. For Military Personnel Only

Pay Grade

Type	Monthly Amount
Base Pay	$
Rations	$
Flight or Hazard	$
Clothing	$
Quarters	$
Pro Pay	$
Overseas or Combat	$
Variable Housing Allowance	$

14. If Overtime or Bonus is Applicable, Is Its Continuance Likely?
Overtime ☐ Yes ☐ No
Bonus ☐ Yes ☐ No

15. If paid hourly — average hours per week

16. Date of applicant's next pay increase

17. Projected amount of next pay increase

18. Date of applicant's last pay increase

19. Amount of last pay increase

20. Remarks (If employee was off work for any length of time, please indicate time period and reason)

Part III — Verification of Previous Employment

21. Date Hired

22. Date Terminated

23. Salary/Wage at Termination Per (Year) (Month) (Week)
Base ________ Overtime ________ Commissions ________ Bonus ________

24. Reason for Leaving	25. Position Held

Part IV — Authorized Signature - Federal statutes provide severe penalties for any fraud, intentional misrepresentation, or criminal connivance or conspiracy purposed to influence the issuance of any guaranty or insurance by the VA Secretary, the U.S.D.A., FmHA/FHA Commissioner, or the HUD/CPD Assistant Secretary.

26. Signature of Employer	27. Title (Please print or type)	28. Date
29. Print or type name signed in Item 26	30. Phone No.	

Fannie Mae
Form 1005 July 96

THE CREDIT REPORT

The credit report is one of the most important documents required by the lender. Lenders determine creditworthiness by evaluating an applicant's attitude toward debt repayment, and this information is reflected in the credit report. If applicants have a history of late or missed payments, lenders will hesitate to approve a mortgage loan application.

The credit report provides information on the current and past credit accounts of the borrower. These accounts are classified as follows: R for revolving, I for installment, M for mortgage, and C for line of credit. In addition, the payment history is rated as follows:

0 Too new to be rated
1 Paying in agreed 30-day time frame
2 30 to 59 days late
3 60 to 89 days late
4 90 to 119 days late
5 120+ days late

Account balance uncollectible:

7 Bankruptcy
8 Asset was repossessed
9 Written off and sent out for collection

All accounts with a balance must have been checked with the creditor within 90 days of the closing, and all inquiries made within the past 90 days must be addressed by the borrower.

In the United States, there are three main credit agencies: Equifax, Experian, and TransUnion. These companies maintain files that contain credit information about individuals in five different areas: personal information (including employment and home addresses going back at least two years); information about current accounts and accounts that are closed; any accounts that have been turned over to a collection agency; liens, bankruptcies, judgments, divorce decrees, and similar legal records; and, finally, a record of who has checked the applicant's credit recently. The Web sites of the major credit agencies are listed below. Lenders may order individual credit reports on a loan applicant from these agencies, or they may order a trimerged or dual merged report, which combines results from different agencies. When lenders rely on a trimerged report to evaluate credit, they use the middle of the three scores. When they use a dual merged report, they use the lower of the two scores.

WEB LINK @

www.equifax.com

www.experian.com

www.transunion.com

As mentioned earlier, underwriters frequently ask applicants to explain any negative information contained in the credit file. It is also important to note that credit files often have errors, and applicants may need to provide the credit agency with the correct information before an underwriter will approve an application.

Lenders use the information in the credit report to make judgments about three areas: character, capacity, and credit. Character is evaluated by information such as how long a person has lived at a particular place, the kind of jobs the person has held, and any legal judgments against the person.

Capacity, which refers to the amount of current debt the applicant has accumulated compared to his or her income, gives some indication of how well the applicant manages credit. Two critical formulas in determining capacity are the **housing expense ratio (HER)**—known as the front-end ratio—and the **total obligations ratio (TOR)**—known as the back-end ratio or **debt-to-income ratio**. HER is calculated by dividing monthly housing expense (proposed new mortgage payments) by monthly income; TOR is calculated by dividing the sum of all obligations longer than ten months plus any lease obligations by monthly income. If the ratio does not meet the requirements set by the lender, the loan is unlikely to be approved. HER and TOR are discussed in detail in chapter 11.

For FHA loans, an applicant's monthly housing expense cannot exceed 31 percent of the gross monthly income. An individual who earns $2,500 a month, for example, would not qualify for any loan requiring more than a $775 per month payment. Under the FHA guidelines, an applicant's total obligations ratio, which is the total monthly obligations divided by monthly gross income, cannot exceed 43 percent.

Eligibility for VA loans is calculated using the total obligations ratio, which, under VA guidelines, cannot exceed 41 percent. For most conventional loans, the maximum housing expense ratio is 28 percent, and the maximum total obligations ratio is 36 percent. Figure 7.4 summarizes the housing expense ratios and total obligations ratios acceptable to FHA, VA, and conventional lenders.

Credit refers to existing credit cards, car loans, and other obligations to financial institutions. In terms of loans, the lender is interested in how close the loan is to its limit and how long the loan has been active. Most, but not all, balances that require payments for more than ten months into the future must be counted as debt in this formula, but balances that will be paid off in ten months or less do not count against the applicant. However, lease payments for housing or automobiles are considered a recurring monthly debt, regardless of the expiration date of the lease. If a debt listed on the credit report does not show a minimum required payment, the lender estimates a payment of 5 percent of the outstanding balance. Overall, credit accounts that near their credit limit soon after the account is opened are not seen positively by lenders.

Most credit reports summarize their findings in terms of a **credit score,** which is numerical representation of the risk associated with a particular borrower. Experian's score name comes from **Fair Isaac Corporation** and is referred to as a FICO score. The factors used by Fair Isaac are payment history (which accounts for 35 percent of an applicant's score); outstanding debt (30 percent); length of the applicant's credit history (15 percent); types of credit (10 percent); and if the applicant is acquiring more debt (10 percent). Credit scores provided by Experian range from 330 to 830. A Beacon score, which ranges from

FIGURE 7.4 ■ Acceptable HER and TOR for FHA, VA, and Conventional Loans

Loan Type	Housing Expense Ratio	Total Obligations Ratio
FHA	31%	43%
VA	N/A	41%
Conventional	28%	36%

300 to 850, comes from Equifax, and Emperica is the name of the score provided by Trans Union, which can range from 150 to 934. The range of credit scores reported on the National Credit Score Disclosure Form discussed in chapter 4 is from 300 to 850.

A **representative credit score** refers to a score derived from credit information from more than one company. Fannie Mae recommends that a lender obtain a minimum of two credit scores for each borrower. Of these two credit scores, the lender must use the lower to evaluate the applicant's creditworthiness. If the lender obtains three scores, the lender is required to use the middle score. In cases where more than one individual is applying for the loan, the lender must use the lowest credit score of those obtained.

When an applicant fails to receive a satisfactory credit report, the lender probably will not approve the loan application. When this occurs, the lender is required under the guidelines of the Fair Credit Reporting Act to notify the applicant and provide a copy of the credit report if requested.

Applicants who have been denied credit can challenge the information contained in their credit report. They can make corrections, as well as file explanations for credit problems in the past.

Reestablishing Credit

According to Fannie Mae guidelines, individuals who have had a property foreclosed or who have been in bankruptcy must wait four years from the completion of the foreclosure or discharge from bankruptcy for a mortgage loan application to be considered. If the applicant can document extenuating circumstances, however, he or she need wait only two years.

To reestablish creditworthiness, individuals who have been discharged from bankruptcy must provide a minimum of four credit references, with at least one of the references being a traditional credit reference and one of the references being housing-related. Three of the four references must have been active in the past 24 months.

In addition, the application must show no more than two installments or revolving debt payments that were 30 days past due in the past 24 months; no installment or revolving debt payments 60 or more days past due since the discharge or completion of the bankruptcy or the completion of the foreclosure-related action; no housing debt payments past due since the discharge or completion of the bankruptcy or the completion of the foreclosure-related action; and no new public records for bankruptcies, foreclosures, deeds-in-lieu of foreclosure, preforeclosure sales, unpaid judgments or collections, garnishments, liens, and so forth, since the discharge or completion of the bankruptcy or the completion of the foreclosure-related action.

Age of the Credit Report

Most lenders prefer to use the most recent credit reports, but sometimes they will accept reports that are already on file if the reports are supplied by three different credit reporting companies and contain at least two years of credit history. As a general rule, all loan documents signed and dated must be no more than 120 days old on the date the borrower signs the mortgage and promissory note.

THE SALES CONTRACT

In cases where the applicant is financing a new purchase—rather than acquiring a second mortgage, refinancing, or obtaining a home equity loan—the lender requires a copy of the sales contract. The sales contract details the financial aspects of the real estate purchase.

Sometimes minor items that do not affect the livability of the structure have not been completed by the time the lender is ready to deliver a mortgage to Fannie Mae. In these cases, the lender must arrange escrow funds—known as a **completion reserve**—amounting to at least 120 percent of the cost to complete the unfinished items. The cost to finish the items cannot exceed 2 percent of the sales price, and finishing cannot require more than 180 days.

The original Contract for Sale and Purchase is retained by the lender after closing.

MORTGAGE PAYMENT HISTORY

In some cases, lenders need to verify that an applicant is fulfilling his or her existing mortgage obligations, as well as the manner in which the applicant handled such obligations in the past. When the applicant's credit report does not contain information about mortgage payments, the lender will require other evidence regarding mortgage payment history.

The lender may ask the company servicing the applicant's existing mortgage to complete a **Verification of Mortgage (VOM) form.** This form asks about the type of mortgage (FHA, VA, or conventional), the original amount of the loan and its current balance, and the monthly payment. Lenders are particularly interested in knowing if payments are current. Under Fannie Mae guidelines, a payment is late if it occurs more than 45 days after the last payment. Also, 12 months is the required period necessary to substantiate a borrower's payment history.

Some other methods lenders use to verify mortgage payment history include the borrower's canceled checks for the 12 months preceding the loan application or the applicant's year-end mortgage account statement. When submitting the year-end statement, applicants should also submit canceled checks covering the period since the statement was generated.

If the applicant is renting, the lender may request verification of the payment of rent using the same form.

Most lenders reserve the right to request any further documentation necessary to make a decision regarding the loan.

SELF-EMPLOYED APPLICANTS

When a loan applicant is self-employed, most lenders require the applicant to submit additional information because lenders consider a VOE form on a self-employed person useless. Lenders consider individuals who own 25 percent or more of a business self-employed.

Not surprisingly, lenders are more cautious regarding loans to self-employed individuals because self-employed borrowers are at the greatest risk for default. In terms of evaluating income, lenders consider income stable if the applicant has been self-employed for at least two years. In most cases, lenders will require all the information described in the first part of this chapter—loan application, VOD form, federal income tax returns, and so forth—as well as additional information regarding the applicant's company. This additional information includes the following:

- Year-to-date statement of profit and loss for the business
- Balance sheet for the previous two fiscal years
- Self-Employed Income Analysis (Form 1084A or 1084B)
- Comparative Income Analysis (Form 1088)
- Federal income tax returns for the business covering the past two years

Self-employed applicants may also be asked to provide documentation of net worth.

FALSIFYING INFORMATION ON A LOAN APPLICATION

By signing Section IX of the mortgage loan application, Acknowledgment and Agreement, both the broker or lender and the applicant are representing that the information on the application is true and correct. Both the applicant and the broker or lender can be held responsible for any misinformation in the application.

Falsifying or omitting information on an application, which is a felony criminal act, violates F.S. 494.0025(4) and (5) and can lead to penalties listed under F.S. 494.0041 and Rule 69V-40.111 and 494.0018. Falsification of information is also a federal crime under Title 18 USC Sec 1001 and can result in administrative or civil action, including revocation of a license or criminal charges.

FORWARDING THE APPLICATION

When the application is complete, the application package goes to the potential lender with a form called the **Uniform Underwriting and Transmittal Summary** (Form 1008). This form, shown in Figure 7.5, summarizes information about the borrower and property, mortgage, underwriting information, seller, contract, contact information, and delivery data. It is always placed on top in the stacking order of loan documents.

FIGURE 7.5 ■ Uniform Underwriting and Transmittal Summary Form

Uniform Underwriting and Transmittal Summary

I. Borrower and Property Information

Borrower Name ____________ SSN ____________
Co-Borrower Name ____________ SSN ____________
Property Address ____________

Property Type
☐ 1 unit
☐ 2-to-4 units
☐ Condominium
☐ PUD ☐ Co-op
☐ Manufactured Housing
☐ Single Wide
☐ Multiwide

Project Classification

Freddie Mac
☐ Streamlined Review
☐ Established Project
☐ New Project
☐ Detached Project
☐ 2-to-4-unit Project
☐ Reciprocal Review

Fannie Mae
☐ P Limited Review New
☐ Q Limited Review Est.
☐ R Expedited Review New
☐ S Expedited Review Est.
☐ T Fannie Mae Review
☐ U FHA-approved
☐ E PUD ☐ 1 Co-op
☐ F PUD ☐ 2 Co-op

Project Name ____________ CMP Project ID# (if any): ____________

Occupancy Status
☐ Primary Residence
☐ Second Home
☐ Investment Property

Additional Property Information
Number of Units ____________
Sales Price $ ____________
Appraised Value $ ____________

Property Rights
☐ Fee Simple
☐ Leasehold

II. Mortgage Information

Loan Type
☐ Conventional
☐ FHA
☐ VA
☐ USDA/RHS

Amortization Type
☐ Fixed Rate–Monthly Payments
☐ Fixed Rate–Biweekly Payments
☐ Balloon
☐ ARM (type) ____________
☐ Other (specify) ____________

Loan Purpose
☐ Purchase
☐ Cash-Out Refinance
☐ Limited Cash-Out Refinance (Fannie)
☐ No Cash-Out Refinance (Freddie)
☐ Home Improvement
☐ Construction to Permanent

Lien Position
☐ First Mortgage
Amount of Subordinate Financing
$ ____________
(If HELOC, include balance and credit limit)
☐ Second Mortgage

Note Information
Original Loan Amount $ ____________
Initial P&I Payment $ ____________
Initial Note Rate ____________ %
Loan Terms (in months) ____________

Mortgage Originator
☐ Seller
☐ Broker
☐ Correspondent
Broker/Correspondent Name and Company Name: ____________

Buydown
☐ Yes
☐ No
Terms ____________

If Second Mortgage
Owner of First Mortgage
☐ Fannie Mae ☐ Freddie Mac
☐ Seller/Other
Original Loan Amount of First Mortgage
$ ____________

III. Underwriting Information

Underwriter's Name ____________ Appraiser's Name/License # ____________ Appraisal Company Name ____________

Stable Monthly Income

	Borrower	Co-Borrower	Total
Base Income	$	$	$
Other Income	$	$	$
Positive Cash Flow (subject property)	$	$	$
Total Income	$	$	$

Present Housing Payment: $ ____________

Proposed Monthly Payments

Borrower's Primary Residence
First Mortgage P&I $ ____________
Second Mortgage P&I $ ____________
Hazard Insurance $ ____________
Taxes $ ____________
Mortgage Insurance $ ____________
HOA Fees $ ____________
Lease/Ground Rent $ ____________
Other $ ____________
Total Primary Housing Expense $ ____________

Other Obligations
Negative Cash Flow (subject property) $ ____________
All Other Monthly Payments $ ____________
Total All Monthly Payments $ ____________

Qualifying Ratios
Primary Housing Expense/Income ____________ %
Total Obligations/Income ____________ %
Debt-to-Housing Gap Ratio (Freddie) ____________ %

Loan-to-Value Ratios
LTV ____________ %
CLTV/TLTV ____________ %
HCLTV/HTLTV ____________ %

Qualifying Rate
☐ Note Rate ____________ %
☐ ____________ % Above Note Rate ____________ %
☐ ____________ % Below Note Rate ____________ %
☐ Bought-Down Rate ____________ %
☐ Other ____________ %

Level of Property Review
☐ Exterior/Interior
☐ Exterior Only
☐ No Appraisal
Form Number: ____________

Risk Assessment
☐ Manual Underwriting
☐ AUS
☐ DU ☐ LP ☐ Other ____________
AUS Recommendation ____________
DU Case ID/LP AUS Key# ____________
LP Doc Class (Freddie) ____________

Escrow (T&I)
☐ Yes ☐ No

Borrower Funds to Close
Required $ ____________
Verified Assets $ ____________
Source of Funds ____________
No. of Months Reserves ____________
Interested Party Contributions ____________ %

Community Lending/Affordable Housing Initiative ☐ Yes ☐ No
Representative Credit/Indicator Score ____________
Home Buyers/Homeownership Education Certificate in file ☐ Yes ☐ No

Underwriter Comments

____

IV. Seller, Contract, and Contact Information

Seller Name ____________
Seller Address ____________
Seller No. ____________ Investor Loan No. ____________
Seller Loan No. ____________

Contact Name ____________
Contact Title ____________
Contact Phone Number ____________ ext. ____________
Contact Signature ____________

Freddie Mac Form 1077 (04/08)
1077/1008 Transmittal Summary 06/08 ~ Encompass™ from Ellie Mae ~ www.elliemae.com

Fannie Mae Form 1008 (04/08)

KEY POINT REVIEW

- Most lenders require applicants for mortgage loans use the Uniform Residential Loan Application (Fannie Mae Form 1003).
- The loan application must state what names appear on the title to the property to be used as collateral and the relationship between the parties because this may affect how the loan is repaid.
- The purpose of the Request for Verification of Deposit form is to determine if the applicant has sufficient funds to pay the down payment and any associated closing costs and reserves to cover any associated closing costs.
- Applicants must provide information about previous employers if they have held their current position less than two years. Income reported on the loan application must be verified for two years.
- Most lenders put more emphasis on stability of an applicant's income than amount of income. Most lenders use the "two years back, three forward" guideline when evaluating income.
- Lenders are particularly interested in an applicant's credit history, which is an indication of a willingness to repay debts.
- Underwriters use information in the credit report to make judgments about an applicant's character, capacity, and credit.
- *Housing expense ratio* (HER) and *total obligations ratio* (TOR) are critical factors in evaluating an applicant's capacity. For FHA loans, HER cannot exceed 31 percent of gross monthly income and TOR cannot exceed 41 percent. For VA loans, TOR cannot exceed 43 percent. Most conventional loans use 28 percent for HER and 36 percent for TOR as benchmarks. TOR is also referred to as the *debt-to-income ratio*.
- Individuals who have had a property in foreclosure or been in bankruptcy must wait four years to have an application considered.
- As a general rule, all loan documents must be no older than 120 days at the time of closing.
- Lenders often require applicants to submit two years of IRS returns, payroll documentation, and the sales contract along with the loan application.
- If an applicant's mortgage payment history is not reported on the credit report, the lender will require a Verification of Mortgage form to make certain that mortgage payments have been current for the past 12 months.
- Self-employed applicants, defined as individuals with 25 percent or more ownership in a business, must provide additional documents, including profit and loss statements, balance sheet, and both personal and business tax returns for the past two years. Self-employed income is considered stable if it has continued for two years or more.

REVIEW QUESTIONS

1. When an application is being prepared, information about the names that will appear on the title and their relationship is important because the
   a. information says exactly who the owners of the property will be.
   b. buyers must be distinguished from the sellers before the application can be reviewed.
   c. legal description cannot be confirmed by the title alone.
   d. relationship between the parties determines if a loan will be FHA, VA, or conventional.

2. In the course of preparing a loan application package on Mr. Dalton, the mortgage broker found that Mr. Dalton had two legal judgments against him. Most likely the mortgage broker found this information on the
   a. Uniform Underwriting and Transmittal Summary form.
   b. Verification of Employment form.
   c. credit report.
   d. Verification of Payment History form.

3. When a loan application is evaluated, the applicant's past income must be verified for at least
   a. six months.
   b. one year.
   c. two years.
   d. three years.

4. Colleen wants the alimony and child support she receives to be considered income to qualify for a mortgage loan. How long must such payments continue after the start of the mortgage?
   a. Six months
   b. One year
   c. Two years
   d. Three years

5. An underwriter who is evaluating existing loans on a loan applicant's credit file is likely to be MOST interested in
   a. the type of company that granted the loan.
   b. the total monthly payments for the borrower's debt-to-income ratio.
   c. a reference letter from the company that granted the loan.
   d. whether the loan is for necessities or luxuries.

6. During the process of evaluating an application, an applicant's debt-to-income ratio is considered part of
   a. character.
   b. capacity.
   c. credit.
   d. all of the above.

7. Mr. Baker wants to apply for a mortgage on a duplex he is buying. Most likely the mortgage company where he applies will require use of the
   a. Standardized Loan Transaction form.
   b. IRS Mortgage Transaction Form 1006.
   c. Uniform Residential Loan Application form.
   d. loan application form that the mortgage broker chooses.

8. The Request for Verification of Employment form
   a. notifies the lender that the borrower has sufficient funds for the down payment.
   b. asks about salary but cannot legally inquire about overtime or bonuses because they are not part of an applicant's regular salary.
   c. can be waived if the applicant signs a notarized Statement of Employment.
   d. cannot be delivered to the lender by the applicant.

9. Thomas would like to reestablish his credit but his car payment for last month was late. With regard to his credit, this information
   a. will not prevent reestablishing his credit because it is unrelated to housing.
   b. could prevent reestablishing his credit because any late payment on an installment account may not be acceptable to a lender.
   c. will prevent reestablishing his credit unless Thomas can provide four credit references, with one related to housing.
   d. will not prevent reestablishing his credit because car payments are usually not counted in the back-end ratio.

10. When evaluating a Verification of Employment form, lenders will most likely emphasize the applicant's
    a. length of employment.
    b. overtime and bonuses.
    c. raises and promotions.
    d. stability of income.

11. Samir has applied for a mortgage, but on the application he states that he is unemployed. The lender
    a. is unlikely to approve Samir's application.
    b. may approve the application if Samir has a satisfactory explanation.
    c. is legally prohibited from discriminating against the unemployed.
    d. will not consider employment status if the applicant has been unemployed less than six months.

12. Which would a lender NOT consider qualifying income?
    a. Overtime and bonuses
    b. Dividends
    c. Salary from a part-time job
    d. Overtime or bonus income received for only nine months

13. Under FHA guidelines, an applicant who plans to buy a condominium cannot have a total obligations ratio greater than
    a. 25 percent.
    b. 30 percent.
    c. 43 percent.
    d. 50 percent.

14. When a lender requests a Verification of Mortgage form, the lender is particularly interested in
    a. whether mortgage payments have been current and on time over the past 12 months.
    b. what lenders have granted a mortgage to the applicant in the past and if payments were made on time.
    c. the applicant's level of credit card debt in comparison with his or her mortgage balance.
    d. whether the information on the Verification of Mortgage form matches information on the credit report.

15. When evaluating a loan application, the lender will consider the kind of jobs an applicant has held as part of
    a. character.
    b. capacity.
    c. credit.
    d. all of the above.

16. Claudia owns Sweetheart Florist Shoppe. When she applies for a mortgage loan, she
    a. must provide the same information as an applicant who is not self-employed.
    b. must provide the same information as an applicant who is not self-employed, plus additional documentation.
    c. will be required to meet completely different requirements because of her self-employed status.
    d. will most likely qualify for an Alt-A loan.

17. When a lender uses dual merged credit reports, the lender
    a. may use either of the scores.
    b. will use the average of the two scores.
    c. must use the lower of the scores.
    d. must use the higher of the scores.

18. For a conventional loan of $250,000, the maximum total obligations ratio is
    a. 28 percent.
    b. 36 percent.
    c. 42 percent.
    d. 52 percent.

19. Applicants who apply for mortgage loans must provide federal income tax returns for the past
    a. year.
    b. two years.
    c. five years.
    d. zero years because tax returns are not required.

20. Mr. Ricardo lists himself on an application as an owner of Ricardo's Tailors. This means that he owns at least what percentage of the business?
    a. 25 percent
    b. 40 percent
    c. 50 percent
    d. 10 percent

21. To qualify for a mortgage loan, a self-employed individual is required to demonstrate how many years of steady income in order for the income to be considered stable?
    a. One
    b. Two
    c. Three
    d. Five

22. An applicant's credit history
    a. is not as important as the survey and appraisal.
    b. can be offset if a property has a high value.
    c. indicates the applicant's willingness to repay debts.
    d. cannot be corrected once it has been entered into the credit file.

23. The Uniform Underwriting and Transmittal Summary form contains
    a. the applicant's credit report, VOE, VOD, and federal income tax return.
    b. information about the borrower, property, and mortgage.
    c. the mortgage broker's recommendation regarding funding the loan.
    d. notice of the lender's approval or rejection of the loan application.

24. A credit score provided by Fair Isaac will put the greatest emphasis on
    a. length of credit history.
    b. outstanding debt.
    c. whether the applicant is acquiring more debt.
    d. payment history.

25. When the lender reviews the applicant's Request for Verification of Deposit form, the lender is looking to confirm that the applicant has
    a. sufficient income from employment to make the mortgage payments.
    b. sufficient cash for the down payment and closing costs.
    c. been truthful on the loan application.
    d. established credit that qualifies him or her for the loan.

CHAPTER

8

UNDERWRITING

LEARNING OBJECTIVES

After finishing chapter 8, you should be able to

1. understand the loan approval process;
2. define loan-to-value ratio;
3. know the requirements for the down payment;
4. understand the property appraisal process;
5. explain automated underwriting;
6. understand how the commitment to the borrower is issued; and
7. understand adverse action.

KEY TERMS

actual age
adverse action
appraisal
automated underwriting system (AUS)
build-up
capitalization rate
Certificate of Reasonable Value (CRV)
certified appraisal
commitment fee
commitment letter
comparables
cost depreciation
depreciation
Desktop Underwriter®
down payment
effective age
external depreciation
Federal Emergency Management Agency (FEMA)
Flexible 97®
Flexible 100®
flood zone
functional depreciation
gift letter
highest and best use
income capitalization
interested party contribution (IPC)
Loan Prospector®
loan-to-value ratio (LTV)
marketing time
market value
overimprovement
payment abatement
physical depreciation
principle of conformity
principle of substitution
reconciliation
sales comparison
standby commitment
subject property
sweat equity
underwriting
Wood Destroying Organism (WDO) Report

INTRODUCTION

When a potential borrower submits a loan application package to a lender, the lender wants to make certain that the level of risk associated with the loan is acceptable to the lender. The process by which lenders analyze risk is called **underwriting.** The job of the underwriter is to review all parts of the application, evaluate the applicant's creditworthiness, and make a judgment of the acceptability of the property—a primary residence, second home, or investment property—being offered as collateral. Although lenders make money by making loans, no law requires a lender to loan money to an individual whose credit does not meet the lender's standards.

EVALUATING PROSPECTIVE BORROWERS

The underwriter reviews an applicant's income, credit history, cash in the bank, securities, other real estate, and businesses owned, along with any other factor that could affect the level of risk to the lender. The underwriter must also resolve any issues relating to the financing of the transaction overall. For example, issues might arise during the underwriting review when the

- applicant fails to receive credit approval from the private mortgage insurance company;
- title search reveals unpaid taxes;
- borrower inexplicably pays off certain debts;
- survey reveals an incurable encroachment; or
- lender requires repairs to the property prior to the closing.

Underwriters pay particular attention to an applicant's credit history. Credit history is a direct indication of an applicant's willingness to repay debts. When a person's credit history shows missed payments on housing, credit card debt, or auto loans, for example, underwriters may not feel confident that the applicant will be committed to making timely payments on a mortgage. In this case, the underwriter may not approve the loan application.

In the process of evaluating an application, many times the underwriter asks the applicant to clarify information included in the application package, as well as to explain any changes that have occurred since he or she applied for the loan. If an applicant changes his or her address or employer, pays off a loan, or acquires new debt, for example, this may affect the underwriter's assessment of the applicant's creditworthiness and the underwriter's willingness to approve the loan.

The basic documents required for an underwriter to assess risk include:

- Uniform Residential Loan Application (HUD-1; Form 1003)
- Appraisal (Form 1004)
- Verification of Employment (Form 1005)
- Verification of Deposit (Form 1006)
- Transmittal Summary (Form 1008)

Although there is no single method for underwriting a loan, most lenders today follow guidelines put forth by the Federal National Mortgage Association (FNMA, or Fannie

Mae), the Federal Home Loan Mortgage Corporation (FHLMC, or Freddie Mac), the Department of Veterans Affairs (VA), or the Federal Housing Administration (FHA). (Fannie Mae and Freddie Mac are discussed in chapter 10.) Underwriters who have received the Direct Endorsement (DE) Underwriter designation from the FHA or VA can approve FHA or VA residential loans up to a specified maximum amount for a lender and proceed to closing. Direct Endorsement is a competitive advantage for the lender who holds the designation, and lenders with DE are careful to make certain not to approve any loans that might jeopardize their holding the DE designation.

LOAN-TO-VALUE RATIO

In most cases, lenders will lend only a certain percentage of the purchase price on a piece of property. Conventional lenders, for example, generally loan 80 percent of a property's value. As you may recall, the **loan-to-value ratio (LTV)** is calculated by dividing the loan amount by either the price of the property or the appraised value, whichever is lower. For example, if Robert buys a home for $200,000 and meets the lender's criteria in terms of credit history, income, and other considerations, he would most likely be eligible for a loan of $160,000 if the lender required a 20 percent down payment. Loan-to-value calculations are reviewed in greater detail in chapter 11.

When the LTV is over 90 percent, the borrower has little equity in the property. That is, the borrower has used personal funds to pay only a small part of the purchase price. In these cases, the borrower may have little motivation to continue to pay the mortgage in case of default. The borrower may be willing to lose his or her equity and be free of the obligation to repay the mortgage by allowing the lender to foreclose on the property. To guard against this situation, most lenders require mortgage insurance when the LTV is over 80 percent. In addition, a high LTV will cause the lender to be more cautious in evaluating the loan application.

Qualifying for Higher Loan-to-Value Ratios

As explained in chapter 7, the benchmark debt-to-income or total obligations ratio (TOR) for conventional mortgages is 36 percent of the borrower's stable monthly income. However, a lender can accept a higher ratio when there are other compensating factors. Some of the factors that might justify a higher ratio include

- the applicant has the ability to devote a greater portion of income toward housing expenses;
- the applicant has demonstrated the ability to accumulate savings and maintain good credit history;
- the applicant has potential for increased earnings and advancement; and
- the applicant's net worth is sufficient to repay the mortgage.

DOWN PAYMENT

One of the best predictors of whether a borrower will default on a mortgage loan is the size of the down payment. The **down payment** is the part of the purchase price paid by the borrower, and it represents the borrower's part of the risk associated with buying a property.

Larger down payments mean lower risk to the lender. Fannie Mae also requires that borrowers with conventional mortgages hold two months of principal, interest, taxes, and insurance (PITI) in liquid reserves.

Underwriters use certain rules to evaluate a borrower's down payment on a property. Although many borrowers use their savings to make a down payment, other sources of down payment include equity in another property, gifts, and money from an individual retirement account (IRA) or 401(k).

Proceeds from the Sale of a Previous Home

Proceeds from the sale of a previous home are acceptable as a down payment on another home if the borrower provides a copy of the closing statement.

First-Time Homebuyer

Certain federal programs offer incentives to encourage individuals to buy their first home. To qualify for these programs, the homebuyer must be the sole purchaser and plan to reside in the property. If there is a coborrower, the coborrower must reside in the property as well. In addition, the homebuyer must have had no ownership interest in a residential property during the three-year period preceding the new home purchase. A displaced homemaker or single parent can also be considered a first-time homebuyer if that person had no ownership interest in a principal residence—other than with a spouse—during the preceding three years. In addition, first-time homebuyers cannot own any income property that is for sale at the time of loan application. Also, if more than one person is applying for a loan to buy a home, only one individual needs to qualify as a first-time homebuyer.

Gift Letters

When an applicant plans to use a gift to help with a home purchase, the applicant must provide a letter from the person supplying the gift. As part of the down payment, the borrower may accept a gift from a relative, domestic partner, or fiancé(e).

A **gift letter** must contain the name and address of the donor, as well as a way to contact that person. The letter must state the precise amount of the gift and make clear that the person who makes the gift does not expect to be repaid.

A sample gift letter is shown in Figure 8.1.

According to Fannie Mae, the borrower's entire down payment can come from a gift if the down payment is at least 20 percent of the property's value. However, if the down payment is less than 20 percent of the property value, at least 5 percent must come from the borrower's own cash resources.

Sweat Equity

In most cases, underwriters do not allow **sweat equity,** which refers to a purchaser's willingness to improve the value of a property by doing work on the property, to be considered as part of the down payment.

FIGURE 8.1 ■ Gift Letter

GIFT LETTER

Applicant(s): Loan Number:

I, ______________________________, do hereby certify the following:
(Donor)

(1) I have made a gift of $ __________ to ______________________________
(Amount) (Recipient)

Whose relationship is: ______________________________
(Relationship)

(2) This gift is to be applied toward the purchase of the property located at:

____
(Property Address)

(3) No repayment of the gift is expected or implied in the form of cash or by future services of the recipient.

(4) The funds given to the homebuyer were not made available to the donor from any person or entity with an interest in the sale of the property including the seller, real estate agent or broker, builder, loan officer, or any entity associated with them.

(5) The source of this gift is: ______________________________
(Source)

____
Donor Signature **Date**

____
Donor Name (Print or Type)

____
Donor Address

( ) ______________________________
Donor Phone Number

____
Borrower Signature

____
Borrower Signature

WARNING: Our signatures above indicate that we fully understand that it is a Federal Crime punishable by fine, imprisonment, or both to knowingly make any false statement concerning any of the above facts as applicable under the provision of Title 18, United States Code, Section 1012 and 1014.

Attachments:

1. **Evidence of Donor's Ability to Provide Funds.**
2. **Evidence of Receipt of Transfer of Funds.**

Calyx Form - giftlttr.frm (05/02)

Source: Form provided by Calyx® Software.

Credit Card Financing

Borrowers cannot charge the down payment amount to their credit card. However, certain costs that must be paid early in the application process, such as a lock-in fee or fees for credit reports or appraisals, can be charged. Closing costs that are less than 1 percent of the mortgage amount, as well as the actual cost of a credit report or appraisal up to $500, can be charged to a credit card account.

Noncitizens

Permanent resident aliens are required to make down payments of at least 5 percent, and nonpermanent resident aliens must make minimum down payments of 10 percent. In general, the same down payment standards applied to U.S. citizens are applied to noncitizens.

Down Payments in Flexible 100® and Flexible 97® Programs

Flexible 100® is a no down payment loan that requires the borrower to pay as little as 3 percent of the purchase price toward closing costs. **Flexible 97®** requires a 3 percent down payment plus a cash down payment to cover closing costs. These funds can come from gifts, grants, or unsecured loans from relatives, employers, or other sources. These loans can be 15-year or 30-year fixed rate or 5-year, 7-year, or 10-year adjustable rate.

Fannie Mae Down Payment Policy

In 2007, Fannie Mae adopted a policy requiring higher down payments for properties in areas designated as declining markets. In 2008, however, this policy was superseded by a new policy stating that Fannie Mae will accept up to 97 percent loan-to-value ratios for conventional, conforming mortgages that are processed through its Desktop Underwriter® system (discussed later in this chapter) and 95 percent loan-to-value for loans underwritten outside of Desktop Underwriter®. These guidelines apply to loans for the purchase of single-family, residential properties.

In some cases, interested parties may assist a borrower in purchasing a home. For example, a builder may offer to make the first six months of mortgage payments for buyers of new homes. In this case, the builder would be making an **interested party contribution (IPC).** This contribution comes in the form of a **payment abatement**, which is an incentive to the buyer. Fannie Mae will not purchase loans with payment abatements.

THE PROPERTY APPRAISAL

The property is the ultimate security for the lender should the buyer be unwilling or unable to make mortgage payments. For this reason, lenders want to be certain that the property's value is verified by an outside expert. Specifically, lenders want to know a property's **market value**, which is defined as the most likely price a property would bring in an open market when an informed buyer and seller without any undue outside influence reach an agreement on price and terms that is based on each party's own best interests.

Lenders determine market value by ordering an **appraisal**, which is an opinion or estimate of a property's value. Appraisers research and document anything that may affect the value of a property, including its age, condition, location, and, most important, the value of surrounding similar properties.

In addition to the lender, both the seller and buyer might want the value of a property to be appraised on the high side so that qualifying for the loan might be easier and to justify the asking price. Lenders want to be certain the value is accurate. Because of this potential for a conflict of interest, appraisals must be ordered by a neutral party such as a mortgage broker or lender, even though they are paid for by the borrower prior to closing. Because Fannie Mae holds the lender responsible for the quality of the appraisal, the lender wants to know that the collateral is worth at least the amount of the loan. Lenders order appraisals only after they have approved a potential borrower's application and supporting documentation.

In most cases, lenders require a certified appraisal rather than a comparative market analysis. A comparative market analysis is an estimate of what a property is worth, and it can be provided by a knowledgeable professional, such as a real estate broker, who is not a certified appraiser. A **certified appraisal,** which is a requirement in all federally related loan transactions, can be done only by an individual who has fulfilled the educational, experience, and examination requirements for licensure as an appraiser. A federally related transaction refers to a transaction in which the property value exceeds $250,000 or involves Fannie Mae, Freddie Mac, the Government National Mortgage Association (GNMA, or Ginnie Mae), the FHA, the VA, the Department of Housing and Urban Development (HUD), or a federally insured financial institution such as a bank, savings association, or credit union. Appendix B contains Fannie Mae Form 1004, the Uniform Residential Appraisal Report.

FHA guidelines suggest that some of the qualifications lenders should consider when hiring an appraiser include education and experience, the quality of sample appraisals, the appraiser's professional affiliations, and his or her references.

In contrast with FHA guidelines for hiring appraisers, VA guidelines require that appraisals for VA loans be done by VA appraisers who are selected on a rotating basis. The VA appraiser issues a **Certificate of Reasonable Value (CRV)** that states the estimated value of the property and is part of the loan approval package.

Despite the fact that the applicant usually pays for the appraisal, the appraisal is the property of the lender. However, lenders are now required to provide a copy of the appraisal to the loan applicant at the time of closing. The maximum age of an appraisal is 12 months from the closing date. If the original appraisal is older than 120 days, a streamlined, or "drive-by," appraisal must be completed. If the drive-by appraisal supports the value estimated in the original appraisal, both are submitted in the loan package. If the drive-by appraisal indicates a lower price than the original, an entirely new appraisal must be completed.

Compensating the Appraiser

Although it may seem reasonable to compensate the appraiser on the basis of the value of the property being appraised, this approach is not considered ethical and is not used by professional appraisers. An appraisal fee based on a percentage of the value of a property creates a conflict of interest for the appraiser—it would be in the appraiser's interest to find a higher value for the property in order to earn a higher commission. For this reason, Fannie Mae guidelines and professional standards require appraisers work on a fee basis only. Professional appraisers follow the *Uniform Standards of Professional Appraisal Practice (USPAP)*, which is a set of standards adopted by appraisal organizations in 1986.

Appraisal Procedures

Appraisers use three approaches when estimating the value of a property: sales comparison, cost depreciation, and income capitalization.

1. Sales comparison. In the **sales comparison** approach, the appraiser first identifies at least three properties sold within the last 12 months that are similar to the property under consideration for purchase. The property the appraiser is valuing is referred to as the **subject property;** the properties being used for comparison are referred to as **comparables,** or comps. Sales comparison is an appraisal technique most often used to establish a value for homes and vacant residential properties. It is viewed as the most reliable method because it reflects several independent buyer-seller transactions in the market.

Properties used in the sales comparison approach must be in the same general market area as the subject property, be similar in size, style, and other features, and have changed ownership as the result of an "arm's length" transaction; that is, the sale of the comparable property involved no special terms or relationships between buyer and seller or was not sold under foreclosure or other special circumstances.

To determine the value of the subject property in comparison with the other properties the appraiser has identified, the appraiser makes a number of adjustments to the sales prices of the comparables, then reconciles the prices to come up with a value for the subject property. When the comparable has a feature that the subject property lacks, the value of that feature is subtracted from the sales price of the comparable to determine an adjusted value. When the subject property has a feature not found in the comparable, the value of that feature is added to the sales price of the comparable to determine an adjusted value. After the appraiser has adjusted the values of all the comparables, he or she then reconciles the adjusted values by weighting each comp's adjusted value according to how closely the appraiser feels the comp is similar to the subject property. See Figure 8.2 for an application of this approach.

Adjustments to comparables cannot exceed certain guidelines. The total *net* adjustments for each comp cannot exceed 15 percent of that comp's sales price. The total *gross* adjustment cannot exceed 25 percent of that comp's sales price. If net and gross adjustments exceed these limits, an underwriter will note that too many adjustments were made to the comp.

2. Cost depreciation. In the **cost depreciation** approach, appraisers estimate the cost of reproducing an already existing property. There are several ways to do this, but the basic procedure consists of estimating what it would cost to reproduce the existing structure as new, then subtracting an amount that reflects the depreciation of the property.

Depreciation, which refers to a loss in value, occurs in three forms. **Physical depreciation** is ordinary wear and tear; **functional depreciation** occurs because of changes in consumer preferences; and **external depreciation** is caused by factors that occur outside the property.

FIGURE 8.2 ■ Sales Comparison Approach

Subject Property	123 Cedar Lane	Three bedrooms, pool, landscaping
Comp #1	2220 Elm Avenue Sales price $249,000	Three bedrooms, no pool, no landscaping
Comp #2	51 Oak Circle Sales price $266,000	Two bedrooms, pool, fireplace, no landscaping
Comp #3	55 Aster Court Sales price $275,000	Three bedrooms, pool, fireplace, landscaping
Value of Features		
Bedroom	$7,000	
Pool	$5,000	
Fireplace	$2,000	
Landscaping	$3,000	

Comparable better, subtract (CBS); Comparable inferior, add (CIA).
Comp #1 = $249,000 + $5,000 (pool) + $3,000 (landscaping) = $257,000
Comp #2 = $266,000 + $7,000 (bedroom) - $2,000 (fireplace) + $3,000 landscaping) = $274,000
Comp #3 = $275,000 - $2,000 (fireplace) = $273,000
Subject property = ($257,000 + $274,000 + $273,000) ÷ 3 = $268,000

Once the appraiser determines the depreciated value of the property, the appraiser makes an estimate of the value of the land—land is not subject to depreciation—often by using a sales comparison approach. The value of the land is added to the value of the depreciated improvements to determine a final value.

3. Income capitalization. The **income capitalization** approach is used for investment properties that create a revenue stream to the owner. The appraiser works with the revenue stream to place a value on this income based on the **capitalization rate,** a number that reflects the rate of return on the owner's investment in the property. In other words, income capitalization calculates how much income the property earns.

Although one appraisal method may appear better suited to a certain kind of property—for example, residential appraisal may work best with sales comparison; income capitalization may be most appropriate for valuing an investment or rental property; and cost depreciation may work best for valuing churches or hospitals—appraisers are required by Fannie Mae to use all three approaches whenever appropriate. Then, through the process of *reconciliation*, they can come up with the most accurate valuation of a property.

Reconciliation

Sometimes appraisers use reconciliation to determine the value of a property. **Reconciliation** is used in all three appraisal approaches, and it is based on the principle of giving more weight to (1) the valuation technique that matches the property type and (2) the similarity between the subject property and the different comparables. The following is an example of reconciliation in a sales comparison appraisal:

EXAMPLE: Appraiser Don wants to use the reconciliation approach to determine a value on the property on Cedar Lane discussed in Figure 8.2. Don makes the adjustments described above, then he decides that Comp #3 at $273,000, which sold two weeks ago, is most similar to the subject property. Comp #2, which sold two months ago and has an adjusted value of $274,000, is the least similar to the subject property, and Comp #1, with an adjusted value of $257,000 and sold three months ago, lies between #3 and #2 in terms of similarity to the subject property.

Don then performs a reconciliation by assigning weights to the adjusted values of the comparable properties based on their similarity to the subject property. Because Comp #3 is the most similar to the subject property, Don assigns a weight of 0.50 to that property. Property #1 is the second most similar, so it gets a weight of 0.30, and property #2 gets a weight of 0.20. Don calculates the value of the subject property as follows:

1. $257,000 × 0.30 = $77,100
2. $274,000 × 0.20 = $54,800
3. $273,000 × 0.50 = $136,500

Value of subject property = $268,400 (The total of 1, 2, and 3)

APPRAISAL TERMINOLOGY

When determining the value of a property, appraisers use a variety of concepts to guide their calculations. Some of the concepts most frequently used are discussed below.

Highest and best use. **Highest and best use** means the most profitable, physically possible, legal use of real property and, in terms of appraisal, properties that are put to their highest and best use are more valuable. For example, a purchaser might plan to build a residence on an empty lot at the corner of a busy intersection, but the highest and best—and more profitable—use of the property might be a gas station or convenience store.

Principle of substitution. This principle, which is the basis for all appraisals, holds that no reasonable buyer will pay more for a property than what the buyer would pay for a reasonably comparable property. For example, the **principle of substitution** holds that a purchaser will not pay more for a home in a subdivision if there is a similar home in a similar location at a lower price.

Overimprovement. **Overimprovement** refers to an improvement in which the cost is greater than the value added to the property.

Principle of conformity. Appraisers generally believe that a property has the greatest value when it fits with the social and economic composition of the neighborhood in which it is located, which is known as the **principle of conformity**.

Build-up. The percentage of land in a neighborhood that has structures or improvements is referred to as **build-up**.

Marketing time. **Marketing time** refers to the average time a property stays on the market before selling. When marketing time exceeds six months, the appraiser needs to offer an explanation.

Actual age and effective age. **Actual age** refers to the age of a property based on when it was built. **Effective age** refers to the age of a property based on the degree of depreciation.

Streamlined Appraisals

In recent years, Fannie Mae and Freddie Mac have developed guidelines for more streamlined appraisals. These streamlined models—which usually require the appraiser to estimate the value of a property by doing a drive-by appraisal—require the appraiser to gather less information and often rely on information already in a database. Streamlined appraisals are used only in situations where the lender feels the risk associated with a loan is not great.

Age of the Appraisal

As stated earlier in this chapter, an appraisal can be no older than 12 months from the date the mortgage loan is closed. If the appraisal report will be more than 4 months old on the date the note and mortgage are signed, the appraiser must reinspect the exterior of the property and review recent sales data for the area where the property is located. If the appraiser determines that the property has not declined in value during the 4-month period, the original appraisal can be accepted by the lender.

If, on the other hand, the appraiser concludes that the value of the property has declined, a new appraisal must be performed.

Wood Destroying Organism (WDO) Report

Most, but not all, lenders require a **Wood Destroying Organism (WDO) Report,** which is an inspection of a property to determine if there is damage caused by wood destroying organisms—such as termites—or if wood destroying organisms are active in the property. In Florida, this inspection must be done by a Florida-licensed pest control inspector. Lenders are unlikely to approve a loan on a property where wood destroying organisms are active, and often they require that any damage be repaired before they approve the loan.

Property Inspection

In contrast with an appraisal, which determines the value of a property, a property inspection determines that all parts of the property are in good repair. Although a property inspection may not be required by the lender, FHA recommends that borrowers arrange for an inspection.

Flood Zone

Lenders also want reassurance that they can recover damages if the property they accept as security for a loan is damaged by floods. As discussed in chapter 4, the likelihood of flood is determined by the **Federal Emergency Management Agency (FEMA),** which identifies flood hazard areas in the United States. If a property is located in an area FEMA designates as a **flood zone,** the lender will require the borrower to obtain special flood insurance and maintain the insurance throughout the life of the loan. FEMA also identifies certain areas as being at risk for velocity or wind-driven storm surge hazard.

Flood insurance covers the amount of the loan minus the value of the land. Borrowers must pay a flood certification fee to determine if the property lies within the flood zone area. Surveyors can determine if a property lies in the flood zone. Lenders require that flood insurance be in effect for the life of the mortgage loan, and the first year premium for flood insurance is paid in advance.

AUTOMATED UNDERWRITING

Historically, underwriters evaluated loan applications by making trained judgments about a borrower's creditworthiness. Lenders had standard criteria they used in evaluating applications, and underwriters simply followed these guidelines. Today, lenders are likely to use an automated underwriting system. An **automated underwriting system (AUS)** compares aspects of an individual's loan application with information that exists in a database of loan portfolios. The loan application receives a score based on this comparison.

Desktop Underwriter® is the automated underwriting system used by Fannie Mae to evaluate mortgage applications; **Loan Prospector®** is Freddie Mac's automated system. Both programs use credit history, down payment, cash on hand, and other factors to determine the amount of risk associated with a particular applicant. Most of this information is taken directly from the applicant's credit report.

Automated underwriting has some particularly attractive features. First, the system evaluates loan risk using statistical data and formulas and thus eliminates any subjectivity or bias on the part of the loan underwriter. Second, the nature of the program allows strengths in certain areas of an applicant's credit history or current situation to compensate for weaknesses elsewhere. Third, AUS can be used for conventional, FHA, or VA loans.

It is important to note that although an AUS makes a recommendation regarding an applicant's creditworthiness, it is ultimately the lender who decides whether to approve a loan. In addition, the lender may be liable for any inaccuracies in the application or errors in underwriting.

Based on the score, the Fannie Mae AUS will make a recommendation: approve/eligible; approve/ineligible; refer/eligible; refer/ineligible; refer with caution; expanded approval; and out of scope, which means that the loan is outside the guidelines of Fannie Mae. When the loan comes back rated approve/eligible, sometimes Fannie Mae will require only three items: a drive-by appraisal, a verbal verification of employment, and a trimerged, infile credit report. Figure 8.3 summarizes the Fannie Mae recommendations.

ISSUING THE COMMITMENT TO THE BORROWER

If the underwriter finds a borrower's application, credit history, and supporting documents acceptable, then the lender will issue a commitment, usually in the form of a letter because a commitment must be in writing to be enforceable. The **commitment letter** is a statement of the terms under which a lender will make a loan to a particular borrower. The loan commitment does not require disclosure of the annual percentage rate of the loan. Some lenders also charge a **commitment fee** as a requirement for guaranteeing specific loan terms at a later date.

A **standby commitment** is a promise from a different lender to make funds available under certain conditions and is used in situations where the borrower may be uncertain that his or her initial application will be approved.

FIGURE 8.3 ■ Fannie Mae Loan Approval Guidelines

Approve/Eligible
Based on the data submitted, the loan meets Fannie Mae, FHA, or VA credit risk and eligibility requirements.

Approve/Ineligible
The loan meets the Fannie Mae, FHA, or VA credit risk requirements based on parameters such as the borrower, product, and maximum LTV ratio. However, the loan does not meet the eligibility requirements specified by Fannie Mae, the FHA, or the VA. An underwriter must determine if the condition that caused the ineligibility creates an additional layering of credit risk that should be considered.

Refer/Eligible
The loan meets the Fannie Mae, FHA, or VA eligibility requirements. Desktop Underwriter® evaluated a combination of risk factors, including assets, each borrower's credit history, each borrower's employment status, the property type, and the purpose of the loan. Based on the data submitted, Desktop Underwriter® is not able to recommend approval for the loan.

Refer/Ineligible
The loan does not meet Fannie Mae, FHA, or VA eligibility requirements. Desktop Underwriter® evaluated a combination of risk factors, and based on the data submitted, the system is not able to recommend approval of the loan. In addition, the risk analysis did not take into consideration any additional credit risk that might be associated with the ineligibility condition.

Refer with Caution
Desktop Underwriter® evaluated a combination of risk factors, and based on the data submitted, the loan does not appear to meet the credit risk of loans that receive a Refer recommendation. This recommendation is not used for government loans.

Out of Scope
Desktop Underwriter® does not contain the rules or models that are necessary to underwrite the product, borrower, or type of loan submitted. Therefore, underwriting may not be valid.

Freddie Mac's AUS provides one of three responses: Approve, Refer, or Caution.

Adverse Action Notice

Adverse action refers to an underwriter denying an individual's loan application. Adverse action is covered by the Equal Credit Opportunity Act and regulated by the Federal Trade Commission (FTC).

The FTC requires that the lender provide the applicant with the reasons the loan was denied. The reasons for denial, along with a list of creditors and other information, must be provided within 30 days of the lender denying the application. The borrower must also receive the name, address, and phone number of the credit agency that provided information to the underwriter.

In addition, an adverse action notice must be given to a borrower within 90 days after a counteroffer has been presented by the lender and the borrower has not responded to the counteroffer.

KEY POINT REVIEW

- *Underwriting* is the analysis of the risk associated with a loan.
- High *loan-to-value ratios* create greater risk for lenders because the frequency of loan default increases when borrowers have little or none of their own cash in the property.
- A gift may be used as part of the down payment if the donor provides a *gift letter* stating that he or she does not expect repayment of the gift. Most lenders will not consider *sweat equity* or cash on hand as part of the down payment.
- An *appraisal* is an opinion of value of a property. The lender is held responsible for the quality and proper analysis of the appraisal.
- Federally related loan transactions require a *certified appraisal;* VA appraisals can only be done by a VA appraiser.
- To avoid conflicts of interest, appraisers are paid on a fee basis, not commission. In addition, an appraisal can only be ordered by a third party, and not the buyer, seller, or real estate sales associate or broker.
- A *sales comparison* appraisal is based on at least three recently sold properties that are similar to the property under consideration that sold within the past 12 months.
- The *cost depreciation* appraisal considers the cost of reproducing the structure, subtracts an amount that reflects the level of depreciation, and then adds back in the value of the land.
- *Income capitalization* places a value on the revenue stream produced by a property. The *capitalization rate* reflects the rate of return on the owner's investment in the property.
- Appraisers are encouraged to use all three approaches—sales comparison, cost depreciation, and income capitalization—when valuing a property.
- *Highest and best use* refers to the most profitable, legal, physically possible use of a property.
- As a general rule, an appraisal can be no older than 120 days from the date the mortgage loan is closed. If the appraisal is more than 4 months old, the appraiser must reinspect the exterior of the property and check sales data.
- The major value of an *automated underwriting system* is that it eliminates bias on the part of the underwriter. But even if a lender uses an automated underwriting system, it is ultimately the lender who decides whether to approve a loan.
- The *commitment letter* is the lender's promise to the borrower to approve a loan.
- If a lender denies a loan—that is, takes *adverse action*—the lender must provide the applicant with reasons why the loan was denied within 30 days of receiving the application.

REVIEW QUESTIONS

1. When a mortgage broker forwards a loan application to the lender to be evaluated, the underwriter will be most interested in making sure
   a. the risk associated with the loan is acceptable.
   b. the loan is brought to closing.
   c. that the borrower has arranged for the loan to be insured.
   d. the value of the property is equal to the loan amount.

2. From the perspective of the lender, the major value of Desktop Underwriter® is that
   a. it eliminates the need for a credit report.
   b. borrowers do not have to complete lengthy applications.
   c. it encourages the underwriter to make subjective judgments.
   d. the program can quickly and efficiently calculate risk associated with a particular applicant.

3. Although Mr. Homebuyer has $250,000 in cash and securities, he wants to make as small a down payment on a property as possible. The lender
   a. will be reassured that Mr. Homebuyer has put little of his cash into buying the property.
   b. may be concerned that Mr. Homebuyer will have little motivation to continue to pay the mortgage.
   c. will require the mortgage broker to identify additional sources of funds to cover any shortage between Mr. Homebuyer's down payment and the loan amount.
   d. will need to reassure the seller that she will receive the full sales price for the property if Mr. Homebuyer makes a small down payment.

4. Once an application package goes to underwriting,
   a. the borrower can no longer make changes to the application package.
   b. the applicant can acquire more debt without jeopardizing approval on a loan already being reviewed.
   c. loan approval is largely guaranteed if the application package has been fully completed.
   d. the applicant needs to explain any changes in financial situation that occur after the submission.

5. Numerous studies of the underwriting process show that one of the best predictors of default is the
   a. age of the borrower.
   b. geographic area in which the property is located.
   c. appraised value of the property.
   d. poor history of debt repayment.

6. Julian wants to buy a house that has a badly damaged roof, which he offers to repair as part of the down payment on the property. The underwriter will agree to this only
   a. if the value of the repair does not exceed 10 percent of the down payment amount.
   b. if an appraiser certifies that the roof needs repair.
   c. if Julian cannot pay the balance of the down payment.
   d. in special cases only.

7. Maria is buying a unit in a building that is being converted to condominiums. The cost of the unit was $165,900. Maria made a down payment of $42,000 and financed the rest, giving her a loan-to-value ratio of
   a. 25 percent.
   b. 72 percent.
   c. 73 percent.
   d. 75 percent.

8. When the purchase of property is a federally related transaction, the lender will require a(n)
   a. opinion of value.
   b. certified appraisal.
   c. warranteed appraisal.
   d. CMA.

9. As part of the underwriting process, the property being sold must be appraised. After the closing, the appraisal is the property of the
   a. lender.
   b. borrower.
   c. mortgage broker.
   d. person who pays for it.

10. Who can use funds from an individual retirement account (IRA) to purchase a home?
    a. Anyone
    b. Retired people only
    c. Anyone who has permission from the FHA
    d. No one

11. West End Appraisers operates at the highest level of professionalism. Therefore, West End compensates its appraisers on
    a. a commission basis.
    b. a fee basis.
    c. the basis of the size of the property being appraised.
    d. a method of compensation that is negotiated with the person paying for the appraisal.

12. When valuing a residential property, which approach is an appraiser from West End most likely to rely on?
    a. Sales comparison
    b. Cost depreciation
    c. Income capitalization
    d. Income averaging

13. Linda's application to All-the-Best Mortgages has been turned down. Linda
    a. is legally prohibited from applying again to that same company.
    b. can appeal to Fannie Mae to have her credit reevaluated.
    c. will receive notification of the reasons for denial within 30 days.
    d. will receive notification of the reasons for denial if she requests such notification in writing.

14. From the underwriter's perspective, the value of the property being mortgaged should be at least equal to the
    a. value of the down payment.
    b. sales price.
    c. loan amount.
    d. first year's payments.

15. When a dispute arises about the value of a property, ultimate responsibility for the appraisal lies with the
    a. seller.
    b. buyer.
    c. lender's underwriter.
    d. mortgage broker.

16. Friendly Appraisals, Inc. is using the sales comparison approach to value a home at 1101 Westwood Drive and has located similar properties within ten blocks of the subject property. Friendly Appraisals will make adjustments to determine value on
    a. both the subject property and the comparables.
    b. the comparables only.
    c. the subject property only.
    d. none of the above because the sales comparison approach does not allow for houses more than five blocks from the property to be used for comparison.

17. In terms of appraisal, the concept highest and best use generally refers to
    a. the most profitable legal use of a property.
    b. the use that most fits with similar kinds of properties.
    c. how the buyer plans to use the property.
    d. the way in which the lender would like to see the property used.

18. What principle holds that no reasonable buyer would pay more for a property than what the buyer would pay for a reasonably comparable property?
    a. Highest and best use
    b. Reasonable valuation
    c. Substitution
    d. Comparative properties

19. When reviewing an application for a VA loan, the underwriter will
    a. not require a certified appraisal.
    b. accept a certified appraisal from any appraiser who holds a Florida license.
    c. require a VA appraisal.
    d. require either an FHA or VA appraiser.

20. Applicants who plan to buy property in flood zones should be aware that flood insurance
    a. is required on all properties regardless of location.
    b. must be maintained for the first five years of the loan.
    c. must be maintained throughout the life of the loan.
    d. is optional if the buyer will post a bond and assume the risk.

21. When valuing an apartment building, which approach is an appraiser most likely to use?
    a. Sales comparison
    b. Cost depreciation
    c. Income capitalization
    d. Income averaging

22. The commitment letter creates a contract between the
    a. borrower and the lender.
    b. lender and the mortgage broker.
    c. borrower and the mortgage broker.
    d. borrower, seller, lender, and mortgage broker.

23. Many underwriters prefer to use an AUS because it
    a. avoids the use of statistical data in evaluating applications.
    b. provides a binding answer to the lender.
    c. eliminates the underwriter's bias.
    d. results in a higher number of loan approvals.

24. When a homebuyer pays full price for a home, has excellent credit, and submits a complete application package, the ultimate responsibility for deciding to fund the loan lies with the
    a. mortgage broker.
    b. lender.
    c. automated underwriting system.
    d. seller.

CHAPTER

9 THE CLOSING

LEARNING OBJECTIVES

After finishing chapter 9, you should be able to

1. understand the HUD-1 Settlement Statement;
2. explain the significance of the note and mortgage;
3. know what buyer funds can be used at closing;
4. explain the Truth-in-Lending Disclosure Form;
5. understand the importance of title insurance;
6. know the requirements for the survey, hazard insurance, WDO clearance letter, and estoppel letter;
7. know what other documents may be required at closing; and
8. understand disbursement procedures and income tax reporting.

KEY TERMS

actual notice
anti-coercion statement
closing
closing agent
cloud on the title
constructive notice
deed restrictions
easement
encroachment
encumbrance
estoppel letter
government survey system
HUD-1 Settlement Statement
involuntary lien
lender's title insurance policy
lot and block description
metes-and-bounds description
owner's title insurance policy
point of beginning (POB)
recording
restrictive covenants
survey
voluntary lien

INTRODUCTION

The **closing** is the process in which a seller delivers title to real property to the buyer, and the buyer accepts the responsibility for repaying the lender for the mortgage loan. The signed mortgage and note create a contract for the repayment of the loan with interest. Furthermore, the mortgage and note also provide the lender with a product to sell on the secondary market.

Lenders will require that all matters regarding any liens on the property be resolved before preparation for the closing can take place. Although all closings follow similar procedures, most states also have specific laws that govern the closing process. The seven steps in a typical loan closing are:

1. Applicant receives notice of loan approval by a commitment letter.
2. Final title report is ordered.
3. Closing is scheduled.
4. Closing agent prepares closing documents.
5. Documents signed at closing.
6. Signed documents returned to the lender.
7. The mortgage is recorded.

The contract for sale and purchase usually specifies the date of the closing. The **closing agent** has responsibility for making sure all documents are ready for the closing, ensuring the accuracy of all documents, and collecting and disbursing all funds associated with the transaction. The closing agent is also required to explain all documents to the buyer and seller. Some closings are done directly by the lender, but many lenders use attorneys or title companies to act as the closing agent.

Documents typically required at closing include the following:

- HUD-1 Settlement Statement
- Lender's title insurance policy
- Deed
- Note and mortgage
- Truth-in-Lending disclosure
- Estoppel letter
- Hazard insurance
- Flood insurance (if required)
- Wood Destroying Organisms (WDO) Inspection Report
- Survey

HUD-1 SETTLEMENT STATEMENT

The **HUD-1 Settlement Statement** details the financial aspects of the real estate transaction and is prepared by the closing agent. According to the Real Estate Settlement Procedures Act (RESPA), the statement must be provided to the parties to the transaction at least one business day in advance of the closing, if requested. This statement, which is provided by the closing agent, lists all known fees related to the transaction. A sample completed HUD-1 Settlement Statement is shown in Figure 9.1.

FIGURE 9.1 ■ Sample HUD-1 Settlement Statement

A. **Settlement Statement**

U.S. Department of Housing and Urban Development

OMB Approval No. 2502-0265 (expires 9/30/2006)

B. Type of Loan

1. [ ] FHA 2. [ ] FmHA 3. [X] Conv. Unins. 4. [ ] VA 5. [ ] Conv. Ins.	6. File Number:	7. Loan Number:	8. Mortgage Insurance Case Number:

C. Note: This form is furnished to give you a statement of actual settlement costs. Amounts paid to and by the settlement agent are shown. Items marked "(p.o.c.)" were paid outside the closing; they are shown here for informational purposes and are not included in the totals.

D. Name & Address of Borrower:	E. Name & Address of Seller:	F. Name & Address of Lender:
Brook Redemann 22 King Court Riverdale, ED 00000	John Iuro and Joanne Iuro 3045 North Racine Avenue Riverdale, ED 00000	Thrift Federal Savings 1100 Fountain Plaza Riverdale, ED 00000

G. Property Location:	H. Settlement Agent:	
3045 North Racine Avenue Riverdale, ED 00000	Open Door Real Estate Co.	
	Place of Settlement: 720 Main Street Riverdale, ED 00000	I. Settlement Date: June 15, 200-

J. Summary of Borrower's Transaction		**K. Summary of Seller's Transaction**	
100. Gross Amount Due From Borrower		**400. Gross Amount Due To Seller**	
101. Contract sales price	$230,000.00	401. Contract sales price	$230,000.00
102. Personal property		402. Personal property	
103. Settlement charges to borrower (line 1400)	9,959.35	403.	
104.		404.	
105.		405.	
Adjustments for items paid by seller in advance		**Adjustments for items paid by seller in advance**	
106. City/town taxes to		406. City/town taxes to	
107. County taxes to		407. County taxes to	
108. Assessments to		408. Assessments to	
109.		409.	
110.		410.	
111.		411.	
112.		412.	
120. Gross Amount Due From Borrower	239,959.35	**420. Gross Amount Due To Seller**	$230,000.00
200. Amounts Paid By Or In Behalf Of Borrower		**500. Reductions In Amount Due To Seller**	
201. Deposit or earnest money	46,000.00	501. Excess deposit (see instructions)	
202. Principal amount of new loan(s)	184,000.00	502. Settlement charges to seller (line 1400)	15,565.00
203. Existing loan(s) taken subject to		503. Existing loan(s) taken subject to	
204.		504. Payoff of first mortgage loan	115,736.60
205.		505. Payoff of second mortgage loan	
206.		506.	
207.		507.	
208.		508.	
209.		509.	
Adjustments for items unpaid by seller		**Adjustments for items unpaid by seller**	
210. City/town taxes to		510. City/town taxes to	
211. County taxes 1/1 to 6/15	1,581.20	511. County taxes 1/1 to 6/15	1,581.20
212. Assessments to		512. Assessments to	
213.		513.	
214.		514.	
215.		515.	
216.		516.	
217.		517.	
218.		518.	
219.		519.	
220. Total Paid By/For Borrower	231,581.20	**520. Total Reduction Amount Due Seller**	132,882.80
300. Cash At Settlement From/To Borrower		**600. Cash At Settlement To/From Seller**	
301. Gross Amount due from borrower (line 120)	239,959.35	601. Gross amount due to seller (line 420)	230,000.00
302. Less amounts paid by/for borrower (line 220)	(231,581.20)	602. Less reductions in amt. due seller (line 520)	(132,882.80)
303. Cash [X] **From** [ ] **To Borrower**	8,378.15	**603. Cash** [X] **To** [ ] **From Seller**	$ 97,117.20

Section 5 of the Real Estate Settlement Procedures Act (RESPA) requires the following: • HUD must develop a Special Information Booklet to help persons borrowing money to finance the purchase of residential real estate to better understand the nature and costs of real estate settlement services; • Each lender must provide the booklet to all applicants from whom it receives or for whom it prepares a written application to borrow money to finance the purchase of residential real estate; • Lenders must prepare and distribute with the Booklet a Good Faith Estimate of the settlement costs that the borrower is likely to incur in connection with the settlement. These disclosures are manadatory.

Section 4(a) of RESPA mandates that HUD develop and prescribe this standard form to be used at the time of loan settlement to provide full disclosure of all charges imposed upon the borrower and seller. These are third party disclosures that are designed to provide the borrower with pertinent information during the settlement process in order to be a better shopper.

The Public Reporting Burden for this collection of information is estimated to average one hour per response, including the time for reviewing instructions, searching existing data sources, gathering and maintaining the data needed, and completing and reviewing the collection of information.

This agency may not collect this information, and you are not required to complete this form, unless it displays a currently valid OMB control number.

The information requested does not lend itself to confidentiality.

Previous editions are obsolete — Page 1 of 2 — form **HUD-1** (3/86) ref Handbook 4305.2

Source: *Modern Real Estate Practice,* 17th Edition. Chicago: Dearborn™ Real Estate Education, 2006.

FIGURE 9.1 ■ Sample HUD-1 Settlement Statement (Continued)

L. Settlement Charges	Paid From Borrowers Funds at Settlement	Paid From Seller's Funds at Settlement
700. Total Sales/Broker's Commission based on price $ 230,000.00 @ 6 % = 13,800.00		
Division of Commission (line 700) as follows:		
701. $ to		
702. $ to		
703. Commission paid at Settlement		$13,800.00
704.		
800. Items Payable In Connection With Loan		
801. Loan Origination Fee %	$2,300.00	
802. Loan Discount %	3,680.00	
803. Appraisal Fee $500.00 to	POC	
804. Credit Report $120.00 to	POC	
805. Lender's Inspection Fee		
806. Mortgage Insurance Application Fee to		
807. Assumption Fee		
808.		
809.		
810.		
811.		
900. Items Required By Lender To Be Paid In Advance		
901. Interest from 6/16 to 6/30 @$ 40.79 /day	611.85	
902. Mortgage Insurance Premium for months to		
903. Hazard Insurance Premium for 1 years to Hite Insurance Co.	690.00	
904. years to		
905.		
1000. Reserves Deposited With Lender		
1001. Hazard insurance 2 months@$ 57.50 per month	115.00	
1002. Mortgage insurance months@$ per month		
1003. City property taxes months@$ per month		
1004. County property taxes 7 months@$ 287.50 per month	2,012.50	
1005. Annual assessments months@$ per month		
1006. months@$ per month		
1007. months@$ per month		
1008. months@$ per month		
1100. Title Charges		
1101. Settlement or closing fee to		
1102. Abstract or title search to		
1103. Title examination to		
1104. Title insurance binder to		20.00
1105. Document preparation to		
1106. Notary fees to		
1107. Attorney's fees to	500.00	600.00
(includes above items numbers:)		
1108. Title insurance to		540.00
(includes above items numbers:)		
1109. Lender's coverage $ 395.00		
1110. Owner's coverage $ 145.00		
1111.		
1112.		
1113.		
1200. Government Recording and Transfer Charges		
1201. Recording fees: Deed $ 25.00 ; Mortgage $ 25.00 ; Releases $ 25.00	50.00	25.00
1202. City/county tax/stamps: Deed $; Mortgage $		
1203. State tax/stamps: Deed $; Mortgage $		230.00
1204. Record 2 documents to clear title		50.00
1205.		
1300. Additional Settlement Charges		
1301. Survey to		200.00
1302. Pest inspection to		100.00
1303.		
1304.		
1305.		
1400. Total Settlement Charges (enter on lines 103, Section J and 502, Section K)	$9,959.35	$15,565.00

Previous editions are obsolete

Page 2 of 2

form **HUD-1** (3/86)
ref Handbook 4305.2

NOTE AND MORTGAGE

When the borrower signs the promissory note, he or she is promising to repay the lender. The note states the loan amount and interest rate, the date when the borrower is expected to start repaying the loan, and the date when the loan will be repaid in full. The note also contains information about any prepayment penalties. From a legal standpoint, it is important that the name on the promissory note be *exactly* the same as the name that appears on all other closing documents.

The mortgage accompanies the promissory note and contains an exact legal description of the property being offered as security for the loan. If a mortgage is assigned from one lender to another, the promissory note is also endorsed in favor of the new lender.

BUYER FUNDS USED AT CLOSING

Lenders use specific guidelines to determine what funds a buyer may use at the closing. Fannie Mae guidelines require borrowers to use their own funds to make a down payment of at least 5 percent of the purchase price. The buyer does not necessarily have to use money, however. Other possible sources of the down payment include gifts, trade equity, rent credit, or disaster relief grant or loan.

The property seller may also give the purchaser *rent credit*, which is credit toward the down payment for a portion of previous rent payments the purchaser made under a documented rental purchase agreement that had a minimum original term of at least 12 months, in an amount up to the difference between the market rent as determined by an appraiser and the actual rent that was paid.

In most cases, buyers are restricted in the amount of donated funds from the seller, builder, selling agent, or other interested party who may benefit financially from the sale.

When any closing or prepaid settlement costs normally paid by the property purchaser are paid by someone else, this payment is considered part of contributions. Contributions are limited to the following:

- **Investment property:** 2 percent of the sales price or the appraised value, whichever is lower
- **Owner-occupied or second home with a loan-to-value ratio (LTV) greater than 90 percent:** 3 percent of the sales price or appraised value, whichever is lower
- **Owner-occupied or second home with an LTV between 76 percent and 90 percent:** 6 percent of the sales price or appraised value, whichever is lower
- **Owner-occupied or second home with an LTV of 75 percent or less:** 9 percent of the sales price or appraised value, whichever is lower

However, a borrower can use a down payment that is a combination of personal funds along with funds received as a gift from a relative who lives with him or her, and who will also live in the home being purchased. In addition, borrowers who make the minimum 5 percent cash down payment from their own funds can supplement that down payment with a gift from a relative or a gift or grant from a religious organization, municipality, or nonprofit organization.

Cash at Closing

Except in the case of certain manufactured home purchases, lenders do not allow a buyer to bring cash to the closing. All funds related to a Fannie Mae transaction must have been deposited in a checking, savings, or other type of account, and the source of the funds be acceptable to the underwriter. A cashier's check, certified check, or a wire transfer of funds are typical sources of funds at the closing, with a wire transfer on the day of closing now considered the most acceptable.

In general, Fannie Mae requires two months of bank statements to prove the borrower has enough cash to close. And, as mentioned earlier, most lenders will not consider "sweat equity," which is a purchaser's willingness to improve the value of a property by doing work on the property, an acceptable part of the buyer's contribution toward the sales price. Borrowers can, however, apply the net proceeds from a loan against the cash value of a life insurance policy as a source of funds for a down payment, closing costs, or financial reserves.

Other possible sources of funds for closing include

- the borrower's deposit on the sales contract;
- money from checking, savings, and trust accounts;
- gifts from relatives;
- sales proceeds;
- bridge loans;
- retirement accounts; and
- stocks and bonds.

The buyer may also use borrowed funds that are secured by an asset such as a certificate of deposit (CD) at closing. Examples of unacceptable borrowed funds for closing include signature loans, lines of credit on credit cards, and overdraft protection on checking accounts.

TRUTH-IN-LENDING DISCLOSURE

As you recall from chapter 4, the federal Truth-in-Lending Act requires that lenders provide borrowers with information regarding the exact cost of borrowing. When the potential borrower applies for the loan initially, the lender provides an *estimate* of loan cost. The figures provided at closing represent the *actual* loan cost.

The Truth-in-Lending Act also gives borrowers a Notice of the Right of Rescission. This right, which is good for three business days not counting the closing date, applies to all persons who have an interest in the property. The right of rescission applies only to refinancing, second mortgages, home equity lines of credit, and loans that add principal as a result of refinancing. It does not apply to first mortgage loans secured by owner-occupied properties if it is for the purchase of the property.

TITLE INSURANCE

An **encumbrance** or **cloud on the title** is a defect that may impair the right of the property owner to sell the property. Typical encumbrances include questions about ownership, physical claims, or financial claims. As you may recall, a lien is a claim that one person has on the property of another. A **voluntary lien** is a pledge of property as security *willingly* offered by a homeowner or purchaser. A mortgage is an example of a voluntary lien. An **involuntary lien** occurs without the consent of the property owner. A tax lien or special assessment is an example of an involuntary lien. In most cases, both voluntary and involuntary liens must be resolved before title to a property can be transferred.

As mentioned earlier, title defects such as involuntary liens must be resolved before a lender will agree to accept a mortgage as security for a loan. Other possible impediments include unpaid real estate taxes and survey exceptions. Physical encumbrances include easements, encroachments, right of way, and deed restrictions. Even when all issues surrounding the title appear to have been resolved, however, lenders still require the purchaser to acquire a lender's title insurance policy.

Title insurance protects buyers and lenders by offering protection from most losses due to problems with the title to real property. The effective date of the title insurance is the date it is recorded. The lender and its successors or assigns are always the first payee.

As discussed earlier, there are two kinds of title insurance: lender's and owner's. Title problems are particularly serious to the lender because if there are questions about the title to a property, the lender may end up having funded a large, unsecured personal loan to a borrower.

The **lender's title insurance policy** protects the lender by insuring the amount of the loan only. The lender's title insurance policy must meet requirements set by the American Land Title Association (ALTA), which is the national trade association for the abstract and title insurance industry. The policy typically has a number of ALTA endorsements. Some of the most important ALTA endorsements include the following:

ALTA 4	**Condominium:** Protects lender against any violations of the condominium rules that would cause the owner to forfeit title to the property
ALTA 5	**Planned Unit Development (PUD):** Protects the lender against liens brought by a homeowners' association
ALTA 6/6.1	**Variable-rate mortgages:** Protects the lender from losses due to a change in interest rates
ALTA 7	**Manufactured Housing Unit:** Includes the manufactured housing unit located on a property as part of the property
ALTA 8.1	**Environmental Protection:** Covers loss or damage due to an environmental protection lien
ALTA 9	**Affirmative Coverage:** Ensures that the property does not violate any restrictions or easements when a survey is not provided

In contrast with the lender's policy, the **owner's title insurance policy** is issued for the amount of the purchase price and cannot be transferred or assigned. This policy protects the buyer in case questions arise about fraud during the purchase and sales transaction or other clouds on the title. Each time the property is sold, the new owner must acquire a new title insurance policy. However, lenders do not require purchasers to buy an owner's title insurance policy.

Title insurance is ordered after the lender has approved the borrower's application and the borrower has accepted the terms of the commitment. Each kind of title insurance has a one-time premium paid at the closing.

Lenders will also require an Indemnity or Closing Protection letter, which protects the lender from loss or damage arising from a breach of the fiduciary duties of the closing agent.

SURVEY

Lenders require exact descriptions of properties they accept as security for a mortgage loan. As part of the approval process, lenders often ask for a **survey,** which defines the exact location and boundaries of a property and describes where structures, driveways, fences, recorded easements, setback lines, neighbor encroachments, and so forth are positioned on the land. When completed, the survey is certified to the lender, title insurance company, or the buyer, but not to the seller. In addition to showing the boundaries of a property, the survey shows the buildings, driveways, and fences, as well as any easements.

Encroachments, Easements, and Deed Restrictions

As explained earlier, an **encroachment** is an unauthorized use of a property. For example, a neighbor may build a fence that encroaches on the property of another. When an encroachment has been in existence for seven years, it becomes an implied easement.

When a survey reveals a serious encroachment, such as a neighbor's building on the property, lenders typically consider this a cloud on the title. The lender will expect the seller of the property to solve this problem before the buyer's loan application can be approved. A cement block wall that is built on the property of a neighbor may be another example of an encroachment that would be considered a cloud on the title.

Other areas of concern to both the purchaser and the lender are easements, deed restrictions, and restrictive covenants. In contrast with an encroachment, which is an unauthorized use of another's property, an **easement** is a right or interest in property that belongs to another person. Utility easements are commonly found on most properties. These are generally permanent, run with the land despite ownership change, and—in contrast with encroachments—are not considered an impediment in the closing process.

Deed restrictions limit the use of a specific property and are part of a deed, and **restrictive covenants** limit the use of all properties in an area such as a subdivision.

Legal Description of Real Property

When a lender makes a loan secured by real property, the lender will require that all documents related to the loan carry an exact description of the property being used as collateral. There are three kinds of legal descriptions: metes-and-bounds, government survey, and lot and block descriptions.

Metes and bounds. Metes refers to distance; bounds refers to direction. A **metes-and-bounds** description of a property starts from a **point of beginning (POB)**. The POB is a permanent marker or monument on the property and serves as the major reference point for locating the property. It is critical that the POB be accurate for the legal description to be accurate. From the POB, the surveyor measures the number of degrees, minutes, and seconds in a particular direction to the first corner of the property. Then the surveyor measures the degrees, minutes, and seconds to the next corner, and so forth, until the surveyor arrives back at the POB. Metes-and-bounds is considered the most accurate method for legal descriptions and is also the best method for identifying irregular-shaped parcels of land.

Government survey system. Created by the Continental Congress in 1785, the government survey system is currently used in all states except Kentucky, Tennessee, Texas, West Virginia, and the original 13 colonies. The **government survey system** uses certain latitudes and longitudes as markers to identify property location. These identifying longitudes are known as principal meridians and latitudes are known as base lines. Along with the principal meridians and base lines, the government survey system relies on range lines, which run parallel to the principal meridians, and township lines, which run parallel to the base lines. Range lines and township lines are six miles apart and create townships that are six miles on a side. Finally, townships are divided into 36 sections that are a mile on each side.

Lot and block. Probably the most common method of identifying property location within a subdvision is by lot and block description. Lot and block is used in areas where the developer has filed a plat map with the local government. Each area on the plat map is divided into blocks, and each block into lots. Lots are usually numbered. The **lot and block description** is recorded using the subdivision name and comes with a book and page number that makes identification easier for the appraiser.

HAZARD INSURANCE

In preparation for the closing, the lender will notify the closing agent that the borrower must obtain hazard insurance for the subject property. The closing agent then informs the buyer. At the closing, the borrower may sign an **anti-coercion statement** stating that the lender did not require the borrower to obtain insurance from a particular insurance company.

Hazard insurance policies must meet the lender's requirements, have the correct names and addresses of all parties, and have the correct form of the loss payable clause to protect the mortgagee. The amount of insurance coverage required is determined by comparing the insurable value of improvements to the unpaid principal balance of the mortgage. If the value of the improvement is less than the unpaid principal balance, the insurable value is the amount required. If the insurable value is greater than, or equal to, the unpaid principal balance, 80 percent of the value is the amount required. Insurance premiums paid from escrow accounts are paid annually in advance.

The lender is the first payee on the hazard insurance. The maximum deductible allowed by Fannie Mae is 5 percent of the total amount of the insurance. The lender also determines the amount of coverage, which can be either 100 percent of the replacement cost of the improvements or the amount of the loan. As mentioned earlier, the deductible for wind damage is twice that amount—$2,000 or 2 percent, whichever is greater.

Finally, Fannie Mae requires insurance coverage for six months of rent loss on investment properties.

WOOD DESTROYING ORGANISMS INSPECTION

Soon after a loan application is approved, the lender will ask for a Wood Destroying Organisms (WDO) Report on the property. In Florida, the most common forms of wood-destroying organisms are termites and wood destroying fungi.

The WDO report may reveal damage that the lender will require to be fixed before the closing. This damage may be due to termites and other pests, weather, or other causes. Usually, the seller is responsible for seeing that the property is repaired.

At the closing, the lender will require a WDO clearance letter issued by a certified inspector that certifies that the property has been repaired and is now clear of any wood-destroying organisms or damage.

ESTOPPEL LETTER

An **estoppel letter** is a statement of any outstanding balances due at the time of a real estate sale. These balances can be related to mortgage payments, interest, taxes, insurance, or other expenses. Because mortgage interest is paid in arrears, interest must be added to the principal balance at the time of payoff.

The estoppel letter gives the precise amount owed on the date the closing takes place. As part of the preparation for the closing, the closing agent orders the estoppel letter and uses information from the letter to prepare the closing statement.

OTHER DOCUMENTS

Depending on the nature of the real estate transaction, the closing agent may be required to provide other kinds of documents. For example, if the property lies in an area with a homeowners' association, the seller is required to give the buyer a copy of the *homeowners' association agreement*. Along the same lines, mortgages with adjustable interest rates require that the borrower sign a document known as an *adjustable-rate rider*.

According to the Truth-in-Lending Act, borrowers who are refinancing or signing for a home equity loan have the right to rescind the transaction within three business days. The closing agent is required to provide this information to the borrower. Finally, individuals occasionally use variations of their name—for example, sometimes signing with a middle initial and sometimes not. At the closing, the lender may require that the borrower sign an affidavit recognizing the differences in name usage.

DISBURSEMENT PROCEDURES

The closing agent is responsible for disbursing funds connected with a closing. These funds include the deposit made by the buyer, the amount of the loan, the commission to the real estate broker, and the various expenses such as title insurance, documentary tax stamps, loan origination and mortgage broker fees, and other fees payable to the lender. The closing agent is also responsible for explaining all closing documents to the buyer and the seller.

In some cases, lenders will provide funds to purchase or close loans by electronic transfer from bank to bank rather than rely on the physical disbursement of checks. In these cases, the funds go directly into the designated recipient's bank account. When checks are used to disburse funds, however, they should be in the form of a cashier's check in order to expedite the transaction.

The final step of the closing process is recording the mortgage at the county courthouse. **Recording** the mortgage creates constructive notice—that is, legal notice—of the transfer of title. **Constructive notice** is created through the recording of documents. **Actual notice**, in contrast, refers to actions typically exercised by the owner: payment of property taxes, maintaining the land, preventing trespass, and so forth. Either method of informing the public of legal ownership is considered sufficient, and both are equally recognized by law.

Although it is the signatures and the notarization that make the document legal, recording the mortgage creates legal notice of the lender's claim to the property should the buyer default on the note and a lien on the property. As mentioned earlier, time of recording establishes the priority of liens within each category, such as mortgages. For example, a first mortgage has first lien position and must be recorded before any other mortgages.

KEY POINT REVIEW

- The *closing agent* has responsibility for making sure all documents are ready for the closing and explaining the documents to the buyer and seller.
- Typical documents at closing include: HUD-1 Settlement Statement, title report, hazard insurance, flood insurance (if required), WDO clearance letter, and survey.
- The *HUD-1 Settlement Statement* must be provided to the interested parties at least one business day prior to closing, if requested.
- Typical borrower expenses include mortgage brokerage fees, discount points, interest charges, insurance premiums, unpaid taxes, tax stamps on the note, and recording fees. Typical seller expenses include the real estate broker's commission, attorney's fees, owner's title insurance, documentary stamps on the deed, and recording fees.
- Figures on the Truth-in-Lending disclosure at closing represent the exact cost of the loan.
- A mortgage is a *voluntary lien*.
- The *lender's title insurance policy* names the lender as the beneficiary for the amount of the loan, and the policy can be transferred to another lender upon sale of the loan. The *owner's title policy* benefits the property owner, is written for the entire purchase price, and is not transferable.
- Title insurance is ordered after the borrower has accepted the terms of the lender's commitment.
- Lenders consider serious *encroachments* to be a cloud on the title.
- Flood insurance and hazard insurance policies cover the amount of the loan minus the value of the land and must remain in effect for the life of the loan.
- If a *Wood Destroying Organisms Report* reveals damage to the property, repairs must be completed prior to closing.
- An *estoppel letter* lists outstanding balances due at the time of a real estate sale.
- The closing agent is responsible for disbursing funds at the closing.
- The final step of the closing process is *recording the mortgage*.

REVIEW QUESTIONS

1. Connie's financing does not come with the right of rescission. This means that Connie's transaction involves
   a. the purchase of a primary residence.
   b. a second mortgage.
   c. a first mortgage refinance.
   d. a home equity line of credit.

2. When a borrower signs the note and mortgage at the closing, this creates
   a. a contract for repayment of the loan amount.
   b. a lien on property.
   c. an obligation on the part of the borrower.
   d. all of the above.

3. The title insurance endorsement that protects the lender from losses due to easements is
   a. ALTA 4.
   b. ALTA 6.
   c. ALTA 8.1.
   d. ALTA 9.

4. Title insurance becomes effective
   a. on the closing date.
   b. on the date it is recorded.
   c. at the time of application.
   d. when the insurance company deposits the purchaser's check.

5. Stefan bought a home in Palatka for $195,000 and made a down payment of $42,000 from an inheritance. With regard to title insurance, the lender will require Stefan to purchase
   a. both owner's and lender's policies.
   b. a lender's policy only.
   c. coverage for the sales price.
   d. sufficient title insurance to cover the difference between the existing policy on the house and the loan amount.

6. A borrower in Gainesville finances the purchase of a town house that he plans to rent to college students. At a minimum, Fannie Mae will require
   a. hazard insurance with a wind loss deductible of the greater of 1 percent of the loan or $1,000.
   b. insurance coverage equal to 80 percent of the loan balance.
   c. six months' rent loss insurance.
   d. all of the above.

7. Lynette has received a gift that the closing agent says is acceptable to use as part of the down payment. This gift was provided by
   a. the builder of the house Lynette is purchasing.
   b. the seller, who is making the gift as part of creative financing.
   c. the real estate broker, who has an interest in seeing the sale close.
   d. Lynette's uncle.

8. The HUD-1 Settlement Statement
   a. must be provided to the parties to the closing three business days before the closing.
   b. reflects the closing agent's best estimate of closing costs.
   c. must be provided to the parties to the closing one business day in advance, if requested.
   d. is not necessary because the closing agent is not obligated to provide an advance copy of the settlement statement.

9. The maximum contribution on the purchase of an investment property is 2 percent of the
   a. purchase price.
   b. lesser of the sales price or appraised value.
   c. appraised value if it is lower than the purchase price.
   d. down payment.

10. When a buyer offers a property as collateral for a loan, the buyer creates a(n)
    a. tax lien.
    b. special assessment.
    c. involuntary lien.
    d. voluntary lien.

11. Mr. and Mrs. Seller are uncertain of the date the sale of their time-share will close. This information can be found in the
    a. commitment letter.
    b. estoppel letter.
    c. contract for sale and purchase.
    d. good faith estimate.

12. When a homebuyer pays for the lender's title insurance, the insurance will guarantee the
    a. amount of the purchase price.
    b. amount of the loan.
    c. difference between the loan amount and the purchase price.
    d. purchase price plus the cost of repairs on any defects in the property.

13. When a homebuyer pays for her owner's title insurance policy, she is
    a. guaranteeing the amount of the loan.
    b. buying a policy that is transferable.
    c. buying a policy that is not transferable.
    d. guaranteeing the purchase price plus the cost of repairing any existing defects in the property.

14. The survey of a property is not certified to the
    a. buyer.
    b. seller.
    c. lender.
    d. title company.

15. When Sally signs the anti-coercion statement, she is affirming that she was not forced to use any particular
    a. loan company.
    b. title insurance company.
    c. appraiser.
    d. flood and hazard insurance provider.

16. Mr. Conigliaro needs to come up with a $25,000 down payment to purchase a condo in Indian Harbour Beach. Which is an acceptable source of Mr. Conigliaro's down payment?
    a. Line of credit
    b. Overdraft protection
    c. Signature loan
    d. Funds from sale of current home

17. As part of the closing process on a home at 2020 Bellevue Place, the closing agent ordered an estoppel letter. The letter
    a. sets the date of the closing.
    b. notifies the seller to stop making mortgage payments on the house he or she has sold.
    c. states any outstanding mortgage balances at the time of a real estate sale.
    d. does all the above.

18. When the closing agent provides the buyer with the Truth-in-Lending disclosure at the closing, the buyer will know
    a. the real cost of the loan.
    b. the estimated cost of the loan over time.
    c. his or her complete credit history and how it affected the interest rate on the loan.
    d. the financial stability of the lender.

19. If a lender plans to resell a loan to Fannie Mae, the lender will usually require a purchaser to use what minimum percentage of his or her own funds to make a down payment?
    a. 5 percent
    b. 10 percent
    c. 20 percent
    d. 3 percent

20. The final step in the real estate transaction is
    a. disbursement of funds.
    b. taking title to the property.
    c. recording the mortgage.
    d. signing all documents.

21. When the survey reveals a utility easement, the closing
    a. cannot go forward until the issue is resolved.
    b. will still go forward in most cases.
    c. can go forward if the utility company provides a waiver of ownership.
    d. can go forward if the utility company signs an acknowledgment of the easement.

22. Jerry Donovan has several alternatives for paying the closing costs on a home he recently bought in Clearwater. Which is NOT an acceptable source of funds to pay Jerry's closing costs?
    a. Bridge loans
    b. Retirement accounts
    c. Trust accounts
    d. Cash on hand

23. When Jerry goes to the closing, which will be an acceptable source of funds for the down payment?
    a. Personal check
    b. Cashier's check
    c. Line of credit
    d. Cash

24. Mr. Doggett has offered $230,000 on a property listed at $249,000. If the seller accepts Mr. Doggett's offer, when will the title insurance be ordered?
    a. After the lender approves Mr. Doggett's application and Mr. Doggett accepts the terms of the lender's commitment
    b. As soon as the seller accepts Mr. Doggett's offer
    c. As soon as the underwriter receives Mr. Doggett's application
    d. After the survey is completed and no encroachments are found

25. The point of beginning is associated with the
    a. initial loan application.
    b. date of the mortgage loan.
    c. lot-and-block system.
    d. metes-and-bounds description.

CHAPTER

10 THE SECONDARY MARKET

LEARNING OBJECTIVES

After finishing chapter 10, you should be able to

1. identify the major participants in the secondary market; and
2. understand recourse, loan servicing, participation, warehousing, table funding, and direct investor funding.

KEY TERMS

assignee
assignor
combined loan-to-value ratio (CLTV)
direct investor funding
mortgage-backed securities (MBSs)
net yield
nonconforming loans
participation
recourse
security holder
servicing released
servicing retained
table funding
warehousing
with full recourse
with normal recourse
without recourse

INTRODUCTION

The relationship between a borrower and a lender creates the primary mortgage market. But when lenders sell mortgages that already exist, they create a secondary mortgage market. The secondary mortgage market came into existence during the Great Depression as a way for the federal government to encourage financial institutions to invest in home mortgages. In the secondary market, a bank that has made a mortgage loan can then sell the loan to an investor such as Fannie Mae. The bank can take the profit from the sale of the mortgage and lend it to another home purchaser.

A second reason for creating the secondary market was to provide funds for mortgage loans in geographical areas that did not have sufficient capital to meet the demand for mortgages. Most commonly, this meant moving funds from the eastern United States to the South and West. By purchasing mortgages everywhere in the country, Fannie Mae and other investors made funds available to more lenders and also helped keep interest rates at similar levels regardless of area.

Today, the secondary market in mortgages has grown from its original mission of increasing liquidity in the mortgage industry to becoming an important part of the American economy. The major secondary market institutions, Fannie Mae and Freddie Mac, are large, publicly traded corporations with capitalizations of billions of dollars. But other major financial institutions participate in the secondary market as well, including commercial banks, mutual funds, pension funds, and foreign investors. In addition to an increased number of participants, the size of offerings in the secondary market has grown enormously. According to the Mortgage Banker's Association, for example, when mortgage-backed securities (discussed below) first appeared in the secondary market in 1983, the total value of securities issued amounted to $69 billion. Today, a single mortgage-backed security can be worth hundreds of billions of dollars.

In the primary market, lenders lend money with the intention of making two kinds of profit: profit on the interest paid by the borrower and profit on the sale of the loan in the secondary market. Assignment of mortgage refers to making an agreement regarding the sale of a mortgage. In these situations, the **assignor** transfers to the **assignee,** who receives the rights associated with the mortgage. The assignee will record the assignment in the public records.

For secondary market investors, profit comes from the combination of the interest rate the borrower pays and the discount at which the investor can buy the loan from the primary lender. This combination of interest rate and discount creates the **net yield** to the investor.

For example, a lender may make a loan of $150,000 at 7.5 percent interest to a homebuyer, then later sell that loan to an investor on the secondary market for $145,000—that is, with a discount of $5,000. The secondary market investor pays $145,000 for a loan still worth $150,000 at 7.5 percent. So in addition to the interest the borrower will pay on the $150,000, the investor receives 7.5 percent interest on the $5,000 discount.

Through prepaid interest, fees, and other charges, the original lender has made a profit on the loan and now has money to lend to the next borrower. But another source of revenue associated with the secondary market is the fees associated with servicing a loan. The original lender may retain servicing, or the lender can sell the servicing to the investor.

Figure 10.1 illustrates the relationship among borrowers, lenders, and the secondary mortgage market. This chapter looks at the major participants in the secondary market, as well as practices related to secondary market operations.

SECONDARY MARKET PARTICIPANTS

Lenders sell or assign loans on the secondary market to private mortgage investors or to government-sponsored enterprises—known as GSEs—such as Fannie Mae or Freddie Mac. Private investors include banks, life insurance companies, pension funds, and other organizations.

Both the private investor and GSE markets have strict regulations regarding procedures for buying and selling mortgages, as well as standards for the quality of mortgages being traded. When a mortgage does not meet these standards, the lender may have difficulty finding a buyer.

One of the major differences between the private investor market and the GSE market has to do with nonconforming loans. **Nonconforming loans** are loans that do not meet Fannie Mae or Freddie Mac guidelines with regard to underwriting or appraising, or they

FIGURE 10.1 ■ Borrowers and Lenders in the Primary and Secondary Market

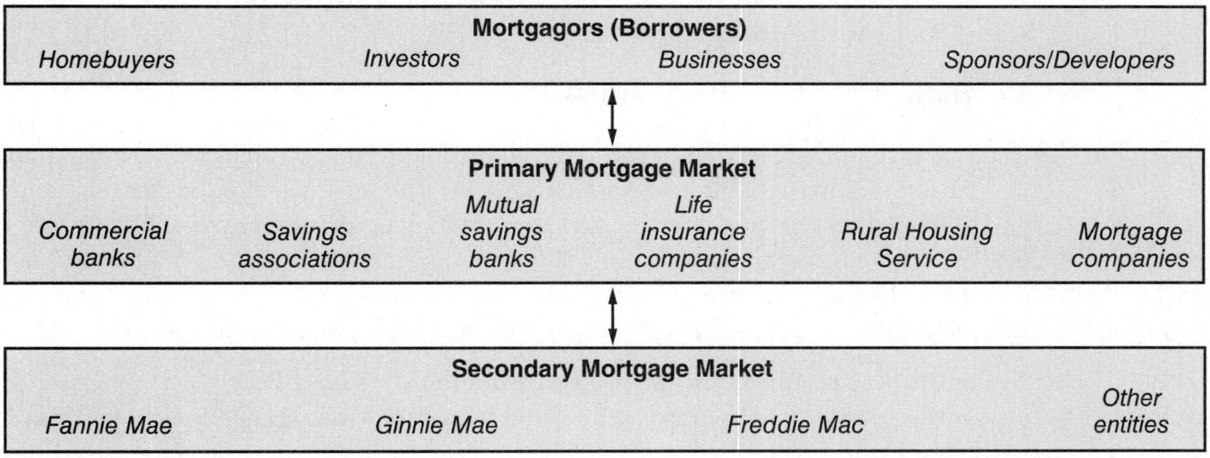

Source: *Florida Real Estate Principles, Practices and Law,* 32nd Edition. Chicago; Dearborn™ Real Estate Education.

exceed the conforming loan limit set by Congress January 1 each year. A nonconforming loan does not necessarily carry greater risk to the investor—it simply does not meet the standards for purchase by the GSEs. In these cases, the lender may try to sell the nonconforming loan to a private investor.

Fannie Mae and Freddie Mac are the major GSEs that purchase mortgages in the secondary market. Because of the large number of mortgages they hold, both institutions are at risk when borrowers default on their loans. As the number of foreclosures increased dramatically in 2008, the U.S. government took control of Fannie Mae and Freddie Mac, placing them under federal conservatorship. At this time, both institutions are undergoing reorganization, but the basic process of lenders in the primary market selling their loans in the secondary market remains the same. Fannie Mae and Freddie Mac, as well as the Government National Mortgage Association, known as Ginnie Mae, are described below.

Fannie Mae

The mission of Fannie Mae is to help more families achieve home ownership by providing financial products and services that make it easier for low-, moderate-, and middle-income families to buy their own homes. Fannie Mae does this in two ways. In addition to buying mortgages from lenders and thus providing lenders with cash to fund other mortgages, Fannie Mae also generates funds by issuing mortgage-backed securities that are sold through securities dealers. **Mortgage-backed securities (MBSs)** are similar to bonds secured by a pool of mortgages.

Although Fannie Mae was initially allowed to purchase only loans made by the Federal Housing Administration (FHA) or Department of Veterans Affairs (VA), today conventional mortgages make up the largest part of Fannie Mae's portfolio. In 1984, Fannie Mae's role in the secondary market was expanded further when Congress authorized Fannie Mae to purchase second mortgages as well. Today, Fannie Mae also buys shorter term mortgages, fixed-rate and adjustable-rate mortgages, and mortgages on multifamily and co-op properties in urban, suburban, or rural areas. Despite this broadening of operations, conventional long-term fixed-rate mortgages still constitute over 75 percent of Fannie Mae's loan portfolio.

Fannie Mae buys mortgages made on residential properties for use by one to four families in which the borrower holds title in fee simple or leasehold. These properties can be a principal residence, a second home, or an investment property. Fannie Mae also purchases conventional mortgages on manufactured homes so long as the home is for one family, the land is owned by the homeowner, and the home is permanently affixed to its site and is legally classified as real property. In 2005, Fannie Mae extended the maximum loan term from 30 to 40 years on certain mortgage products. The 40-year term applies to fully amortizing first mortgages on principal residences, second homes, and investment properties.

Fannie Mae requires that the mortgages it purchases have been made to *natural persons* only; it does not purchase mortgages owned by corporations, general partnerships, limited partnerships, or real estate syndicates. Fannie Mae can buy mortgages granted to aliens who are lawful permanent residents of the United States—that is, who hold a *green card*—as long as they can provide proof of their Immigration and Naturalization (INS) status. A nonpermanent resident alien needs to make a down payment of at least 10 percent. Under Fannie Mae guidelines, there is no maximum age limit for a borrower on the loans it purchases.

As suggested earlier, Fannie Mae purchases only conforming loans. Mortgages with a title impediment, such as delinquent or unpaid real estate taxes or survey exceptions, are not acceptable to Fannie Mae.

Fannie Mae also has standards for loan-to-value ratios (LTVs) on the loans it purchases. For example, Fannie Mae will purchase both fixed-rate mortgages and adjustable-rate mortgages (ARMs) with a 95 percent LTV if the owner occupies the property. Some other LTV guidelines used by Fannie Mae to purchase loans include a 95 percent LTV if it is the principal residence or a second home, a limited cash-out refinance on a principal residence and the homeowner can be either a citizen or permanent resident alien; a 90 percent LTV if the loan is for an investment property or a cash-out refinance on a principal residence and the homeowner is a citizen or nonpermanent resident alien; and an 85 percent LTV if the loan is a cash-out refinance to an investor.

Sometimes lenders calculate the LTV using the **combined loan-to-value ratio (CLTV)**. CLTV is the total value of the loans issued divided by a property's value. Fannie Mae's maximum CLTV is 95 percent, which is the same as its LTV maximum.

Finally, Fannie Mae restricts the number of mortgages that are secured by a borrower's principal residence. If the mortgage is secured by a second home or an investment property, the borrower may not own more than ten properties—including his or her principal residence—that are currently being financed.

Freddie Mac

In 1970, Congress created the Federal Home Loan Mortgage Corporation—Freddie Mac—with the mission of providing secondary market services to members of the Federal Home Loan Bank System, which are largely savings institutions. Like Fannie Mae, Freddie Mac has the mission of making home ownership available to a wider segment of the population, and it is also a publicly owned corporation with its shares traded on the New York Stock

Exchange. One difference between Freddie Mac and Fannie Mae is in the reason they were created. Freddie Mac's original mission was to purchase conventional loans from savings and loan associations, whereas Fannie Mae was organized to purchase conventional loans from commercial channels. Today, these two compete directly with one another and each purchases many types of conforming loans.

Ginnie Mae

In 1968, Congress split Fannie Mae into two separate organizations, thus creating the Government National Mortgage Association, or Ginnie Mae. Unlike Fannie Mae and Freddie Mac, Ginnie Mae is not an independent corporation but a division of the Department of Housing and Urban Development (HUD).

Ginnie Mae has the mission of guaranteeing securities that are backed by pools of FHA, VA, or FmHA (Farmer's Home Administration) mortgages (FmHA mortgages are originated through the Rural Housing Service). Ginnie Mae does not guarantee conventional mortgages, nor does it buy or sell mortgages of any kind or issue mortgage-backed securities. Rather, its role is to *guarantee* MBSs issued by approved securities dealers such as banks and mortgage companies. Purchasers of Ginnie Mae mortgage-backed securities are identified as **security holders**, and they are guaranteed monthly payment of the principal and interest. For the most part, MBSs guaranteed by Ginnie Mae are purchased by commercial banks, investment bankers, Fannie Mae, or Freddie Mac.

Suppose, for example, that a lender has a pool of mortgages and wishes to issue and sell a security backed by those mortgages to investors. The lender requests Ginnie Mae issue a guarantee on the MBS the lender plans to issue. If Ginnie Mae agrees, the lender places the mortgages in a special account as collateral for the MBS, then the security is issued and sold to investors. Because the security is guaranteed by Ginnie Mae, it has the full faith and credit of the U.S. government and carries zero risk to its purchaser. Investors in Ginnie Mae–backed securities can count on timely payments of principal and interest. Almost 10 percent of the nation's mortgages are currently backed by a Ginnie Mae guarantee.

Farmer's Home Administration

As you may recall from chapter 6, FmHA loans are made through the Rural Housing Service of the Department of Agriculture to individuals who are ineligible for most other kinds of loans. In the secondary market, FmHA purchases loans on properties where land represents more than 30 percent of the appraised value of the property. FmHA also makes loans directly to borrowers.

WEB LINK

@

www.fanniemae.com

www.freddiemac.com

www.ginniemae.gov

www.fsa.usda.gov

SECONDARY MARKET OPERATIONS

The secondary market has a number of special features not generally associated with primary market lending. These include selling loans with or without recourse, selling a loan with or without servicing, investor participation, the practice of warehousing, and table funding versus direct investor funding. These aspects of the secondary market are discussed below.

Recourse

Recourse refers to the requirements regarding the repurchase of a loan. On the secondary market, mortgages can be sold *with full recourse*, *without recourse*, or *with normal recourse*. A loan sold **with full recourse** means that the seller must repurchase the loan if the borrower defaults. Loans sold **without recourse** do not require the seller to repurchase the loan in case of default. Loans sold without recourse create higher yields to investors because investors pay less due to their higher risk.

A loan sold **with normal recourse** means that the seller is required to repurchase the loan if the borrower defaults and the default is due to the seller underwriting the loan in a faulty manner.

Loan Servicing

Although loan servicing is usually thought of as collecting a borrower's monthly payments and disbursing payments for taxes and insurance, servicing actually involves several other functions. These include handling all communication with parties who have an interest in the loan, monitoring any liens or encumbrances on a property, making certain that a homeowner has sufficient insurance to protect the lender's interest, and handling a foreclosure when necessary. The loan servicer can be paid a fee or a designated portion of the interest the borrower pays. Sometimes a loan servicer is allowed to keep any late payment fees paid by the borrower.

Mortgage brokers should advise borrowers that the servicing on their loan is likely to change, and that both the old and new servicer must notify the borrower of the change in writing. When the mortgage loan servicer changes, the mortgage payment must be mailed to the new servicer. There is no limit on the number of times a loan servicer may change.

Lenders who sell loans on the secondary market can sell their loans with either servicing released or servicing retained. When a secondary market investor buys a loan with **servicing released,** that means that the seller of the loan releases responsibility for servicing the loan to the secondary market investor. The investor then takes responsibility for all the service requirements associated with the loan. Under Florida law, loan servicing requires a separate set of books and accounts, as well as an annual audit.

The primary market lender can also sell loans with **servicing retained,** which means that the buyer takes ownership of the loan, but the seller continues to perform the servicing for some form of compensation.

The servicer of a mortgage loan can change several times during the term of the loan, and part of the closing requires that borrowers be notified that servicing of their loan may be transferred from their original lender. Who provides the servicing does not affect the terms of repayment, however. That is, the length of the repayment period, interest rate, and principal to be repaid do not change when the loan servicer changes.

Participation

A third aspect of loans sold on the secondary market is that they offer investors the opportunity of **participation** at different levels of ownership. That is, a secondary market investor can acquire a whole loan, which gives the investor complete ownership of the mortgage, along with all rights and responsibilities that go with the mortgage.

A second possibility for the investor is to participate in buying a loan and thereby own a percentage of the loan. Along with the other participants, the investor has an undivided interest in the rights and responsibilities associated with the loan. A final way to participate in the secondary market is by acquiring mortgage-backed securities. The income associated with a pool of mortgage-backed securities creates a revenue stream for the investor.

Warehousing

Warehousing, or *warehouse lending,* refers to the practice of a lender or correspondent lender using a short-term loan from a commercial bank to fund its loan commitments. The loan is usually in the form of a line of credit with a term of 90 to 180 days. The term *warehousing* comes from the earlier practice of banks providing storage for a lender's documentation.

Warehousing is used to fund loan production. Because even mortgage bankers operate with little capitalization, the warehouse line provides the money to fund new loans. When a borrower accepts a loan, the lender may obtain the funds for the loan from a warehouse lender. The loan the borrower has accepted is long term and probably carries a higher interest rate than the short-term loan the lender can arrange through warehousing, so the lender earns a profit on the difference in rates. And because of the loan's short term, the bank can adjust the interest rate to reflect changes in the economic climate.

From the bank's perspective, the warehouse loan offers little risk. The lender offers the promissory note as security, the interest rate reflects market rates, and the term of the loan is six months or less. Government loans, on the other hand, are seen by warehouse lenders as more risky because the borrower has made a lower down payment on the property and lower down payments are associated with greater default risks. At a minimum, the bank will require the lender to assign the mortgage to the bank, along with the promissory note.

Table Funding and Direct Investor Funding

Table funding is the practice of a lender or correspondent lender closing a loan with either the lender's own funds or the warehouse line. Through table funding the lender can more quickly acquire loans to sell on the secondary market.

In contrast, **direct investor funding** is the process of borrowers working directly with lenders. Working with the assistance of a mortgage broker, a lender funds the loan directly to the borrower. As with table funding, the lender can more quickly acquire loans to sell on the secondary market.

KEY POINT REVIEW

- In the *secondary mortgage market,* investors sell existing mortgages.
- The secondary market was created to provide cash and liquidity to primary market participants that invest in home mortgages.
- *Nonconforming loans* do not meet Fannie Mae or Freddie Mac guidelines.
- The mission of *Fannie Mae* is to help more families achieve home ownership by providing financial products and services that make it possible for low-, moderate-, and middle-income families to buy homes.
- Fannie Mae buys conventional, FHA, VA, and second mortgages.
- *Ginnie Mae* guarantees securities that are backed by packages of mortgages. GNMA is a government institution that is part of the Department of Housing and Urban Development.
- Ginnie Mae does not buy or sell mortgages or issue mortgage-backed securities; rather, it guarantees securities issued by approved investors.
- A loan sold *with full recourse* means the seller must repurchase the loan if the buyer defaults. Loans sold *without recourse* do not require the seller to repurchase in case of default. *Normal recourse* means that the seller must repurchase the loan only if the default resulted from an error in the seller's underwriting.
- Loans sold with *servicing released* means that the secondary market investor will take responsibility for collecting payments and paying escrowed items. *Servicing retained* means the seller will continue to do the servicing.
- *Warehousing* refers to the practice of a lender using funds borrowed on a line of credit from a financial institution to fund its loan commitments.
- *Table funding* is the practice of a lender closing a loan in the lender's own name. *Direct investor funding* is the process of a mortgage broker working directly with borrowers with loans funded by a lender or correspondent lender.

REVIEW QUESTIONS

1. Most Freddie Mac loans were initially originated in
   a. banks.
   b. savings associations.
   c. the secondary market.
   d. mortgage brokerages.

2. Olympic Mortgage has sold a loan with full recourse to Athena Mortgage. This means that
   a. Olympic Mortgage must repurchase the loan if the borrower defaults.
   b. Olympic Mortgage is not required to repurchase the loan if the borrower defaults.
   c. Olympic Mortgage must repurchase the loan but only if the borrower's default is the result of faulty underwriting.
   d. Athena Mortgage may redeem the mortgage at any time.

3. Which is NOT an activity of Fannie Mae?
   a. Making loans to homebuyers
   b. Providing funds to the primary mortgage market
   c. Buying and selling VA mortgages
   d. Buying and selling FHA mortgages

4. Bill's First Rate Mortgages specializes in warehousing. This means that Bill's First Rate Mortgages
   a. accumulates mortgage applications and transfers all of them to a secondary lender.
   b. has joined several lenders to form a consortium.
   c. creates mortgage-backed securities for sale to the public.
   d. uses funds borrowed on a line of credit to fund loan commitments.

5. Twenty-First Century Mortgages closes loans in its own name with funds provided by Venture Capital, Inc. This practice is known as
   a. warehousing.
   b. table funding.
   c. direct investor funding.
   d. commitment funding.

6. The secondary mortgage market was originally created to
   a. provide a way for borrowers to go directly to the source of funds.
   b. remove the government from the mortgage business.
   c. provide cash and liquidity to institutions that invest in home mortgages by providing a market to buy and sell existing mortgages.
   d. create jobs during the Great Depression.

7. John has been offered a nonconforming loan by Alligator Mortgages. Alligator Mortgages can sell the loan to
   a. Fannie Mae or Freddie Mac only.
   b. Fannie Mae but not Freddie Mac.
   c. neither Fannie Mae nor Freddie Mac.
   d. Fannie Mae, Freddie Mac, or a private investor.

8. The organization that holds more residential mortgages than any other organization in the world is
   a. the Department of Housing and Urban Development.
   b. the FHA.
   c. Fannie Mae.
   d. Ginnie Mae.

9. Fannie Mae can purchase mortgages made to
   a. corporations.
   b. limited partnerships.
   c. natural persons.
   d. any of the above.

10. Although more than one quasigovernmental institution purchases mortgages, only one institution is part of the federal government. That institution is
    a. Ginnie Mae.
    b. Fannie Mae.
    c. Freddie Mac.
    d. the VA.

11. Fannie Mae cannot purchase mortgages on
    a. investment property.
    b. manufactured homes.
    c. vacation homes.
    d. shopping centers.

12. Orlando Mortgage has sold a loan in the secondary market and released servicing. This means that the
    a. firm that originated the loan will not continue to service the loan.
    b. mortgage broker will retain servicing.
    c. terms of the loan may change.
    d. loan cannot be sold again for 180 days.

13. The mission of Ginnie Mae is to
    a. sell mortgage-backed securities.
    b. buy and sell mortgages.
    c. loan money to investors.
    d. guarantee mortgage-backed securities.

14. When an investor evaluates the net yield on a loan, the investor is considering
    a. the interest rate and discount.
    b. funds generated by interest payments and negative amortization.
    c. the total interest paid, minus the servicing expenses.
    d. the total interest paid, minus fees to the mortgage broker.

CHAPTER

11

BASIC CONCEPTS OF MORTGAGE FINANCE

LEARNING OBJECTIVES

After finishing chapter 11, you should be able to

1. understand loan-to-value ratio calculations;
2. explain how amortization and monthly loan payments are calculated;
3. calculate front-end and back-end ratios;
4. understand proration;
5. know the different kinds of Florida real estate taxes;
6. calculate fees associated with gross loans and net loans; and
7. change weekly or monthly income to yearly income.

KEY TERMS

amortization
back-end ratio
debt-to-income ratio
discount points
documentary stamp tax on deeds
documentary stamp tax on notes
escrowed items
front-end ratio
gross loan
housing expense ratio (HER)
intangible tax on new mortgages
late fee
loan-to-value ratio (LTV)
mills
net loan
prorations
residual income
total obligations ratio (TOR)
yield

INTRODUCTION

Although lenders now use computer programs to do most of the calculations regarding mortgage loans, mortgage professionals need to understand these calculations so they can explain them to borrowers. Chapter 11 reviews some of the mathematical concepts introduced in earlier chapters and introduces some other concepts related to mortgage finance.

LOAN-TO-VALUE CALCULATIONS

One of the most important calculations in a mortgage transaction is the loan-to-value ratio. As you may recall, **loan-to-value ratio (LTV)** is determined by dividing the amount of the mortgage loan by the lesser of the sales price or the appraised value of the property. The higher the ratio, the smaller the borrower's down payment, the greater the cash outlay from the lender, and the greater the risk to the lender. This is because buyers in these transactions have little equity in the property, so they may be willing to lose their equity in order to avoid future mortgage payments.

Different lenders have different standards for determining acceptable LTVs. Because conventional loans, which are neither insured by FHA nor guaranteed by the VA, carry higher risk, conventional lenders typically require an LTV of no more than 80 percent. The FHA and VA accept higher ratios, but virtually all conventional lenders will require private mortgage insurance (PMI) when the ratio exceeds 80 percent. Furthermore, high LTVs almost always require a more careful analysis of the borrower's application and credit history.

Calculating Loan-to-Value Ratio

The formula for loan-to-value is as follows:

LTV = Amount of loan ÷ Lesser of the purchase price or appraised value of property

EXAMPLE: Roger finds a house priced at $240,000. Roger has $25,000 in savings that he plans to use as a down payment. What will be the loan-to-value ratio on the mortgage he will apply for?

Mortgage amount = Price – Down payment
= $240,000 – $25,000
= $215,000

Loan-to-value ratio = $215,000 ÷ $240,000
= 89.6%

Any conventional lender who funds Roger's loan will require private mortgage insurance, which Roger will be obliged to carry as long as his LTV exceeds 80 percent. As Roger repays the mortgage principal over time, of course, his LTV will go down.

AMORTIZATION AND MONTHLY LOAN PAYMENTS

Amortization refers to the payment of a loan and its interest over a specified period of time. Although the very first amortized loans were typically for 20 years, lenders now make loans for 30, 15, or even 50 years.

Mortgages with a fixed interest rate have equal monthly payments over the term of the loan. Payments on adjustable-rate mortgages (ARMs), on the other hand, change to reflect movements in interest rates.

Regardless of the type of amortized mortgage, part of each monthly payment goes toward the principal and part goes toward the interest. In the first years of a mortgage loan, almost all of the payment goes toward paying interest. In later years, more of the payment goes toward repaying the principal. Mortgage payments are typically calculated by computer, but they can also be calculated using a monthly mortgage table.

To find what part of a mortgage payment goes toward principal and what part toward interest, the outstanding balance on the mortgage, the interest rate, and the monthly payment amount must be known. The calculation is as follows:

Current month's interest = (Loan balance × Interest rate) ÷ 12 months
Principal payment = Monthly payment amount – Current month's interest
New principal balance = Beginning loan balance – Principal payment

EXAMPLE: Jessica owes $165,000 on a 30-year mortgage with an interest rate of 6.5 percent. Her monthly payment on the mortgage is $1,042.91. To find out how much of the payment goes toward the principal, Jessica would need to work the formulas listed above.

Current month's interest = ($165,000 × 0.065) ÷ 12
= $893.75
Principal payment = $1,042.91 – 893.75
= $149.16
New principal balance = $165,000 – 149.16
= $164,850.84

To find the amounts that go to principal and interest in the following month, Jessica would need to use the same procedures starting with the new principal balance:

Second month interest = ($164,850.84 × 0.065) ÷ 12
= $892.94
Principal payment = $1,042.91 – 892.94
= $149.97
New principal balance = $164,850.84 – 149.97
= $164,700.87

Escrowed Items

As you may recall, the monthly mortgage payment covers principal, interest, and escrowed items. **Escrowed items** are typically property taxes and hazard insurance. To determine the amount of the monthly payment going to the escrow account, the annual tax bill or hazard insurance amount is divided by 12 and added to the monthly payment.

In the example above, Jessica's monthly payment of principal and interest amounts to $1,042.91. If her property taxes are $1,300 and hazard insurance premium $800, her total PITI (principal, interest, taxes, and insurance) payment would be calculated as follows:

Total PITI payment = Monthly PI payment + (Annual property taxes ÷ 12)
+ (Annual hazard insurance premium ÷ 12)
= $1,042.91 + $108.33 + $66.67
= $1,217.91

Late Fee

If Jessica is late with her monthly mortgage payment, conventional lenders typically charge a 5 percent penalty on the principal and interest part of the PITI only. (The late fee on an FHA loan is 4 percent.) So Jessica's payment on her conventional loan, including **late fee,** would be calculated as follows:

Total late payment = [(Principal + Interest) × Late fee] + Regular payment
= ($1,042.91 × .05) + $1,217.91
= $52.15 + $1,217.91
= $1,270.06

Taxes and insurance amount to $175 ($108.33 + $66.67), so Jessica's total payment including late fee amounts to $1,270.06.

FRONT-END AND BACK-END RATIOS

When a lender makes a mortgage loan, one of the most important considerations is whether the borrower has sufficient monthly income to make the required monthly payment (PITI). The two critical formulas to determine a borrower's ability to pay—referred to as capacity—are the front-end ratio and back-end ratio. The **front-end ratio**, as you may recall, is the **housing expense ratio (HER)**, and the **back-end ratio** is the **total obligations ratio (TOR)**. Fannie Mae also uses the term **debt-to-income ratio**, which is the sum of housing expense, installment debt, and other liabilities, divided by total monthly income.

The front-end ratio, or HER, is calculated by dividing an applicant's monthly housing expense—mortgage payments—by gross monthly income. The back-end ratio, or TOR, is calculated by dividing the sum of the monthly housing payment plus all the applicant's recurring debt exceeding ten months plus any leases to include housing expense by gross monthly income. If a borrower's credit card account does not require a minimum monthly payment, the underwriter will consider payments equal to 5 percent of the outstanding balance. Also, lenders work only with current year information regarding homestead exemptions, and only overtime and bonuses that have been received in the last 12 months can be considered part of gross monthly income.

As you may recall, different lenders have different standards for acceptability of HER and TOR, and if the ratio does not meet the lender's requirements, the loan may not be approved. For FHA loans, an applicant's monthly housing expense cannot exceed 31 percent of the gross monthly income, and an applicant's total obligations ratio cannot exceed 43 percent.

Eligibility for VA loans is calculated using an overall ratio that cannot exceed 41 percent. The VA also uses a ratio known as **residual income,** which refers to a set of adjustments based on the number of family members and the area where the property is located.

For most conventional loans, the maximum HER, or front-end ratio, is 28 percent, and the maximum TOR, or back-end ratio, is 36 percent.

EXAMPLE: Marie's monthly income is $3,750. Her housing cost is $800, and she has monthly payments amounting to $225 on an auto loan, $65 on credit card debt, and $90 to a furniture company. Marie's HER and TOR would be calculated as follows:

Gross monthly income	$3,750
Housing expenses	800
Auto loan	225
Credit card	65
Furniture payment	90
Total monthly payments	$1,180

Housing expense ratio = Housing payment ÷ Gross monthly income
= $800 ÷ $3,750
= 21.33%

Total obligations ratio = Total obligations ÷ Gross monthly income
= $1,180 ÷ $3,750
= 31.47%

Under FHA, VA, or conventional loan guidelines, Marie would qualify for a loan based on both her front-end ratio and back-end ratio.

PRORATION

At the time of closing, the buyer and seller are each responsible for certain expenses. The seller may owe the buyer property taxes for the months that he or she lived in the property, as well as any rent collected from tenants living in an investment property. To determine the amount owed, lenders calculate **prorations,** which refer to expenses shared by the buyer and seller. In most cases, because property taxes are paid in arrears, mortgage interest is paid in arrears, and rents are paid in advance, these funds need to be prorated at the closing and credited to or debited from the buyer or seller.

EXAMPLE: Brian agrees to pay $175,000 for a house and to close on April 20, with the day of closing belonging to the buyer. Unpaid property taxes for the year are $2,700. At the closing, the seller owes Brian his share of the unpaid taxes for the period the seller lived in the house. The formula for calculating prorated taxes is as follows:

Prorated taxes = Annual tax bill ÷ 365 × Number of days lived in the property

= ($2,700 ÷ 365) × Number of days
= $7.40 × Number of days

Number of days = January 31
February 28
March 31
April 19
109

Prorated taxes = $7.40 × 109
= $806.60

Because the taxes are unpaid, this amount would be owed by the seller to the buyer.

If Brian were buying a house that the seller had rented to a tenant at $775 per month, the rent proration would be as follows:

Prorated rent = Monthly rent – (Rent ÷ Number of days in month × Days seller owned property)
= $775 – ($775 ÷ 30 × 19)
= $284.17

Because the seller had already collected the full rent, \$284.17 would be credited to Brian and debited from the seller.

If Brian had not applied for a new mortgage but assumed the seller's mortgage, interest would be prorated as follows:

$$\begin{aligned}\text{Prorated interest} &= \text{Daily interest rate} \times \text{Days interest owed}\\ \text{Daily interest rate} &= (\text{Mortgage balance} \times \text{Interest rate}) \div 365\\ &= (\$175{,}000 \times .065) \div 365\\ &= \$31.16\\ \text{Prorated interest} &= \$31.16 \times 19\\ &= \$592.04\end{aligned}$$

FLORIDA REAL ESTATE TAXES

In Florida, the standard homestead exemption is \$25,000. However, under a new law approved in 2008, homeowners may qualify for an additional exemption. Homes assessed at \$50,000 or less are eligible for the standard exemption only, but properties with an assessed value between \$50,001 and \$74,999 can receive both the standard exemption and a proportionate additional exemption for the value over \$50,000. Homes assessed at \$75,000 and up are eligible for the standard exemption plus a second \$25,000 exemption. In all three cases, school board taxes are calculated on the assessed value of a home minus the first \$25,000 exemption only.

To qualify for the exemption, the homeowner need not live in the home year-round, but the home must be the principal place of residence. In addition, the borrower must have held title since at least January 1 of the current year and have applied for the exemption prior to March 1. Homestead exemptions are granted when the homeowner provides the county appraiser with proof that he or she owns the home.

Taxes on Real Property

Taxable value is calculated by deducting any allowable exemptions from the assessed value of a home.

EXAMPLE: If the assessed value of a home with a homestead exemption is \$200,000, its taxable value would be \$150,000 (\$200,000 – \$50,000).

In addition to the homestead exemption, Florida law also provides additional smaller exemptions for disabled and blind persons, as well as a surviving spouse.

How Florida Property Taxes Are Calculated

Ad valorem is a Latin term meaning "according to value," and it refers to the way in which property taxes are calculated. In Florida, calculation of property taxes starts with the county property appraiser determining the taxable value of a homeowner's property, including both the land and its improvements. The taxable value is multiplied by a tax rate—usually expressed in **mills** or one-thousandths of one dollar—to determine the homeowner's tax bill. For example, if a home is valued at \$220,000 and the tax rate is 10 mills, the taxes on the property amount to \$2,200 (\$220,000 × .010).

In Florida, real estate taxes can be paid at a discount starting November 1. November's discount is 4 percent, and the discount declines 1 percent each month until March. Taxes not paid by April 1 become delinquent and are assessed a 3 percent penalty through May 31. After May 31, the unpaid property taxes are sold to the public as a tax deed certificate. Unpaid property taxes are considered a lien on a property that creates a cloud on the title that could prevent a lender from funding a loan.

Taxes Relating to the Purchase and Sale of Real Property

Florida law requires that certain taxes be collected at the time of a real estate closing: a documentary stamp tax on the deed to the property; a documentary stamp tax on all promissory notes related to the real estate transaction; and an intangible tax on new mortgages. These taxes are actually paid to the state at the time or recording.

Documentary stamp taxes on deeds are assessed at the rate of $.70 for each $100 or fraction thereof of the total purchase price of a property. When the purchase price on a property is not evenly divisible by 100—for example, $74,550 as opposed to $74,600—the amount of the sale is rounded upward to the nearest 100 and taxes are calculated on that amount.

Although documentary stamp taxes on the deed are usually paid by the seller, this payment is negotiable and the party responsible is specified in the sales contract.

Parties to a real estate closing must also pay **documentary stamp taxes on notes** related to a transaction. These taxes apply to both new and assumed mortgages. The rate for this tax is $.35 per $100 of the amount of each note. For purposes of calculating taxes, this amount must also be rounded up to the next 100. The documentary stamp tax is generally paid by the borrower.

Finally, Florida requires payment of an **intangible tax on new mortgages,** which is also usually paid by the borrower. The rate for this tax is two mills, or $.002 for each dollar of the new mortgage. Intangible taxes do not apply to the assumed portion of a loan. Figure 11.1 illustrates a sample calculation of Florida taxes on real estate transactions.

These taxes are paid as part of the closing. At the end of the closing, the title company or the closing agent typically records the different legal documents in the appropriate government offices, which may require a separate fee.

NET LOANS AND GROSS LOANS

As you may recall from chapter 1, mortgage loan amounts can be expressed as a *net loan* or a *gross loan*, depending on the fees associated with the loan. A **gross loan** is the amount of a loan *plus* any additional fees charged.

When a gross loan amount is over $5,750, the maximum fee is the mortgage amount divided by 11 plus $227.27. For loan amounts that fall between $5,650 and $5,750, the maximum fee is the amount over $5,000. The maximum fee on loans from $1,000 to $5,650 is the loan amount plus $1,500, with the sum divided by 11. Fees on gross loans up to $1,000 cannot exceed $250.

A **net loan** refers to the amount of the loan *less* costs and fees. On loans over $5,000, the broker can charge the mortgage amount divided by 10 plus $250. For loans between $2,000 and $5,000, the broker can charge $350 on the first $2,000 of the loan and

FIGURE 11.1 ■ Florida Tax on Real Estate

Suppose Connie buys a house for $225,000. She makes a down payment of $50,000, assumes a mortgage for $80,000, and acquires new financing for the balance. Taxes on the transaction would be as follows:

Purchase price	$225,000
Less down payment	– 50,000
Loan amount	$175,000
Doc. stamp tax on deed	$225,000 ÷ 100 × .70 = $1,575
Doc. stamp tax on mortgage	$80,000 ÷ 100 × .35 = $280
	$95,000 ÷ 100 × .35 = $332.50
Total tax on mortgage	$280 + $332.50 = $612.50
Intangible tax on new mortgage	$95,000 × .002 = $190

10 percent on the remaining balance. For loans from $1,000 to $2,000, the maximum fee is $250 on the first $1,000 plus 10 percent of the balance. For loans of less than $1,000, the maximum fee is $250.

Formulas for the maximum net and gross loans are as follows:

Net loan	= Loan amount ÷ 10 + $250 *or* Loan amount + $2,500 ÷ 10
Gross loan	= Loan amount ÷ 11 + $227.27 *or* Loan amount + $2,500 ÷ 11

Examples of Net and Gross Loans

- What would be the fee on a gross loan of $101,000?
- What would be the fee on a net loan of the same amount?
- What is the fee on a net loan of $6,200?
- What is the maximum fee on a gross loan of $95,500?

$9,409.09 ($101,000 ÷ 11 + $227.27)
$10,350 ($101,000 ÷ 10 + $250)
$870 ($6,200 ÷ 10 + $250)
$8,909.09 ($95,500 ÷ 11 + $227.27)

YIELD AND DISCOUNT POINTS

As you may also recall, **yield** is the return to an investor on a mortgage loan and generally refers to the interest rate the lender is charging. **Discount points** increase the lender's yield by about one-eighth of 1 percent (.125 percent) per discount point paid. One discount point is equal to 1 percent of the loan amount to be charged to the borrower on additional up-front closing costs.

FIGURE 11.2 ■ Summary of Basic Mortgage Finance Formulas

Loan-to-Value

Amount of loan ÷ Lesser of purchase price of property or appraised value

Amortization

Current month's interest = (Loan balance × Interest rate) ÷ 12 months

Principal payment = Monthly payment amount – Current month's interest

New principal balance = Beginning loan balance – Principal payment

Total PITI Payment

Monthly PI payment + (Annual property taxes ÷ 12) + (Annual hazard insurance premium ÷ 12)

Total late payment = Principal + Interest + (Principal + Interest × Late fee) + Monthly taxes + Monthly insurance payment

Housing Expense Ratio (HER)

Housing payment ÷ Gross monthly income

Total Obligations or Debt-to-Income Ratio

Total obligations ÷ Gross monthly income

Prorated Taxes

Annual tax bill ÷ 365 × Number of days lived in the property

Prorated Rent

Rent – (Rent ÷ Number of days in month × Days seller owned house in the month)

Prorated Interest

Daily interest rate × Days interest owed

Daily interest rate = [(Mortgage balance × interest rate) ÷ 365]

Taxable value

Assessed value – Total exemptions

Documentary stamp tax on deed

Sales price ÷ 100 × $.70

Documentary stamp tax on mortgages

Total mortgages ÷ 100 × $.35

Intangible tax on new mortgages

New mortgages × $.002

Maximum net loan fee

Loan amount ÷ 10 + $250

Maximum gross loan fee

Loan amount ÷ 11 + $227.27

CONVERTING INCOME

Lenders often require an applicant to report monthly or yearly income. Weekly income is converted to annual income by multiplying weekly income by 52. Monthly income is calculated by dividing annual income by 12. Hourly income is converted to monthly income by multiplying the salary times the number of hours worked in a month.

Basic mortgage finance formulas are summarized in Figure 11.2.

KEY POINT REVIEW

- *Loan-to-value ratio* is determined by dividing the amount of the mortgage loan by the sales price of the property. The higher the loan-to-value ratio, the greater the risk to the lender.
- Conventional loans with a loan-to-value ratio of more than 80 percent require private mortgage insurance.
- *Amortization* refers to the payment of a loan and its interest over a specified period of time.
- *Fixed-rate mortgages* have equal monthly payments over the term of the loan. Payments on *adjustable-rate mortgages* change to reflect movements in interest rates.
- The monthly mortgage payment typically includes principal, interest, and *escrowed items* such as taxes and insurance. Payments for escrowed items are determined by dividing the annual payment by 12 and adding that amount to the monthly principal and interest payment.
- *Late payment fees* are typically 5 percent of the principal and interest payment only on conventional loans and 4 percent of the principal and interest on government loans.
- The *front-end ratio*, or *housing expense ratio*, is the monthly housing expense divided by the gross monthly income. The *back-end ratio*, or *total obligations ratio*, is the sum of obligations divided by gross monthly income. The back-end ratio is also known as the *debt-to-income ratio*.
- For FHA loans, the housing expense ratio cannot exceed 31 percent and the total obligations ratio cannot exceed 43 percent. For VA loans, the TOR cannot exceed 41 percent. Most conventional loans require a HER of less than 28 percent and a TOR of less than 36 percent.
- *Proration* refers to expenses shared by the buyer and seller and is paid at the time of closing.
- Florida homestead law allows homeowners a $25,000 to $50,000 tax deduction from the assessed value of a principal place of residence. Real estate taxes are due November 1 but do not become delinquent until April 1.
- In Florida, three kinds of taxes are paid at closing: the rate for *documentary stamp taxes on deeds* is $.70 per $100 or fraction thereof of the sales price; for *documentary stamp taxes on notes*, the rate is $.35 per $100 or fraction thereof of the value of all mortgages; and the *intangible tax on new mortgages* is $.002 for each dollar of new mortgage.
- A *gross loan* is the amount of a loan plus any additional fees and charges. *Net loans* refer to the amount of the loan less costs and fees.
- *Yield* is the return to an investor on a mortgage loan.
- *Discount points* increase the lender's yield on a loan by about .00125 percent per point.

REVIEW QUESTIONS

1. Mr. Ortega qualifies for a loan with a high loan-to-value ratio. This means that Mr. Ortega's lender will
   a. have greater risk.
   b. have lower risk.
   c. have equal risk with the borrower.
   d. require Mr. Ortega to make a large down payment.

2. Virtually all conventional lenders require mortgage insurance when the loan-to-value ratio exceeds
   a. 50 percent.
   b. 75 percent.
   c. 78 percent.
   d. 80 percent.

3. Joanne bought a house for $350,000 with a down payment of $40,000 and financed the rest by paying 3 points to get a mortgage interest rate of 5.75 percent. Joanne's loan-to-value ratio will be
   a. 11 percent.
   b. 97 percent.
   c. 89 percent.
   d. 57.5 percent.

4. Marian made a down payment of $30,000 on a house for which she received 90 percent financing. What was the value of the house?
   a. $270,000
   b. $300,000
   c. $360,000
   d. $290,000

5. What is the maximum fee on a $105,000 net loan?
   a. $10,750
   b. $9,772.72
   c. $9,795.45
   d. $10,727.27

6. Freddie bought a manufactured home for $125,000. He made a down payment of $35,000, assumed a mortgage of $65,000, and financed the rest. What are the intangible taxes on this transaction?
   a. $875
   b. $625
   c. $350
   d. $50

7. Stewart recently financed the purchase of a second home for $235,500 with a conventional mortgage at 7.125 percent and 2 points. Total points on Stewart's loan will cost
   a. $4,700.
   b. 5.125 percent.
   c. $2,000.
   d. $4,710.

8. To calculate the part of Stewart's monthly mortgage payment that goes toward principal, which is NOT needed?
   a. Mortgage balance
   b. Interest rate
   c. Amount of monthly payment
   d. Term of mortgage

9. What is the maximum amount a mortgage brokerage business can charge on a $175,000 gross loan?
   a. $17,750.00
   b. $17,727.27
   c. $17,527.27
   d. $16,136.36

10. If Vicki acquires a 30-year mortgage for $275,000 with an interest rate of 6.45 percent and monthly payments of $1,729.15, how much of the payment will go toward the principal in the first month?
    a. $1,478.13
    b. $251.03
    c. $111.53
    d. $591.25

11. How much of Vicki's payment will go toward the principal in the second month?
    a. $1,476.78
    b. $252.37
    c. $113.89
    d. $595.82

12. If Vicki's annual tax bill on her 30-year amortized mortgage is $975 and her insurance premium is $700, what will be her monthly tax payment?
    a. $32.50
    b. $139.58
    c. $58.33
    d. $81.25

13. If Claire makes a monthly payment of $215.15 principal, $622 interest, $75 taxes, and $65 insurance, and is late in paying her conventional mortgage, how much will the late fee be?
    a. $10.76
    b. $48.86
    c. $41.86
    d. $7.00

14. On a gross loan of $5,775, the maximum fee is
    a. $570.00.
    b. $700.27.
    c. $820.00.
    d. $752.27.

15. The front-end ratio refers to
    a. the loan-to-value ratio.
    b. total obligations.
    c. housing expense.
    d. total obligations plus housing expense.

16. A net loan refers to the amount of the loan
    a. plus brokerage fees.
    b. without brokerage fees.
    c. including all closing costs.
    d. without closing costs.

17. Residual income is a ratio associated with
    a. FHA loans.
    b. VA loans.
    c. conventional loans.
    d. all types of loans.

18. If Paul has a monthly income of $2,500 and housing expense of $850, his housing expense ratio is
    a. 34 percent.
    b. 2.94 percent.
    c. $1,650.
    d. 41 percent.

19. If Paul also has car payments of $225 and a student loan with a $125 monthly payment, his debt-to-income ratio is
    a. 14 percent.
    b. 41 percent.
    c. 34 percent.
    d. 48 percent.

20. Under what program would Paul qualify for a mortgage loan?
    a. Conventional
    b. FHA
    c. VA
    d. None of the above

21. Taxes are generally paid
    a. only when a property is sold.
    b. in arrears.
    c. in advance.
    d. by the buyer to the seller.

22. Prorated taxes to be paid at closing by the seller are calculated by
    a. dividing the total tax bill by 12 months.
    b. dividing the tax bill by 365 days.
    c. dividing the tax bill by 365 and multiplying by the number of days lived in the property.
    d. multiplying last year's tax rate plus the amount of increase in the year the property is sold.

23. Maria sold her house and is planning to close on May 1 with the day of closing belonging to the buyer. Her annual tax bill is $1,200. At the closing Maria can expect to be
    a. credited $295.89.
    b. credited $394.52.
    c. debited $295.89.
    d. debited $394.52.

24. Homestead exemptions are granted when
    a. property taxes are paid.
    b. property is sold to a new owner.
    c. the mortgage is paid in full.
    d. the homeowner provides proof of ownership to the county property appraiser.

25. Mr. Landlord sold a duplex with an assumable mortgage of $155,125 at 7.25 percent interest. The closing is on December 23. How much prorated interest does the buyer owe Mr. Landlord?
    a. $277.31
    b. $417.00
    c. $659.90
    d. $199.89

26. James has housing expenses of $675 and other obligations totaling $305 per month. He works in a bookstore 150 hours a month and earns $8.25 per hour. What is James's front-end ratio?
    a. 36%
    b. 29%
    c. 79%
    d. 55%

27. What kind of loan might James qualify for?
    a. FHA
    b. Conventional
    c. Either of the above
    d. None of the above

28. The intangible tax rate on a new mortgage is
    a. $.75 per $100.
    b. $.35 per $100.
    c. $.002 per $100.
    d. $.002 times the value of any new mortgage.

29. In Florida, taxes become delinquent
    a. January 1.
    b. April 1.
    c. November 1.
    d. December 31.

30. Sellers typically pay
    a. the documentary stamp tax on deed.
    b. the documentary stamp tax on mortgage.
    c. the intangible tax.
    d. no taxes because all taxes are paid by the borrower.

31. Tom buys a property for $220,000. He has a down payment of $45,000 from the sale of his previous home, a new mortgage of $20,000, and the balance of the sales price assumed under the seller's previous mortgage. What are the documentary stamp taxes on the deed for this transaction?
    a. $1,225
    b. $1,400
    c. $1,540
    d. $1,995

32. What are the documentary stamp taxes on the note?
    a. $612.50
    b. $70.00
    c. $770.00
    d. $840.50

33. What are the intangible taxes?
    a. $770
    b. $90
    c. $40
    d. $310

34. Intangible taxes are paid on
    a. the deed.
    b. all mortgages associated with a transaction.
    c. existing mortgages only.
    d. new mortgages only.

35. *Ad valorem* means
    a. according to value.
    b. added value.
    c. actual value.
    d. and additional value.

36. At the closing on a four-bedroom house in St. Petersburg, the $3,345 property tax bill had not been paid. If the closing is on June 2, the prorated taxes due from the seller will be
    a. $1,392.99.
    b. $1,401.48.
    c. $1,502.02.
    d. $1,581.17.

37. Alicia is assuming a $212,000 mortgage at 6.75 percent. If the closing is on March 15, how much interest does Alicia owe?
    a. $2,901.21
    b. $666.49
    c. $588.08
    d. $1,462.88

38. A home has been appraised at $185,000 but sells for $182,250. The buyer makes a down payment of $45,000, assumes a loan of $105,000, and gets a new mortgage for the balance. What are the taxes on the deed?
    a. $1,295.00
    b. $1,276.10
    c. $1,275.75
    d. $960.75

39. Mr. Van Helsing owns a rundown Victorian home in a remote part of Florida. His annual tax bill is $2,125. If he pays his taxes on December 5, he will need to write a check for
    a. $1,992.82.
    b. $2,061.25.
    c. $2,090.06.
    d. $2,121.50.

APPENDIX A

SAMPLE FLORIDA MORTGAGE DOCUMENT

After Recording Return To:

____

____

____

____

__________________ **[Space Above This Line for Recording Data]** ______________________

MORTGAGE

DEFINITIONS

Words used in multiple sections of this document are defined below and other words are defined in Sections 3, 11, 13, 18, 20 and 21. Certain rules regarding the usage of words used in this document are also provided in Section 16.

(A) "Security Instrument" means this document, which is dated _________________________, ________, together with all Riders to this document.
(B) "Borrower" is ____. Borrower is the mortgagor under this Security Instrument.
(C) "Lender" is ____. Lender is a ____ organized and existing under the laws of ____. Lender's address is ____. Lender is the mortgagee under this Security Instrument.
(D) "Note" means the promissory note signed by Borrower and dated ______________________, _____. The Note states that Borrower owes Lender ____________________________________ Dollars (U.S. $____________________) plus interest. Borrower has promised to pay this debt in regular Periodic Payments and to pay the debt in full not later than ____________________________.
(E) "Property" means the property that is described below under the heading "Transfer of Rights in the Property."
(F) "Loan" means the debt evidenced by the Note, plus interest, any prepayment charges and late charges due under the Note, and all sums due under this Security Instrument, plus interest.
(G) "Riders" means all Riders to this Security Instrument that are executed by Borrower. The following Riders are to be executed by Borrower [check box as applicable]:

☐ Adjustable Rate Rider	☐ Condominium Rider	☐ Second Home Rider
☐ Balloon Rider	☐ Planned Unit Development Rider	☐ Other(s) [specify] ________
☐ 1-4 Family Rider	☐ Biweekly Payment Rider	

(H) "Applicable Law" means all controlling applicable federal, state and local statutes, regulations, ordinances and administrative rules and orders (that have the effect of law) as well as all applicable final, non-appealable judicial opinions.
(I) "Community Association Dues, Fees, and Assessments" means all dues, fees, assessments and other charges that are imposed on Borrower or the Property by a condominium association, homeowners association or similar organization.
(J) "Electronic Funds Transfer" means any transfer of funds, other than a transaction originated by check, draft, or similar paper instrument, which is initiated through an electronic terminal, telephonic instrument, computer, or magnetic tape so as to order, instruct, or authorize a financial institution to debit or credit an account. Such term includes, but is not limited to, point-of-sale transfers, automated teller machine transactions, transfers initiated by telephone, wire transfers, and automated clearinghouse transfers.
(K) "Escrow Items" means those items that are described in Section 3.
(L) "Miscellaneous Proceeds" means any compensation, settlement, award of damages, or proceeds paid by any third party (other than insurance proceeds paid under the coverages described in Section 5) for: (i) damage to, or destruction of, the Property; (ii) condemnation or other taking of all or any part of the Property; (iii) conveyance in lieu of condemnation; or (iv) misrepresentations of, or omissions as to, the value and/or condition of the Property.
(M) "Mortgage Insurance" means insurance protecting Lender against the nonpayment of, or default on, the Loan.
(N) "Periodic Payment" means the regularly scheduled amount due for (i) principal and interest under the Note, plus (ii) any amounts under Section 3 of this Security Instrument.
(O) "RESPA" means the Real Estate Settlement Procedures Act (12 U.S.C. §2601 et seq.) and its implementing regulation, Regulation X (24 C.F.R. Part 3500), as they might be amended from time to time, or any additional or successor legislation or regulation that governs the same subject matter. As used in this Security Instrument, "RESPA" refers to all requirements and restrictions that are imposed in regard to a "federally related mortgage loan" even if the Loan does not qualify as a "federally related mortgage loan" under RESPA.
(P) "Successor in Interest of Borrower" means any party that has taken title to the Property, whether or not that party has assumed Borrower's obligations under the Note and/or this Security Instrument.

TRANSFER OF RIGHTS IN THE PROPERTY

This Security Instrument secures to Lender: (i) the repayment of the Loan, and all renewals, extensions and modifications of the Note; and (ii) the performance of Borrower's covenants and agreements under this Security Instrument and the Note. For this purpose, Borrower does hereby

mortgage, grant and convey to Lender, the following described property located in the ______________________ of ______________________:
[Type of Recording Jurisdiction] [Name of Recording Jurisdiction]

which currently has the address of ______________________
[Street]
______________________, Florida ______________ ("Property Address"):
[City] [Zip Code]

TOGETHER WITH all the improvements now or hereafter erected on the property, and all easements, appurtenances, and fixtures now or hereafter a part of the property. All replacements and additions shall also be covered by this Security Instrument. All of the foregoing is referred to in this Security Instrument as the "Property."

BORROWER COVENANTS that Borrower is lawfully seised of the estate hereby conveyed and has the right to mortgage, grant and convey the Property and that the Property is unencumbered, except for encumbrances of record. Borrower warrants and will defend generally the title to the Property against all claims and demands, subject to any encumbrances of record.

THIS SECURITY INSTRUMENT combines uniform covenants for national use and non-uniform covenants with limited variations by jurisdiction to constitute a uniform security instrument covering real property.

UNIFORM COVENANTS. Borrower and Lender covenant and agree as follows:

1. Payment of Principal, Interest, Escrow Items, Prepayment Charges, and Late Charges. Borrower shall pay when due the principal of, and interest on, the debt evidenced by the Note and any prepayment charges and late charges due under the Note. Borrower shall also pay funds for Escrow Items pursuant to Section 3. Payments due under the Note and this Security Instrument shall be made in U.S. currency. However, if any check or other instrument received by Lender as payment under the Note or this Security Instrument is returned to Lender unpaid, Lender may require that any or all subsequent payments due under the Note and this Security Instrument be made in one or more of the following forms, as selected by Lender: (a) cash; (b) money order; (c) certified check, bank check, treasurer's check or cashier's check, provided any such check is drawn upon an institution whose deposits are insured by a federal agency, instrumentality, or entity; or (d) Electronic Funds Transfer.

Payments are deemed received by Lender when received at the location designated in the Note or at such other location as may be designated by Lender in accordance with the notice provisions in Section 15. Lender may return any payment or partial payment if the payment or partial payments are insufficient to bring the Loan current. Lender may accept any payment or partial payment insufficient to bring the Loan current, without waiver of any rights hereunder or prejudice to its rights to refuse such payment or partial payments in the future, but Lender is not obligated to apply such payments at the time such payments are accepted. If each Periodic Payment is applied as of its scheduled due date, then Lender need not pay interest on unapplied funds. Lender may hold such unapplied funds until Borrower makes payment to bring the Loan current. If Borrower does not do so within a reasonable period of time, Lender shall either apply such funds or return them to Borrower. If not applied earlier, such funds will be applied to the outstanding principal balance under the Note immediately prior to foreclosure. No offset or claim which Borrower might have now or in the future against Lender shall relieve Borrower from making payments due under the Note and this Security Instrument or performing the covenants and agreements secured by this Security Instrument.

2. Application of Payments or Proceeds. Except as otherwise described in this Section 2, all payments accepted and applied by Lender shall be applied in the following order of priority: (a) interest due under the Note; (b) principal due under the Note; (c) amounts due under Section 3. Such payments shall be applied to each Periodic Payment in the order in which it became due. Any remaining amounts shall be applied first to late charges, second to any other amounts due under this Security Instrument, and then to reduce the principal balance of the Note.

If Lender receives a payment from Borrower for a delinquent Periodic Payment which includes a sufficient amount to pay any late charge due, the payment may be applied to the delinquent payment and the late charge. If more than one Periodic Payment is outstanding, Lender may apply any payment received from Borrower to the repayment of the Periodic Payments if, and to the extent that, each payment can be paid in full. To the extent that any excess exists after the payment is applied to the full payment of one or more Periodic Payments, such excess may be applied to any late charges due. Voluntary prepayments shall be applied first to any prepayment charges and then as described in the Note.

Any application of payments, insurance proceeds, or Miscellaneous Proceeds to principal due under the Note shall not extend or postpone the due date, or change the amount, of the Periodic Payments.

3. Funds for Escrow Items. Borrower shall pay to Lender on the day Periodic Payments are due under the Note, until the Note is paid in full, a sum (the "Funds") to provide for payment of amounts due for: (a) taxes and assessments and other items which can attain priority over this Security Instrument as a lien or encumbrance on the Property; (b) leasehold payments or ground rents on the Property, if any; (c) premiums for any and all insurance required by Lender under Section 5; and (d) Mortgage Insurance premiums, if any, or any sums payable by Borrower to Lender in lieu of the payment of Mortgage Insurance premiums in accordance with the provisions of Section 10. These items are called "Escrow Items." At origination or at any time during the term of the Loan, Lender may require that Community Association Dues, Fees, and Assessments, if any, be escrowed by Borrower, and such dues, fees and assessments shall be an Escrow Item. Borrower shall promptly furnish to Lender all notices of amounts to be paid under this Section. Borrower shall pay Lender the Funds for Escrow Items unless Lender waives Borrower's obligation to pay the

Funds for any or all Escrow Items. Lender may waive Borrower's obligation to pay to Lender Funds for any or all Escrow Items at any time. Any such waiver may only be in writing. In the event of such waiver, Borrower shall pay directly, when and where payable, the amounts due for any Escrow Items for which payment of Funds has been waived by Lender and, if Lender requires, shall furnish to Lender receipts evidencing such payment within such time period as Lender may require. Borrower's obligation to make such payments and to provide receipts shall for all purposes be deemed to be a covenant and agreement contained in this Security Instrument, as the phrase "covenant and agreement" is used in Section 9. If Borrower is obligated to pay Escrow Items directly, pursuant to a waiver, and Borrower fails to pay the amount due for an Escrow Item, Lender may exercise its rights under Section 9 and pay such amount and Borrower shall then be obligated under Section 9 to repay to Lender any such amount. Lender may revoke the waiver as to any or all Escrow Items at any time by a notice given in accordance with Section 15 and, upon such revocation, Borrower shall pay to Lender all Funds, and in such amounts, that are then required under this Section 3.

Lender may, at any time, collect and hold Funds in an amount (a) sufficient to permit Lender to apply the Funds at the time specified under RESPA, and (b) not to exceed the maximum amount a lender can require under RESPA. Lender shall estimate the amount of Funds due on the basis of current data and reasonable estimates of expenditures of future Escrow Items or otherwise in accordance with Applicable Law.

The Funds shall be held in an institution whose deposits are insured by a federal agency, instrumentality, or entity (including Lender, if Lender is an institution whose deposits are so insured) or in any Federal Home Loan Bank. Lender shall apply the Funds to pay the Escrow Items no later than the time specified under RESPA. Lender shall not charge Borrower for holding and applying the Funds, annually analyzing the escrow account, or verifying the Escrow Items, unless Lender pays Borrower interest on the Funds and Applicable Law permits Lender to make such a charge. Unless an agreement is made in writing or Applicable Law requires interest to be paid on the Funds, Lender shall not be required to pay Borrower any interest or earnings on the Funds. Borrower and Lender can agree in writing, however, that interest shall be paid on the Funds. Lender shall give to Borrower, without charge, an annual accounting of the Funds as required by RESPA.

If there is a surplus of Funds held in escrow, as defined under RESPA, Lender shall account to Borrower for the excess funds in accordance with RESPA. If there is a shortage of Funds held in escrow, as defined under RESPA, Lender shall notify Borrower as required by RESPA, and Borrower shall pay to Lender the amount necessary to make up the shortage in accordance with RESPA, but in no more than 12 monthly payments. If there is a deficiency of Funds held in escrow, as defined under RESPA, Lender shall notify Borrower as required by RESPA, and Borrower shall pay to Lender the amount necessary to make up the deficiency in accordance with RESPA, but in no more than 12 monthly payments.

Upon payment in full of all sums secured by this Security Instrument, Lender shall promptly refund to Borrower any Funds held by Lender.

4. Charges; Liens. Borrower shall pay all taxes, assessments, charges, fines, and impositions attributable to the Property which can attain priority over this Security Instrument, leasehold payments or ground rents on the Property, if any, and Community Association Dues, Fees, and Assessments, if any. To the extent that these items are Escrow Items, Borrower shall pay them in the manner provided in Section 3.

Borrower shall promptly discharge any lien which has priority over this Security Instrument unless Borrower: (a) agrees in writing to the payment of the obligation secured by the lien in a manner acceptable to Lender, but only so long as Borrower is performing such agreement; (b) contests the lien in good faith by, or defends against enforcement of the lien in, legal proceedings which in Lender's opinion operate to prevent the enforcement of the lien while those proceedings are pending, but only until such proceedings are concluded; or (c) secures from the holder of the lien an agreement satisfactory to Lender subordinating the lien to this Security Instrument. If Lender determines that any part of the Property is subject to a lien which can attain priority over this Security Instrument, Lender may give Borrower a notice identifying the lien. Within 10 days of the date on which that notice is given, Borrower shall satisfy the lien or take one or more of the actions set forth above in this Section 4.

Lender may require Borrower to pay a one-time charge for a real estate tax verification and/or reporting service used by Lender in connection with this Loan.

5. Property Insurance. Borrower shall keep the improvements now existing or hereafter erected on the Property insured against loss by fire, hazards included within the term "extended coverage," and any other hazards including, but not limited to, earthquakes and floods, for which Lender requires insurance. This insurance shall be maintained in the amounts (including deductible levels) and for the periods that Lender requires. What Lender requires pursuant to the preceding sentences can change during the term of the Loan. The insurance carrier providing the insurance shall be chosen by Borrower subject to Lender's right to disapprove Borrower's choice, which right shall not be exercised unreasonably. Lender may require Borrower to pay, in connection with this Loan, either: (a) a one-time charge for flood zone determination, certification and tracking services; or (b) a one-time charge for flood zone determination and certification services and subsequent charges each time remappings or similar changes occur which reasonably might affect such determination or certification. Borrower shall also be responsible for the payment of any fees imposed by the Federal Emergency Management Agency in connection with the review of any flood zone determination resulting from an objection by Borrower.

If Borrower fails to maintain any of the coverages described above, Lender may obtain insurance coverage, at Lender's option and Borrower's expense. Lender is under no obligation to purchase any particular type or amount of coverage. Therefore, such coverage shall cover Lender, but might or might not protect Borrower, Borrower's equity in the Property, or the contents of the Property, against any risk, hazard or liability and might provide greater or lesser coverage than was previously in effect. Borrower acknowledges that the cost of the insurance coverage so obtained might significantly exceed the cost of insurance that Borrower could have obtained. Any amounts disbursed by Lender under this Section 5 shall become additional debt of Borrower secured by this Security Instrument. These amounts shall bear interest at the Note rate from the date of disbursement and shall be payable, with such interest, upon notice from Lender to Borrower requesting payment.

All insurance policies required by Lender and renewals of such policies shall be subject to Lender's right to disapprove such policies, shall include a standard mortgage clause, and shall name Lender as mortgagee and/or as an additional loss payee. Lender shall have the right to hold the policies and renewal certificates. If Lender requires, Borrower shall promptly give to Lender all receipts of paid premiums and renewal notices. If Borrower obtains any form of insurance coverage, not otherwise required by Lender, for damage to, or destruction of, the Property, such policy shall include a standard mortgage clause and shall name Lender as mortgagee and/or as an additional loss payee.

In the event of loss, Borrower shall give prompt notice to the insurance carrier and Lender. Lender may make proof of loss if not made promptly by Borrower. Unless Lender and Borrower otherwise agree in writing, any insurance proceeds, whether or not the underlying insurance was required by Lender, shall be applied to restoration or repair of the Property, if the restoration or repair is economically feasible and Lender's security is not lessened. During such repair and restoration period, Lender shall have the right to hold such insurance proceeds until Lender has had an opportunity to inspect such Property to ensure the work has been completed to Lender's satisfaction, provided that such inspection shall be undertaken promptly. Lender may disburse proceeds for the repairs and restoration in a single payment or in a series of progress payments as the work is completed. Unless an agreement is made in writing or Applicable Law requires interest to be paid on such insurance proceeds, Lender shall not be required to pay Borrower any interest or earnings on such proceeds. Fees for public adjusters, or other third parties, retained by Borrower shall not be paid out of the insurance proceeds and shall be the sole obligation of Borrower. If the restoration or repair is not economically feasible or Lender's security would be lessened, the insurance proceeds shall be applied to the sums secured by this Security Instrument, whether or not then due, with the excess, if any, paid to Borrower. Such insurance proceeds shall be applied in the order provided for in Section 2.

If Borrower abandons the Property, Lender may file, negotiate and settle any available insurance claim and related matters. If Borrower does not respond within 30 days to a notice from Lender that the insurance carrier has offered to settle a claim, then Lender may negotiate and settle the claim. The 30-day period will begin when the notice is given. In either event, or if Lender acquires the Property under Section 22 or otherwise, Borrower hereby assigns to Lender (a) Borrower's rights to any insurance proceeds in an amount not to exceed the amounts unpaid under the Note or this Security Instrument, and (b) any other of Borrower's rights (other than the right to any refund of unearned premiums paid by Borrower) under all insurance policies covering the Property, insofar as such rights are applicable to the coverage of the Property. Lender may use the insurance proceeds either to repair or restore the Property or to pay amounts unpaid under the Note or this Security Instrument, whether or not then due.

6. Occupancy. Borrower shall occupy, establish, and use the Property as Borrower's principal residence within 60 days after the execution of this Security Instrument and shall continue to occupy the Property as Borrower's principal residence for at least one year after the date of occupancy, unless Lender otherwise agrees in writing, which consent shall not be unreasonably withheld, or unless extenuating circumstances exist which are beyond Borrower's control.

7. Preservation, Maintenance and Protection of the Property; Inspections. Borrower shall not destroy, damage or impair the Property, allow the Property to deteriorate or commit waste on the Property. Whether or not Borrower is residing in the Property, Borrower shall maintain the Property in order to prevent the Property from deteriorating or decreasing in value due to its condition. Unless it is determined pursuant to Section 5 that repair or restoration is not economically feasible, Borrower shall promptly repair the Property if damaged to avoid further deterioration or damage. If insurance or condemnation proceeds are paid in connection with damage to, or the taking of, the Property, Borrower shall be responsible for repairing or restoring the Property only if Lender has released proceeds for such purposes. Lender may disburse proceeds for the repairs and restoration in a single payment or in a series of progress payments as the work is completed. If the insurance or condemnation proceeds are not sufficient to repair or restore the Property, Borrower is not relieved of Borrower's obligation for the completion of such repair or restoration.

Lender or its agent may make reasonable entries upon and inspections of the Property. If it has reasonable cause, Lender may inspect the interior of the improvements on the Property. Lender shall give Borrower notice at the time of or prior to such an interior inspection specifying such reasonable cause.

8. Borrower's Loan Application. Borrower shall be in default if, during the Loan application process, Borrower or any persons or entities acting at the direction of Borrower or with Borrower's knowledge or consent gave materially false, misleading, or inaccurate information or statements to Lender (or failed to provide Lender with material information) in connection with the Loan. Material representations include, but are not limited to, representations concerning Borrower's occupancy of the Property as Borrower's principal residence.

9. Protection of Lender's Interest in the Property and Rights Under this Security Instrument. If (a) Borrower fails to perform the covenants and agreements contained in this Security Instrument, (b) there is a legal proceeding that might significantly affect Lender's interest in the Property and/or rights under this Security Instrument (such as a proceeding in bankruptcy, probate, for condemnation or forfeiture, for enforcement of a lien which may attain priority over this Security Instrument or to enforce laws or regulations), or (c) Borrower has abandoned the Property, then Lender may do and pay for whatever is reasonable or appropriate to protect Lender's interest in the Property and rights under this Security Instrument, including protecting and/or assessing the value of the Property, and securing and/or repairing the Property. Lender's actions can include, but are not limited to: (a) paying any sums secured by a lien which has priority over this Security Instrument; (b) appearing in court; and (c) paying reasonable attorneys' fees to protect its interest in the Property and/or rights under this Security Instrument, including its secured position in a bankruptcy proceeding. Securing the Property includes, but is not limited to, entering the Property to make repairs, change locks, replace or board up doors and windows, drain water from pipes, eliminate building or other code violations or dangerous conditions, and have utilities turned on or off. Although Lender may take action under this Section 9, Lender does not have to do so and is not under any duty or obligation to do so. It is agreed that Lender incurs no liability for not taking any or all actions authorized under this Section 9.

Any amounts disbursed by Lender under this Section 9 shall become additional debt of Borrower secured by this Security Instrument. These amounts shall bear interest at the Note rate from the date of disbursement and shall be payable, with such interest, upon notice from Lender to Borrower requesting payment.

If this Security Instrument is on a leasehold, Borrower shall comply with all the provisions of the lease. If Borrower acquires fee title to the Property, the leasehold and the fee title shall not merge unless Lender agrees to the merger in writing.

10. Mortgage Insurance. If Lender required Mortgage Insurance as a condition of making the Loan, Borrower shall pay the premiums required to maintain the Mortgage Insurance in effect. If, for any reason, the Mortgage Insurance coverage required by Lender ceases to be available from the mortgage insurer that previously provided such insurance and Borrower was required to make separately designated payments toward the premiums for Mortgage Insurance, Borrower shall pay the premiums required to obtain coverage substantially equivalent to the Mortgage Insurance previously in effect, at a cost substantially equivalent to the cost to Borrower of the Mortgage Insurance previously in effect, from an alternate mortgage insurer selected by Lender. If substantially equivalent Mortgage Insurance coverage is not available, Borrower shall continue to pay to Lender the amount of the separately designated payments that were due when the insurance coverage ceased to be in effect. Lender will accept, use and retain these payments as a non-refundable loss reserve in lieu of Mortgage Insurance. Such loss reserve shall be non-refundable, notwithstanding the fact that the Loan is ultimately paid in full, and Lender shall not be required to pay Borrower any interest or earnings on such loss reserve. Lender can no longer require loss reserve payments if Mortgage Insurance coverage (in the amount and for the period that Lender requires) provided by an insurer selected by Lender again becomes available, is obtained, and Lender requires separately designated payments toward the premiums for Mortgage Insurance. If Lender required Mortgage Insurance as a condition of making the Loan and Borrower was required to make separately designated payments toward the premiums for Mortgage Insurance, Borrower shall pay the premiums required to maintain Mortgage Insurance in effect, or to provide a non-refundable loss reserve, until Lender's requirement for Mortgage Insurance ends in accordance with any written agreement between Borrower and Lender providing for such termination or until termination is required by Applicable Law. Nothing in this Section 10 affects Borrower's obligation to pay interest at the rate provided in the Note.

Mortgage Insurance reimburses Lender (or any entity that purchases the Note) for certain losses it may incur if Borrower does not repay the Loan as agreed. Borrower is not a party to the Mortgage Insurance.

Mortgage insurers evaluate their total risk on all such insurance in force from time to time, and may enter into agreements with other parties that share or modify their risk, or reduce losses. These agreements are on terms and conditions that are satisfactory to the mortgage insurer and the other party (or parties) to these agreements. These agreements may require the mortgage insurer to make payments using any source of funds that the mortgage insurer may have available (which may include funds obtained from Mortgage Insurance premiums).

As a result of these agreements, Lender, any purchaser of the Note, another insurer, any reinsurer, any other entity, or any affiliate of any of the foregoing, may receive (directly or indirectly) amounts that derive from (or might be characterized as) a portion of Borrower's payments for Mortgage Insurance, in exchange for sharing or modifying the mortgage insurer's risk, or reducing losses. If such agreement provides that an affiliate of Lender takes a share of the insurer's risk in exchange for a share of the premiums paid to the insurer, the arrangement is often termed "captive reinsurance." Further:

(a) Any such agreements will not affect the amounts that Borrower has agreed to pay for Mortgage Insurance, or any other terms of the Loan. Such agreements will not increase the amount Borrower will owe for Mortgage Insurance, and they will not entitle Borrower to any refund.

(b) Any such agreements will not affect the rights Borrower has – if any – with respect to the Mortgage Insurance under the Homeowners Protection Act of 1998 or any other law. These rights may include the right to receive certain disclosures, to request and obtain cancellation of the Mortgage Insurance, to have the Mortgage Insurance terminated

automatically, and/or to receive a refund of any Mortgage Insurance premiums that were unearned at the time of such cancellation or termination.

11. Assignment of Miscellaneous Proceeds; Forfeiture. All Miscellaneous Proceeds are hereby assigned to and shall be paid to Lender.

If the Property is damaged, such Miscellaneous Proceeds shall be applied to restoration or repair of the Property, if the restoration or repair is economically feasible and Lender's security is not lessened. During such repair and restoration period, Lender shall have the right to hold such Miscellaneous Proceeds until Lender has had an opportunity to inspect such Property to ensure the work has been completed to Lender's satisfaction, provided that such inspection shall be undertaken promptly. Lender may pay for the repairs and restoration in a single disbursement or in a series of progress payments as the work is completed. Unless an agreement is made in writing or Applicable Law requires interest to be paid on such Miscellaneous Proceeds, Lender shall not be required to pay Borrower any interest or earnings on such Miscellaneous Proceeds. If the restoration or repair is not economically feasible or Lender's security would be lessened, the Miscellaneous Proceeds shall be applied to the sums secured by this Security Instrument, whether or not then due, with the excess, if any, paid to Borrower. Such Miscellaneous Proceeds shall be applied in the order provided for in Section 2.

In the event of a total taking, destruction, or loss in value of the Property, the Miscellaneous Proceeds shall be applied to the sums secured by this Security Instrument, whether or not then due, with the excess, if any, paid to Borrower.

In the event of a partial taking, destruction, or loss in value of the Property in which the fair market value of the Property immediately before the partial taking, destruction, or loss in value is equal to or greater than the amount of the sums secured by this Security Instrument immediately before the partial taking, destruction, or loss in value, unless Borrower and Lender otherwise agree in writing, the sums secured by this Security Instrument shall be reduced by the amount of the Miscellaneous Proceeds multiplied by the following fraction: (a) the total amount of the sums secured immediately before the partial taking, destruction, or loss in value divided by (b) the fair market value of the Property immediately before the partial taking, destruction, or loss in value. Any balance shall be paid to Borrower.

In the event of a partial taking, destruction, or loss in value of the Property in which the fair market value of the Property immediately before the partial taking, destruction, or loss in value is less than the amount of the sums secured immediately before the partial taking, destruction, or loss in value, unless Borrower and Lender otherwise agree in writing, the Miscellaneous Proceeds shall be applied to the sums secured by this Security Instrument whether or not the sums are then due.

If the Property is abandoned by Borrower, or if, after notice by Lender to Borrower that the Opposing Party (as defined in the next sentence) offers to make an award to settle a claim for damages, Borrower fails to respond to Lender within 30 days after the date the notice is given, Lender is authorized to collect and apply the Miscellaneous Proceeds either to restoration or repair of the Property or to the sums secured by this Security Instrument, whether or not then due. "Opposing Party" means the third party that owes Borrower Miscellaneous Proceeds or the party against whom Borrower has a right of action in regard to Miscellaneous Proceeds.

Borrower shall be in default if any action or proceeding, whether civil or criminal, is begun that, in Lender's judgment, could result in forfeiture of the Property or other material impairment of Lender's interest in the Property or rights under this Security Instrument. Borrower can cure such a default and, if acceleration has occurred, reinstate as provided in Section 19, by causing the action or proceeding to be dismissed with a ruling that, in Lender's judgment, precludes forfeiture of the Property or other material impairment of Lender's interest in the Property or rights under this Security Instrument. The proceeds of any award or claim for damages that are attributable to the impairment of Lender's interest in the Property are hereby assigned and shall be paid to Lender.

All Miscellaneous Proceeds that are not applied to restoration or repair of the Property shall be applied in the order provided for in Section 2.

12. Borrower Not Released; Forbearance By Lender Not a Waiver. Extension of the time for payment or modification of amortization of the sums secured by this Security Instrument granted by Lender to Borrower or any Successor in Interest of Borrower shall not operate to release the liability of Borrower or any Successors in Interest of Borrower. Lender shall not be required to commence proceedings against any Successor in Interest of Borrower or to refuse to extend time for payment or otherwise modify amortization of the sums secured by this Security Instrument by reason of any demand made by the original Borrower or any Successors in Interest of Borrower. Any forbearance by Lender in exercising any right or remedy including, without limitation, Lender's acceptance of payments from third persons, entities or Successors in Interest of Borrower or in amounts less than the amount then due, shall not be a waiver of or preclude the exercise of any right or remedy.

13. Joint and Several Liability; Co-signers; Successors and Assigns Bound. Borrower covenants and agrees that Borrower's obligations and liability shall be joint and several. However, any Borrower who co-signs this Security Instrument but does not execute the Note (a "co-signer"): (a) is co-signing this Security Instrument only to mortgage, grant and convey the co-signer's interest in the Property under the terms of this Security Instrument; (b) is not personally obligated to pay the sums secured by this Security Instrument; and (c) agrees that Lender and any other Borrower can agree to extend, modify, forbear or make any accommodations with regard to the terms of this Security Instrument or the Note without the co-signer's consent.

Subject to the provisions of Section 18, any Successor in Interest of Borrower who assumes Borrower's obligations under this Security Instrument in writing, and is approved by Lender, shall obtain all of Borrower's rights and benefits under this Security Instrument. Borrower shall not be released from Borrower's obligations and liability under this Security Instrument unless Lender agrees to such release in writing. The covenants and agreements of this Security Instrument shall bind (except as provided in Section 20) and benefit the successors and assigns of Lender.

14. Loan Charges. Lender may charge Borrower fees for services performed in connection with Borrower's default, for the purpose of protecting Lender's interest in the Property and rights under this Security Instrument, including, but not limited to, attorneys' fees, property inspection and valuation fees. In regard to any other fees, the absence of express authority in this Security Instrument to charge a specific fee to Borrower shall not be construed as a prohibition on the charging of such fee. Lender may not charge fees that are expressly prohibited by this Security Instrument or by Applicable Law.

If the Loan is subject to a law which sets maximum loan charges, and that law is finally interpreted so that the interest or other loan charges collected or to be collected in connection with the Loan exceed the permitted limits, then: (a) any such loan charge shall be reduced by the amount necessary to reduce the charge to the permitted limit; and (b) any sums already collected from Borrower which exceeded permitted limits will be refunded to Borrower. Lender may choose to make this refund by reducing the principal owed under the Note or by making a direct payment to Borrower. If a refund reduces principal, the reduction will be treated as a partial prepayment without any prepayment charge (whether or not a prepayment charge is provided for under the Note). Borrower's acceptance of any such refund made by direct payment to Borrower will constitute a waiver of any right of action Borrower might have arising out of such overcharge.

15. Notices. All notices given by Borrower or Lender in connection with this Security Instrument must be in writing. Any notice to Borrower in connection with this Security Instrument shall be deemed to have been given to Borrower when mailed by first class mail or when actually delivered to Borrower's notice address if sent by other means. Notice to any one Borrower shall constitute notice to all Borrowers unless Applicable Law expressly requires otherwise. The notice address shall be the Property Address unless Borrower has designated a substitute notice address by notice to Lender. Borrower shall promptly notify Lender of Borrower's change of address. If Lender specifies a procedure for reporting Borrower's change of address, then Borrower shall only report a change of address through that specified procedure. There may be only one designated notice address under this Security Instrument at any one time. Any notice to Lender shall be given by delivering it or by mailing it by first class mail to Lender's address stated herein unless Lender has designated another address by notice to Borrower. Any notice in connection with this Security Instrument shall not be deemed to have been given to Lender until actually received by Lender. If any notice required by this Security Instrument is also required under Applicable Law, the Applicable Law requirement will satisfy the corresponding requirement under this Security Instrument.

16. Governing Law; Severability; Rules of Construction. This Security Instrument shall be governed by federal law and the law of the jurisdiction in which the Property is located. All rights and obligations contained in this Security Instrument are subject to any requirements and limitations of Applicable Law. Applicable Law might explicitly or implicitly allow the parties to agree by contract or it might be silent, but such silence shall not be construed as a prohibition against agreement by contract. In the event that any provision or clause of this Security Instrument or the Note conflicts with Applicable Law, such conflict shall not affect other provisions of this Security Instrument or the Note which can be given effect without the conflicting provision.

As used in this Security Instrument: (a) words of the masculine gender shall mean and include corresponding neuter words or words of the feminine gender; (b) words in the singular shall mean and include the plural and vice versa; and (c) the word "may" gives sole discretion without any obligation to take any action.

17. Borrower's Copy. Borrower shall be given one copy of the Note and of this Security Instrument.

18. Transfer of the Property or a Beneficial Interest in Borrower. As used in this Section 18, "Interest in the Property" means any legal or beneficial interest in the Property, including, but not limited to, those beneficial interests transferred in a bond for deed, contract for deed, installment sales contract or escrow agreement, the intent of which is the transfer of title by Borrower at a future date to a purchaser.

If all or any part of the Property or any Interest in the Property is sold or transferred (or if Borrower is not a natural person and a beneficial interest in Borrower is sold or transferred) without Lender's prior written consent, Lender may require immediate payment in full of all sums secured by this Security Instrument. However, this option shall not be exercised by Lender if such exercise is prohibited by Applicable Law.

If Lender exercises this option, Lender shall give Borrower notice of acceleration. The notice shall provide a period of not less than 30 days from the date the notice is given in accordance with Section 15 within which Borrower must pay all sums secured by this Security Instrument. If Borrower fails to pay these sums prior to the expiration of this period, Lender may invoke any remedies permitted by this Security Instrument without further notice or demand on Borrower.

19. Borrower's Right to Reinstate After Acceleration. If Borrower meets certain conditions, Borrower shall have the right to have enforcement of this Security Instrument discontinued at any time prior to the earliest of: (a) five days before sale of the Property pursuant to any power of sale contained in this Security Instrument; (b) such other period as Applicable Law might specify for the termination of Borrower's right to reinstate; or (c) entry of a judgment enforcing this Security Instrument. Those conditions are that Borrower: (a) pays Lender all sums which then would be due under this Security Instrument and the Note as if no acceleration had occurred; (b) cures any default of any other covenants or agreements; (c) pays all expenses incurred in enforcing this Security Instrument, including, but not limited to, reasonable attorneys' fees, property inspection and valuation fees, and other fees incurred for the purpose of protecting Lender's interest in the Property and rights under this Security Instrument; and (d) takes such action as Lender may reasonably require to assure that Lender's interest in the Property and rights under this Security Instrument, and Borrower's obligation to pay the sums secured by this Security Instrument, shall continue unchanged. Lender may require that Borrower pay such reinstatement sums and expenses in one or more of the following forms, as selected by Lender: (a) cash; (b) money order; (c) certified check, bank check, treasurer's check or cashier's check, provided any such check is drawn upon an institution whose deposits are insured by a federal agency, instrumentality or entity; or (d) Electronic Funds Transfer. Upon reinstatement by Borrower, this Security Instrument and obligations secured hereby shall remain fully effective as if no acceleration had occurred. However, this right to reinstate shall not apply in the case of acceleration under Section 18.

20. Sale of Note; Change of Loan Servicer; Notice of Grievance. The Note or a partial interest in the Note (together with this Security Instrument) can be sold one or more times without prior notice to Borrower. A sale might result in a change in the entity (known as the "Loan Servicer") that collects Periodic Payments due under the Note and this Security Instrument and performs other mortgage loan servicing obligations under the Note, this Security Instrument, and Applicable Law. There also might be one or more changes of the Loan Servicer unrelated to a sale of the Note. If there is a change of the Loan Servicer, Borrower will be given written notice of the change which will state the name and address of the new Loan Servicer, the address to which payments should be made and any other information RESPA requires in connection with a notice of transfer of servicing. If the Note is sold and thereafter the Loan is serviced by a Loan Servicer other than the purchaser of the Note, the mortgage loan servicing obligations to Borrower will remain with the Loan Servicer or be transferred to a successor Loan Servicer and are not assumed by the Note purchaser unless otherwise provided by the Note purchaser.

Neither Borrower nor Lender may commence, join, or be joined to any judicial action (as either an individual litigant or the member of a class) that arises from the other party's actions pursuant to this Security Instrument or that alleges that the other party has breached any provision of, or any duty owed by reason of, this Security Instrument, until such Borrower or Lender has notified the other party (with such notice given in compliance with the requirements of Section 15) of such alleged breach and afforded the other party hereto a reasonable period after the giving of such notice to take corrective action. If Applicable Law provides a time period which must elapse before certain action can be taken, that time period will be deemed to be reasonable for purposes of this paragraph. The notice of acceleration and opportunity to cure given to Borrower pursuant to Section 22 and the notice of acceleration given to Borrower pursuant to Section 18 shall be deemed to satisfy the notice and opportunity to take corrective action provisions of this Section 20.

21. Hazardous Substances. As used in this Section 21: (a) "Hazardous Substances" are those substances defined as toxic or hazardous substances, pollutants, or wastes by Environmental Law and the following substances: gasoline, kerosene, other flammable or toxic petroleum products, toxic pesticides and herbicides, volatile solvents, materials containing asbestos or formaldehyde, and radioactive materials; (b) "Environmental Law" means federal laws and laws of the jurisdiction where the Property is located that relate to health, safety or environmental protection; (c) "Environmental Cleanup" includes any response action, remedial action, or removal action, as defined in Environmental Law; and (d) an "Environmental Condition" means a condition that can cause, contribute to, or otherwise trigger an Environmental Cleanup.

Borrower shall not cause or permit the presence, use, disposal, storage, or release of any Hazardous Substances, or threaten to release any Hazardous Substances, on or in the Property. Borrower shall not do, nor allow anyone else to do, anything affecting the Property (a) that is in violation of any Environmental Law, (b) which creates an Environmental Condition, or (c) which, due to the presence, use, or release of a Hazardous Substance, creates a condition that adversely affects the value of the Property. The preceding two sentences shall not apply to the presence, use, or storage on the Property of small quantities of Hazardous Substances that are generally recognized to be appropriate to normal residential uses and to maintenance of the Property (including, but not limited to, hazardous substances in consumer products).

Borrower shall promptly give Lender written notice of (a) any investigation, claim, demand, lawsuit or other action by any governmental or regulatory agency or private party involving the Property and any Hazardous Substance or Environmental Law of which Borrower has actual knowledge, (b) any Environmental Condition, including but not limited to, any spilling, leaking, discharge, release or threat of release of any Hazardous Substance, and (c) any condition caused by the presence, use or release of a Hazardous Substance which adversely affects the value of the Property. If Borrower learns, or is notified by any governmental or regulatory authority, or any private party, that any removal or other remediation of any Hazardous Substance affecting the Property is necessary, Borrower shall promptly take all necessary remedial actions in accordance with Environmental Law. Nothing herein shall create any obligation on Lender for an Environmental Cleanup.

NON-UNIFORM COVENANTS. Borrower and Lender further covenant and agree as follows:

22. Acceleration; Remedies. Lender shall give notice to Borrower prior to acceleration following Borrower's breach of any covenant or agreement in this Security Instrument (but not prior to acceleration under Section 18 unless Applicable Law provides otherwise). The notice shall specify: (a) the default; (b) the action required to cure the default; (c) a date, not less than 30 days from the date the notice is given to Borrower, by which the default must be cured; and (d) that failure to cure the default on or before the date specified in the notice may result in acceleration of the sums secured by this Security Instrument, foreclosure by judicial proceeding and sale of the Property. The notice shall further inform Borrower of the right to reinstate after acceleration and the right to assert in the foreclosure proceeding the non-existence of a default or any other defense of Borrower to acceleration and foreclosure. If the default is not cured on or before the date specified in the notice, Lender at its option may require immediate payment in full of all sums secured by this Security Instrument without further demand and may foreclose this Security Instrument by judicial proceeding. Lender shall be entitled to collect all expenses incurred in pursuing the remedies provided in this Section 22, including, but not limited to, reasonable attorneys' fees and costs of title evidence.

23. Release. Upon payment of all sums secured by this Security Instrument, Lender shall release this Security Instrument. Borrower shall pay any recordation costs. Lender may charge Borrower a fee for releasing this Security Instrument, but only if the fee is paid to a third party for services rendered and the charging of the fee is permitted under Applicable Law.

24. Attorneys' Fees. As used in this Security Instrument and the Note, attorneys' fees shall include those awarded by an appellate court and any attorneys' fees incurred in a bankruptcy proceeding.

25. Jury Trial Waiver. The Borrower hereby waives any right to a trial by jury in any action, proceeding, claim, or counterclaim, whether in contract or tort, at law or in equity, arising out of or in any way related to this Security Instrument or the Note.

BY SIGNING BELOW, Borrower accepts and agrees to the terms and covenants contained in this Security Instrument and in any Rider executed by Borrower and recorded with it.

Signed, sealed and delivered in the presence of:

_______________________ _______________________(Seal)
- Borrower

_______________________ _______________________(Seal)
- Borrower

_______________ **[Space Below This Line for Acknowledgment]** _______________

UNIFORM RESIDENTIAL APPRAISAL REPORT

Uniform Residential Appraisal Report

File #

The purpose of this summary appraisal report is to provide the lender/client with an accurate, and adequately supported, opinion of the market value of the subject property.

SUBJECT

Property Address City State Zip Code
Borrower Owner of Public Record County
Legal Description
Assessor's Parcel # Tax Year R.E. Taxes $
Neighborhood Name Map Reference Census Tract
Occupant ☐ Owner ☐ Tenant ☐ Vacant Special Assessments $ ☐ PUD HOA $ ☐ per year ☐ per month
Property Rights Appraised ☐ Fee Simple ☐ Leasehold ☐ Other (describe)
Assignment Type ☐ Purchase Transaction ☐ Refinance Transaction ☐ Other (describe)
Lender/Client Address
Is the subject property currently offered for sale or has it been offered for sale in the twelve months prior to the effective date of this appraisal? ☐ Yes ☐ No
Report data source(s) used, offering price(s), and date(s).

CONTRACT

I ☐ did ☐ did not analyze the contract for sale for the subject purchase transaction. Explain the results of the analysis of the contract for sale or why the analysis was not performed.

Contract Price $ Date of Contract Is the property seller the owner of public record? ☐Yes ☐No Data Source(s)
Is there any financial assistance (loan charges, sale concessions, gift or downpayment assistance, etc.) to be paid by any party on behalf of the borrower? ☐ Yes ☐ No
If Yes, report the total dollar amount and describe the items to be paid.

NEIGHBORHOOD

Note: Race and the racial composition of the neighborhood are not appraisal factors.

Neighborhood Characteristics	One-Unit Housing Trends	One-Unit Housing		Present Land Use %
Location ☐ Urban ☐ Suburban ☐ Rural	Property Values ☐ Increasing ☐ Stable ☐ Declining	PRICE	AGE	One-Unit %
Built-Up ☐ Over 75% ☐ 25–75% ☐ Under 25%	Demand/Supply ☐ Shortage ☐ In Balance ☐ Over Supply	$ (000)	(yrs)	2-4 Unit %
Growth ☐ Rapid ☐ Stable ☐ Slow	Marketing Time ☐ Under 3 mths ☐ 3–6 mths ☐ Over 6 mths	Low		Multi-Family %
Neighborhood Boundaries		High		Commercial %
		Pred.		Other %

Neighborhood Description

Market Conditions (including support for the above conclusions)

SITE

Dimensions Area Shape View
Specific Zoning Classification Zoning Description
Zoning Compliance ☐ Legal ☐ Legal Nonconforming (Grandfathered Use) ☐ No Zoning ☐ Illegal (describe)
Is the highest and best use of the subject property as improved (or as proposed per plans and specifications) the present use? ☐ Yes ☐ No If No, describe

Utilities	Public	Other (describe)		Public	Other (describe)	Off-site Improvements—Type	Public	Private
Electricity	☐	☐	Water	☐	☐	Street	☐	☐
Gas	☐	☐	Sanitary Sewer	☐	☐	Alley	☐	☐

FEMA Special Flood Hazard Area ☐ Yes ☐ No FEMA Flood Zone FEMA Map # FEMA Map Date
Are the utilities and off-site improvements typical for the market area? ☐ Yes ☐ No If No, describe
Are there any adverse site conditions or external factors (easements, encroachments, environmental conditions, land uses, etc.)? ☐ Yes ☐ No If Yes, describe

IMPROVEMENTS

General Description	Foundation	Exterior Description materials/condition	Interior materials/condition
Units ☐ One ☐ One with Accessory Unit	☐ Concrete Slab ☐ Crawl Space	Foundation Walls	Floors
# of Stories	☐ Full Basement ☐ Partial Basement	Exterior Walls	Walls
Type ☐ Det. ☐ Att. ☐ S-Det./End Unit	Basement Area sq. ft.	Roof Surface	Trim/Finish
☐ Existing ☐ Proposed ☐ Under Const.	Basement Finish %	Gutters & Downspouts	Bath Floor
Design (Style)	☐ Outside Entry/Exit ☐ Sump Pump	Window Type	Bath Wainscot
Year Built	Evidence of ☐ Infestation	Storm Sash/Insulated	Car Storage ☐ None
Effective Age (Yrs)	☐ Dampness ☐ Settlement	Screens	☐ Driveway # of Cars
Attic ☐ None	Heating ☐ FWA ☐ HWBB ☐ Radiant	Amenities ☐ Woodstove(s) #	Driveway Surface
☐ Drop Stair ☐ Stairs	☐ Other Fuel	☐ Fireplace(s) # ☐ Fence	☐ Garage # of Cars
☐ Floor ☐ Scuttle	Cooling ☐ Central Air Conditioning	☐ Patio/Deck ☐ Porch	☐ Carport # of Cars
☐ Finished ☐ Heated	☐ Individual ☐ Other	☐ Pool ☐ Other	☐ Att. ☐ Det. ☐ Built-in

Appliances ☐Refrigerator ☐Range/Oven ☐Dishwasher ☐Disposal ☐Microwave ☐Washer/Dryer ☐Other (describe)
Finished area **above** grade contains: Rooms Bedrooms Bath(s) Square Feet of Gross Living Area Above Grade
Additional features (special energy efficient items, etc.)

Describe the condition of the property (including needed repairs, deterioration, renovations, remodeling, etc.).

Are there any physical deficiencies or adverse conditions that affect the livability, soundness, or structural integrity of the property? ☐ Yes ☐ No If Yes, describe

Does the property generally conform to the neighborhood (functional utility, style, condition, use, construction, etc.)? ☐ Yes ☐ No If No, describe

Uniform Residential Appraisal Report

File #

There are comparable properties currently offered for sale in the subject neighborhood ranging in price from $ to $.

There are comparable sales in the subject neighborhood within the past twelve months ranging in sale price from $ to $.

SALES COMPARISON APPROACH

FEATURE	SUBJECT	COMPARABLE SALE # 1		COMPARABLE SALE # 2		COMPARABLE SALE # 3	
Address							
Proximity to Subject							
Sale Price	$		$		$		$
Sale Price/Gross Liv. Area	$ sq. ft.	$ sq. ft.		$ sq. ft.		$ sq. ft.	
Data Source(s)							
Verification Source(s)							
VALUE ADJUSTMENTS	DESCRIPTION	DESCRIPTION	+(-) $ Adjustment	DESCRIPTION	+(-) $ Adjustment	DESCRIPTION	+(-) $ Adjustment
Sale or Financing Concessions							
Date of Sale/Time							
Location							
Leasehold/Fee Simple							
Site							
View							
Design (Style)							
Quality of Construction							
Actual Age							
Condition							
Above Grade Room Count	Total / Bdrms. / Baths	Total / Bdrms. / Baths		Total / Bdrms. / Baths		Total / Bdrms. / Baths	
Gross Living Area	sq. ft.	sq. ft.		sq. ft.		sq. ft.	
Basement & Finished Rooms Below Grade							
Functional Utility							
Heating/Cooling							
Energy Efficient Items							
Garage/Carport							
Porch/Patio/Deck							
Net Adjustment (Total)		☐ + ☐ -	$	☐ + ☐ -	$	☐ + ☐ -	$
Adjusted Sale Price of Comparables		Net Adj. % Gross Adj. %	$	Net Adj. % Gross Adj. %	$	Net Adj. % Gross Adj. %	$

I ☐ did ☐ did not research the sale or transfer history of the subject property and comparable sales. If not, explain

My research ☐ did ☐ did not reveal any prior sales or transfers of the subject property for the three years prior to the effective date of this appraisal.

Data source(s)

My research ☐ did ☐ did not reveal any prior sales or transfers of the comparable sales for the year prior to the date of sale of the comparable sale.

Data source(s)

Report the results of the research and analysis of the prior sale or transfer history of the subject property and comparable sales (report additional prior sales on page 3).

ITEM	SUBJECT	COMPARABLE SALE # 1	COMPARABLE SALE # 2	COMPARABLE SALE # 3
Date of Prior Sale/Transfer				
Price of Prior Sale/Transfer				
Data Source(s)				
Effective Date of Data Source(s)				

Analysis of prior sale or transfer history of the subject property and comparable sales

Summary of Sales Comparison Approach

Indicated Value by Sales Comparison Approach $

RECONCILIATION

Indicated Value by: Sales Comparison Approach $ Cost Approach (if developed) $ Income Approach (if developed) $

This appraisal is made ☐ "as is", ☐ subject to completion per plans and specifications on the basis of a hypothetical condition that the improvements have been completed, ☐ subject to the following repairs or alterations on the basis of a hypothetical condition that the repairs or alterations have been completed, or ☐ subject to the following required inspection based on the extraordinary assumption that the condition or deficiency does not require alteration or repair:

Based on a complete visual inspection of the interior and exterior areas of the subject property, defined scope of work, statement of assumptions and limiting conditions, and appraiser's certification, my (our) opinion of the market value, as defined, of the real property that is the subject of this report is $, as of , which is the date of inspection and the effective date of this appraisal.

Uniform Residential Appraisal Report

File #

ADDITIONAL COMMENTS

COST APPROACH

COST APPROACH TO VALUE (not required by Fannie Mae)

Provide adequate information for the lender/client to replicate the below cost figures and calculations.

Support for the opinion of site value (summary of comparable land sales or other methods for estimating site value)

ESTIMATED ☐ REPRODUCTION OR ☐ REPLACEMENT COST NEW	OPINION OF SITE VALUE .... =$
Source of cost data	Dwelling Sq. Ft. @ $ .... =$
Quality rating from cost service Effective date of cost data	Sq. Ft. @ $ .... =$
Comments on Cost Approach (gross living area calculations, depreciation, etc.)	
	Garage/Carport Sq. Ft. @ $ .... =$
	Total Estimate of Cost-New .... = $
	Less Physical Functional External
	Depreciation =$( )
	Depreciated Cost of Improvements............ =$
	"As-is" Value of Site Improvements............ =$
Estimated Remaining Economic Life (HUD and VA only) Years	Indicated Value By Cost Approach .... =$

INCOME

INCOME APPROACH TO VALUE (not required by Fannie Mae)

Estimated Monthly Market Rent $ X Gross Rent Multiplier = $ Indicated Value by Income Approach

Summary of Income Approach (including support for market rent and GRM)

PUD INFORMATION

PROJECT INFORMATION FOR PUDs (if applicable)

Is the developer/builder in control of the Homeowners' Association (HOA)? ☐ Yes ☐ No Unit type(s) ☐ Detached ☐ Attached

Provide the following information for PUDs ONLY if the developer/builder is in control of the HOA and the subject property is an attached dwelling unit.

Legal name of project

Total number of phases Total number of units Total number of units sold

Total number of units rented Total number of units for sale Data source(s)

Was the project created by the conversion of an existing building(s) into a PUD? ☐ Yes ☐ No If Yes, date of conversion

Does the project contain any multi-dwelling units? ☐ Yes ☐ No Data source(s)

Are the units, common elements, and recreation facilities complete? ☐ Yes ☐ No If No, describe the status of completion.

Are the common elements leased to or by the Homeowners' Association? ☐ Yes ☐ No If Yes, describe the rental terms and options.

Describe common elements and recreational facilities

Uniform Residential Appraisal Report

File #

This report form is designed to report an appraisal of a one-unit property or a one-unit property with an accessory unit; including a unit in a planned unit development (PUD). This report form is not designed to report an appraisal of a manufactured home or a unit in a condominium or cooperative project.

This appraisal report is subject to the following scope of work, intended use, intended user, definition of market value, statement of assumptions and limiting conditions, and certifications. Modifications, additions, or deletions to the intended use, intended user, definition of market value, or assumptions and limiting conditions are not permitted. The appraiser may expand the scope of work to include any additional research or analysis necessary based on the complexity of this appraisal assignment. Modifications or deletions to the certifications are also not permitted. However, additional certifications that do not constitute material alterations to this appraisal report, such as those required by law or those related to the appraiser's continuing education or membership in an appraisal organization, are permitted.

SCOPE OF WORK: The scope of work for this appraisal is defined by the complexity of this appraisal assignment and the reporting requirements of this appraisal report form, including the following definition of market value, statement of assumptions and limiting conditions, and certifications. The appraiser must, at a minimum: (1) perform a complete visual inspection of the interior and exterior areas of the subject property, (2) inspect the neighborhood, (3) inspect each of the comparable sales from at least the street, (4) research, verify, and analyze data from reliable public and/or private sources, and (5) report his or her analysis, opinions, and conclusions in this appraisal report.

INTENDED USE: The intended use of this appraisal report is for the lender/client to evaluate the property that is the subject of this appraisal for a mortgage finance transaction.

INTENDED USER: The intended user of this appraisal report is the lender/client.

DEFINITION OF MARKET VALUE: The most probable price which a property should bring in a competitive and open market under all conditions requisite to a fair sale, the buyer and seller, each acting prudently, knowledgeably and assuming the price is not affected by undue stimulus. Implicit in this definition is the consummation of a sale as of a specified date and the passing of title from seller to buyer under conditions whereby: (1) buyer and seller are typically motivated; (2) both parties are well informed or well advised, and each acting in what he or she considers his or her own best interest; (3) a reasonable time is allowed for exposure in the open market; (4) payment is made in terms of cash in U. S. dollars or in terms of financial arrangements comparable thereto; and (5) the price represents the normal consideration for the property sold unaffected by special or creative financing or sales concessions* granted by anyone associated with the sale.

*Adjustments to the comparables must be made for special or creative financing or sales concessions. No adjustments are necessary for those costs which are normally paid by sellers as a result of tradition or law in a market area; these costs are readily identifiable since the seller pays these costs in virtually all sales transactions. Special or creative financing adjustments can be made to the comparable property by comparisons to financing terms offered by a third party institutional lender that is not already involved in the property or transaction. Any adjustment should not be calculated on a mechanical dollar for dollar cost of the financing or concession but the dollar amount of any adjustment should approximate the market's reaction to the financing or concessions based on the appraiser's judgment.

STATEMENT OF ASSUMPTIONS AND LIMITING CONDITIONS: The appraiser's certification in this report is subject to the following assumptions and limiting conditions:

1. The appraiser will not be responsible for matters of a legal nature that affect either the property being appraised or the title to it, except for information that he or she became aware of during the research involved in performing this appraisal. The appraiser assumes that the title is good and marketable and will not render any opinions about the title.

2. The appraiser has provided a sketch in this appraisal report to show the approximate dimensions of the improvements. The sketch is included only to assist the reader in visualizing the property and understanding the appraiser's determination of its size.

3. The appraiser has examined the available flood maps that are provided by the Federal Emergency Management Agency (or other data sources) and has noted in this appraisal report whether any portion of the subject site is located in an identified Special Flood Hazard Area. Because the appraiser is not a surveyor, he or she makes no guarantees, express or implied, regarding this determination.

4. The appraiser will not give testimony or appear in court because he or she made an appraisal of the property in question, unless specific arrangements to do so have been made beforehand, or as otherwise required by law.

5. The appraiser has noted in this appraisal report any adverse conditions (such as needed repairs, deterioration, the presence of hazardous wastes, toxic substances, etc.) observed during the inspection of the subject property or that he or she became aware of during the research involved in performing this appraisal. Unless otherwise stated in this appraisal report, the appraiser has no knowledge of any hidden or unapparent physical deficiencies or adverse conditions of the property (such as, but not limited to, needed repairs, deterioration, the presence of hazardous wastes, toxic substances, adverse environmental conditions, etc.) that would make the property less valuable, and has assumed that there are no such conditions and makes no guarantees or warranties, express or implied. The appraiser will not be responsible for any such conditions that do exist or for any engineering or testing that might be required to discover whether such conditions exist. Because the appraiser is not an expert in the field of environmental hazards, this appraisal report must not be considered as an environmental assessment of the property.

6. The appraiser has based his or her appraisal report and valuation conclusion for an appraisal that is subject to satisfactory completion, repairs, or alterations on the assumption that the completion, repairs, or alterations of the subject property will be performed in a professional manner.

Uniform Residential Appraisal Report

File #

APPRAISER'S CERTIFICATION: The Appraiser certifies and agrees that:

1. I have, at a minimum, developed and reported this appraisal in accordance with the scope of work requirements stated in this appraisal report.

2. I performed a complete visual inspection of the interior and exterior areas of the subject property. I reported the condition of the improvements in factual, specific terms. I identified and reported the physical deficiencies that could affect the livability, soundness, or structural integrity of the property.

3. I performed this appraisal in accordance with the requirements of the Uniform Standards of Professional Appraisal Practice that were adopted and promulgated by the Appraisal Standards Board of The Appraisal Foundation and that were in place at the time this appraisal report was prepared.

4. I developed my opinion of the market value of the real property that is the subject of this report based on the sales comparison approach to value. I have adequate comparable market data to develop a reliable sales comparison approach for this appraisal assignment. I further certify that I considered the cost and income approaches to value but did not develop them, unless otherwise indicated in this report.

5. I researched, verified, analyzed, and reported on any current agreement for sale for the subject property, any offering for sale of the subject property in the twelve months prior to the effective date of this appraisal, and the prior sales of the subject property for a minimum of three years prior to the effective date of this appraisal, unless otherwise indicated in this report.

6. I researched, verified, analyzed, and reported on the prior sales of the comparable sales for a minimum of one year prior to the date of sale of the comparable sale, unless otherwise indicated in this report.

7. I selected and used comparable sales that are locationally, physically, and functionally the most similar to the subject property.

8. I have not used comparable sales that were the result of combining a land sale with the contract purchase price of a home that has been built or will be built on the land.

9. I have reported adjustments to the comparable sales that reflect the market's reaction to the differences between the subject property and the comparable sales.

10. I verified, from a disinterested source, all information in this report that was provided by parties who have a financial interest in the sale or financing of the subject property.

11. I have knowledge and experience in appraising this type of property in this market area.

12. I am aware of, and have access to, the necessary and appropriate public and private data sources, such as multiple listing services, tax assessment records, public land records and other such data sources for the area in which the property is located.

13. I obtained the information, estimates, and opinions furnished by other parties and expressed in this appraisal report from reliable sources that I believe to be true and correct.

14. I have taken into consideration the factors that have an impact on value with respect to the subject neighborhood, subject property, and the proximity of the subject property to adverse influences in the development of my opinion of market value. I have noted in this appraisal report any adverse conditions (such as, but not limited to, needed repairs, deterioration, the presence of hazardous wastes, toxic substances, adverse environmental conditions, etc.) observed during the inspection of the subject property or that I became aware of during the research involved in performing this appraisal. I have considered these adverse conditions in my analysis of the property value, and have reported on the effect of the conditions on the value and marketability of the subject property.

15. I have not knowingly withheld any significant information from this appraisal report and, to the best of my knowledge, all statements and information in this appraisal report are true and correct.

16. I stated in this appraisal report my own personal, unbiased, and professional analysis, opinions, and conclusions, which are subject only to the assumptions and limiting conditions in this appraisal report.

17. I have no present or prospective interest in the property that is the subject of this report, and I have no present or prospective personal interest or bias with respect to the participants in the transaction. I did not base, either partially or completely, my analysis and/or opinion of market value in this appraisal report on the race, color, religion, sex, age, marital status, handicap, familial status, or national origin of either the prospective owners or occupants of the subject property or of the present owners or occupants of the properties in the vicinity of the subject property or on any other basis prohibited by law.

18. My employment and/or compensation for performing this appraisal or any future or anticipated appraisals was not conditioned on any agreement or understanding, written or otherwise, that I would report (or present analysis supporting) a predetermined specific value, a predetermined minimum value, a range or direction in value, a value that favors the cause of any party, or the attainment of a specific result or occurrence of a specific subsequent event (such as approval of a pending mortgage loan application).

19. I personally prepared all conclusions and opinions about the real estate that were set forth in this appraisal report. If I relied on significant real property appraisal assistance from any individual or individuals in the performance of this appraisal or the preparation of this appraisal report, I have named such individual(s) and disclosed the specific tasks performed in this appraisal report. I certify that any individual so named is qualified to perform the tasks. I have not authorized anyone to make a change to any item in this appraisal report; therefore, any change made to this appraisal is unauthorized and I will take no responsibility for it.

20. I identified the lender/client in this appraisal report who is the individual, organization, or agent for the organization that ordered and will receive this appraisal report.

Uniform Residential Appraisal Report

File #

21. The lender/client may disclose or distribute this appraisal report to: the borrower; another lender at the request of the borrower; the mortgagee or its successors and assigns; mortgage insurers; government sponsored enterprises; other secondary market participants; data collection or reporting services; professional appraisal organizations; any department, agency, or instrumentality of the United States; and any state, the District of Columbia, or other jurisdictions; without having to obtain the appraiser's or supervisory appraiser's (if applicable) consent. Such consent must be obtained before this appraisal report may be disclosed or distributed to any other party (including, but not limited to, the public through advertising, public relations, news, sales, or other media).

22. I am aware that any disclosure or distribution of this appraisal report by me or the lender/client may be subject to certain laws and regulations. Further, I am also subject to the provisions of the Uniform Standards of Professional Appraisal Practice that pertain to disclosure or distribution by me.

23. The borrower, another lender at the request of the borrower, the mortgagee or its successors and assigns, mortgage insurers, government sponsored enterprises, and other secondary market participants may rely on this appraisal report as part of any mortgage finance transaction that involves any one or more of these parties.

24. If this appraisal report was transmitted as an "electronic record" containing my "electronic signature," as those terms are defined in applicable federal and/or state laws (excluding audio and video recordings), or a facsimile transmission of this appraisal report containing a copy or representation of my signature, the appraisal report shall be as effective, enforceable and valid as if a paper version of this appraisal report were delivered containing my original hand written signature.

25. Any intentional or negligent misrepresentation(s) contained in this appraisal report may result in civil liability and/or criminal penalties including, but not limited to, fine or imprisonment or both under the provisions of Title 18, United States Code, Section 1001, et seq., or similar state laws.

SUPERVISORY APPRAISER'S CERTIFICATION: The Supervisory Appraiser certifies and agrees that:

1. I directly supervised the appraiser for this appraisal assignment, have read the appraisal report, and agree with the appraiser's analysis, opinions, statements, conclusions, and the appraiser's certification.

2. I accept full responsibility for the contents of this appraisal report including, but not limited to, the appraiser's analysis, opinions, statements, conclusions, and the appraiser's certification.

3. The appraiser identified in this appraisal report is either a sub-contractor or an employee of the supervisory appraiser (or the appraisal firm), is qualified to perform this appraisal, and is acceptable to perform this appraisal under the applicable state law.

4. This appraisal report complies with the Uniform Standards of Professional Appraisal Practice that were adopted and promulgated by the Appraisal Standards Board of The Appraisal Foundation and that were in place at the time this appraisal report was prepared.

5. If this appraisal report was transmitted as an "electronic record" containing my "electronic signature," as those terms are defined in applicable federal and/or state laws (excluding audio and video recordings), or a facsimile transmission of this appraisal report containing a copy or representation of my signature, the appraisal report shall be as effective, enforceable and valid as if a paper version of this appraisal report were delivered containing my original hand written signature.

APPRAISER

Signature ____________________
Name ____________________
Company Name ____________________
Company Address ____________________
____
Telephone Number ____________________
Email Address ____________________
Date of Signature and Report ____________________
Effective Date of Appraisal ____________________
State Certification # ____________________
or State License # ____________________
or Other (describe) ____________ State # ____________
State ____________________
Expiration Date of Certification or License ____________________

ADDRESS OF PROPERTY APPRAISED

____
____

APPRAISED VALUE OF SUBJECT PROPERTY $ ____________

LENDER/CLIENT

Name ____________________
Company Name ____________________
Company Address ____________________
____
Email Address ____________________

SUPERVISORY APPRAISER (ONLY IF REQUIRED)

Signature ____________________
Name ____________________
Company Name ____________________
Company Address ____________________
____
Telephone Number ____________________
Email Address ____________________
Date of Signature ____________________
State Certification # ____________________
or State License # ____________________
State ____________________
Expiration Date of Certification or License ____________________

SUBJECT PROPERTY

- ☐ Did not inspect subject property
- ☐ Did inspect exterior of subject property from street
  Date of Inspection ____________________
- ☐ Did inspect interior and exterior of subject property
  Date of Inspection ____________________

COMPARABLE SALES

- ☐ Did not inspect exterior of comparable sales from street
- ☐ Did inspect exterior of comparable sales from street
  Date of Inspection ____________________

1. A closing is scheduled for the first Tuesday of the month. Before the closing can occur, the closing agent
   a. must make certain that the transfer of servicing disclosure form is signed by the lender, borrower, and closing agent.
   b. must provide the HUD-1 Settlement Statement to the buyer, if requested.
   c. is required to provide the good faith estimate of costs to the borrower one business day before closing.
   d. is responsible for providing the *Homeownership and You* brochure to the borrower.

2. A borrower has agreed to pay four discount points on a loan of $325,000 at 6.125 percent. The cost of the points will be
   a. 10.125 percent.
   b. $4,000.
   c. $7,250.
   d. $13,000.

3. When a borrower signs the anti-coercion statement, the borrower is acknowledging that
   a. he or she has not been forced to accept a high interest rate.
   b. the provisions of the loan do not violate the Florida Fair Lending Act.
   c. the lender is not making a subprime loan.
   d. the buyer chose his or her insurance.

4. A person who has *control* of a business
   a. largely influences decisions that affect the business.
   b. largely fulfills job requirements.
   c. makes decisions that affect the business.
   d. requires licensure.

5. Broker Bob has collected a $300 fee for an appraisal from a loan applicant. Regarding this fee,
   a. the closing agent will forward it to the appraiser at the time of closing.
   b. Bob must deposit it into a segregated account within seven business days.
   c. Bob may hold the check until the underwriter notifies him that the loan has been approved.
   d. the fee must be deposited into a segregated account within ten business days.

6. Ron Johnson makes mortgage loans but under the terms of his license cannot service the loans for more than four months. The type of license Ron Johnson holds is as a
   a. mortgage broker.
   b. mortgage lender.
   c. mortgage brokerage business.
   d. correspondent lender.

7. Loan applicants are considered self-employed if they own what percentage of a business that provides their income?
   a. At least 10 percent
   b. At least 25 percent
   c. At least 50 percent
   d. A percentage stipulated by the mortgage lender

8. A borrower has made enough payments on his $200,000 mortgage loan so that the mortgage insurance is automatically canceled. The balance on this mortgage is
   a. $160,000.
   b. $170,000.
   c. $168,000.
   d. $156,000.

9. A borrower has arranged for a property she is buying to be appraised. The borrower can expect to pay the appraiser
   a. a commission.
   b. either a fee or a commission, depending on the appraiser's contract.
   c. a fee.
   d. unless the lender declines to fund the loan.

10. FICO stands for
    a. Federal Insurance Corporation.
    b. Florida Insurance Corporation.
    c. Fair Isaac Corporation.
    d. First International Credit Organization.

11. The amount of time the borrower has to find financing is usually specified on the
    a. Truth-in-Lending disclosure form.
    b. sales contract.
    c. good faith estimate.
    d. mortgage brokerage agreement.

12. In order for a VA loan to be approved by a lender, the VA will require
    a. a Certificate of Reasonable Value.
    b. a VA or FHA appraisal.
    c. veteran status.
    d. all of the above.

13. Bill's loan payment consists of $742.42 interest, $213.80 principal, $147 taxes, and $94.35 insurance. If Bill's payment is late, a penalty will be assessed against the
    a. principal only.
    b. interest only.
    c. principal and interest only.
    d. principal, interest, taxes, and insurance.

14. When the underwriter reviews an applicant's front-end ratio, the underwriter will need to know
    a. the applicant's total debts.
    b. the amount of the loan divided by the value of the property.
    c. the estimate of total closing costs.
    d. housing expenses.

15. When a revolving credit account fails to state a required minimum monthly payment, the underwriter will assume the monthly obligation is
    a. 1 percent of the balance.
    b. 5 percent of the balance.
    c. a minimum of $50.
    d. at least the amount of the monthly interest.

16. All Florida Mortgages has just discovered that the firm cannot meet the minimum net worth requirements. All Florida
    a. has seven days to comply with the requirements.
    b. must stop accepting loan applications until requirements are met.
    c. is out of the mortgage business until an investigation is completed.
    d. must meet the requirements within 30 days to maintain licensure.

17. Mr. Buyer has arranged a mortgage to buy a home from Mr. Seller. In this transaction, Mr. Buyer is the
    a. mortgagee.
    b. mortgagor.
    c. investor.
    d. grantor.

18. An ad for a mortgage offers an adjustable rate starting at 5.45 percent. The rate is based on the 11th District of the Federal Home Loan Bank rate. The part of this mortgage loan that cannot change is the
    a. principal payment.
    b. margin.
    c. interest payment.
    d. prime rate.

19. According to the FAR/BAR contract, a marketable title must be provided by the
    a. seller.
    b. buyer.
    c. lender.
    d. mortgage broker.

20. Escrowed funds must be refunded by loan servicers when the surplus reaches
    a. $25.
    b. $50.
    c. $100.
    d. $250.

21. Roger's offer to buy Maria's property with a loan from Ace Mortgage involves hypothecation. Hypothecation refers to
    a. the process of Roger applying for a loan.
    b. Ace Mortgage providing Roger with a good faith estimate.
    c. Roger pledging the property as security for a loan without giving up possession.
    d. Ace Mortgage agreeing to Roger placing a name on the mortgage that is not on the promissory note.

22. In Florida, the laws that determine who will hold title to a property purchased with a mortgage loan make Florida a
    a. lien theory state.
    b. title theory state.
    c. deed of trust state.
    d. contract for deed state.

23. In the event of a foreclosure, the priority in which the liens will be addressed is determined by
    a. the amount of the lien.
    b. the order in which the liens are signed.
    c. the time of recording.
    d. who records the lien.

24. Tom paid his $150,000 mortgage down to $125,000, then borrowed back $20,000 without reapplying to his mortgage lender. What kind of mortgage does Tom have?
    a. Term
    b. Package
    c. Exculpatory
    d. Open-end

25. Sally Anne has owner's title insurance on her property in Rolling Acres subdivision. If Sally sells her house, the title insurance
    a. will transfer to the new owner.
    b. will transfer back to the lender.
    c. can be transferred but only if it is paid in full.
    d. cannot be transferred.

26. A property that was appraised for $215,000 was later found to be worth $205,000. The ultimate responsibility for the appraisal lies with the
    a. buyer.
    b. seller.
    c. mortgage broker.
    d. lender.

27. Fannie Mae *cannot* purchase a mortgage on a
    a. second home at the beach.
    b. one- to four-unit residence located in a flood zone.
    c. doctor's office at the entrance to a subdivision.
    d. manufactured home in a subdivision for the elderly.

28. The AUS used by Fannie Mae is called
    a. Loan Prospector®.
    b. Desktop Underwriter®.
    c. Mortgage Calculator®.
    d. Loan Advantage®.

29. Mr. Lopez is closing on a home he purchased on August 27, but the closing for the home he is selling is not until October 10. In order for both closings to occur, Mr. Lopez will need a
    a. standby commitment.
    b. second mortgage.
    c. HELOC.
    d. bridge loan.

30. *Ad valorem* means
    a. added value.
    b. according to value.
    c. with value.
    d. assessed value.

31. An important distinction between VA and other types of financing is that VA loans are
    a. insured.
    b. partially guaranteed.
    c. partially insured.
    d. warranteed.

32. The commitment letter
    a. states the loan terms and the APR.
    b. is written by the broker to the borrower.
    c. is written by the borrower to the lender.
    d. states the loan terms without the APR.

33. The DFS has discovered that All-Purpose Mortgages, Inc. is using the good faith estimate in place of a mortgage brokerage agreement. This practice is
    a. legal.
    b. legal but only if All-Purpose fulfills the three-day notification requirements.
    c. illegal in any case.
    d. legal if the borrower agrees.

34. A question about a transaction regarding the statute of frauds has arisen. What would this question concern?
    a. Whether a contract is enforceable
    b. A prohibited practice regarding a high-cost home loan
    c. The good faith estimate of costs
    d. Usury

35. A completion reserve refers to
   a. withholding taxes on a real estate sale.
   b. a loan made on a house not yet completely constructed.
   c. money the lender holds to ensure full payment of the mortgage.
   d. escrowed taxes and insurance.

36. Mr. Buyer is considering the purchase of a newly constructed home using a subprime loan. Mr. Buyer should be aware that subprime loans
   a. usually have higher interest rates.
   b. are illegal in Florida.
   c. can be used for commercial, but not residential, properties.
   d. require high payments up front that drop after a certain level of equity is reached.

37. Under the laws of Florida, the homestead exemption
   a. can be applied to any property owned by a Florida resident.
   b. can be applied to a vacation home.
   c. is subtracted from the assessed value of a primary residence.
   d. is based on the market value of a primary residence.

38. RESPA requires that the HUD-1 form be used at closing
   a. except when the seller has no closing costs.
   b. except when the buyer has no closing costs.
   c. except when the buyer's down payment is greater than 20 percent.
   d. in all cases.

39. F.S. 494 directs licensees to make certain disclosures when a conflict of interest occurs. An example of a conflict of interest would be when a
   a. mortgage broker represents several lenders at the same time.
   b. lender denies a loan based on a borrower's default on another mortgage.
   c. mortgage broker and a borrower disagree about mortgage terms.
   d. mortgage broker owns more than 10 percent of a business that provides services to a borrower.

40. Larry is a salaried employee who works for Money Mortgages, Inc., a lender. Larry takes loan applications and assists in arranging appraisals, surveys, and WDO inspections. In this case, Larry
   a. needs a mortgage broker license.
   b. does not need a mortgage broker license.
   c. can be paid on commission.
   d. should not be taking loan applications.

41. The total gross adjustment an appraiser can make to a comparable property's sales price should not be greater than
   a. 10 percent.
   b. 15 percent.
   c. 25 percent.
   d. a figure set by the underwriter.

42. Jack is selling his home to Susan using a purchase-money mortgage. Under the terms of the mortgage, Jack will lend Susan $42,000 at 7.5 percent interest, to be paid biweekly. Under the terms of this agreement, Jack
    a. is acting as a lender and needs a license.
    b. needs a license only if he accepts a fee for services.
    c. does not need a license.
    d. does not live in Florida because purchase-money mortgages are illegal in Florida.

43. A buyer has a large amount of cash in his safe deposit box at the bank that he would like to use at closing. Under Fannie Mae guidelines,
    a. this would be acceptable because the money has been in a bank.
    b. the money can be used only if the seller consents.
    c. the money can be used only if it has been deposited in a bank account for at least 30 days.
    d. the buyer cannot use this cash.

44. The Department of Financial Services has learned that mortgage broker Wilson may be defrauding elderly borrowers with loans that violate the Florida Fair Lending Act. Under what conditions can the DFS investigate mortgage broker Wilson?
    a. Only if there is a formal complaint
    b. Only if he has violated state laws regarding mortgage lending
    c. Without a formal complaint being filed
    d. Only if he is a mortgage broker but not a lender or correspondent lender

45. Mr. Bradford, a principal representative for Edgar Mortgages, has been served with a subpoena duces tecum. This means that Mr. Bradford
    a. must stop making mortgage loans until the matter is resolved.
    b. has been summoned to testify in a trial.
    c. must appear and produce all records requested.
    d. is the person filing the lawsuit.

46. When a licensee is found guilty of a pattern of misconduct according to F.S. 494, the licensee has committed
    a. any violation of Florida mortgage lending law.
    b. three violations in one year.
    c. one violation in a three-year period.
    d. a total of three violations during one licensing period.

47. A mortgage lender that *cannot* meet the net worth requirements must report its situation to the DFS within
    a. 24 hours.
    b. one week.
    c. three business days.
    d. 48 hours.

48. A-1 Mortgages ran a series of newspaper ads promoting its unique loan products. According to F.S. 494, A-1 must keep samples of its advertising for at least
    a. six months after the ad appears.
    b. one year.
    c. two years.
    d. three years.

49. Regulation B concerns
    a. the true cost of borrowing funds.
    b. flood zones.
    c. access to credit.
    d. mortgage insurance.

50. What is the maximum fee a mortgage brokerage business can charge on a net loan of $6,200?
    a. $250
    b. $500
    c. $870
    d. $1,100

51. Mr. Byrd works as a real estate attorney. Occasionally his clients ask him to help them find mortgages to finance their purchases. Under what conditions would Mr. Byrd need a mortgage broker license?
    a. If he is regularly dealing in mortgages within his normal practice
    b. If he is acting as both the real estate broker and the mortgage broker
    c. If he is acting in a fiduciary capacity
    d. Under no circumstances because attorneys do not need a license to deal in mortgages

52. If a mortgage brokerage business fails to file the Principal Broker Designation Form within 30 days, the penalty will be
    a. a Notice of Noncompliance.
    b. a fine of $5,000.
    c. a suspension of license.
    d. all of the above.

53. Vera submitted her financial information to a lender in preparation for buying a property without identifying a specific property she wished to buy. Vera's submission
    a. qualifies as a mortgage loan application.
    b. does not qualify as a mortgage loan application.
    c. will not be considered by the lender without identification of a specific property.
    d. constitutes mortgage fraud.

54. The application fee for licensure as a mortgage brokerage business is
    a. $215.
    b. $315.
    c. $525.
    d. $425.

55. When a transaction is complete, Florida law requires that documents for each mortgage transaction be maintained for a period of at least
    a. 60 days.
    b. one year.
    c. three years.
    d. five years.

56. Many brokers regard Direct Endorsement status as desirable because Direct Endorsement allows
    a. a mortgage broker to offer a loan as soon as the application is completed.
    b. loan approval without requiring a survey or appraisal.
    c. the broker to sell loans directly to the secondary market.
    d. expedited underwriting.

57. When a mortgage brokerage business forwards the Quarterly Report Transmittal form to the DFS, the person who completes the form must list
    a. each mortgage application accepted by the broker.
    b. transactions performed by the lender.
    c. names of individuals who have done business with the brokerage firm during that period.
    d. all new or terminated associates of the brokerage firm.

58. Ms. Broker has just opened Log Cabin Mortgages. She will need to renew the company license
    a. annually.
    b. before September 1 of even-numbered years.
    c. before September 1 of odd-numbered years.
    d. two years after the date of Log Cabin's initial licensure.

59. A mortgage brokerage business would like to make a commitment to Paul and Sheila, first-time homebuyers. Paul and Sheila have good jobs, excellent credit history, and a large down payment. Given these considerations, the broker can make the commitment when the
    a. loan application is signed.
    b. loan application is approved.
    c. brokerage fee is paid.
    d. lender makes a commitment.

60. How often must transactions be entered in the transaction journal?
    a. Quarterly
    b. Daily
    c. Monthly
    d. Within seven days

61. The major purpose of the secondary market is to
    a. loan money to the primary market.
    b. loan money to borrowers.
    c. buy existing mortgages.
    d. act as mortgage brokers.

62. Mr. Vinh has arranged a loan that requires mortgage insurance. Mr. Vinh's loan is
    a. an FHA loan.
    b. a VA loan.
    c. either an FHA or a VA loan.
    d. either a VA or a conventional loan.

63. The primary beneficiary of the yield spread premium is the
    a. lender.
    b. borrower.
    c. secondary market.
    d. mortgage brokerage business.

64. A borrower and a lender have arranged a nonconforming loan for $779,500. Under current guidelines, the nonconforming nature of this loan means that it
    a. cannot be sold on the secondary market.
    b. cannot be bought by the GSEs.
    c. has a cloud on the title.
    d. has irregularities in the way it was granted.

65. The difference between an encroachment and an easement is that an encroachment is
    a. implied whereas an easement is authorized.
    b. a restriction on how a property is used whereas an easement is interest in another's property.
    c. a right or interest in another's property whereas an easement is public land.
    d. unauthorized use of a property whereas an easement is granted with the owner's permission.

66. Veronica would like to assume the mortgage on a house she just bought. Which clause in the mortgage contract will determine if Veronica can do this?
    a. Defeasance
    b. Exculpatory
    c. Open-end
    d. Alienation

67. The role of Ginnie Mae in the secondary market is to
    a. partially guarantee mortgages.
    b. insure mortgages.
    c. guarantee mortgage-backed securities.
    d. issue mortgage-backed securities.

68. When an underwriter determines a loan cannot be funded, the borrower must be notified within
    a. one week.
    b. two weeks.
    c. 30 days.
    d. 60 days.

69. Joe and Sharon would like to buy a home, but in the early years of their marriage, they filed for bankruptcy. According to Fannie Mae guidelines, how long after the bankruptcy would Joe and Sharon need to wait to have their loan application considered assuming there were no extenuating circumstances?
    a. One year
    b. Two years
    c. Three years
    d. Four years

70. The form of co-ownership that limits the number of co-owners is
    a. tenancy by the entireties.
    b. joint tenancy.
    c. tenants in common.
    d. community property.

71. Mortgage brokers
    a. bring borrowers and lenders together but do not loan money.
    b. bring borrowers and lenders together and sometimes loan money.
    c. can make loans for up to four months before selling them on the secondary market.
    d. sell their loans on the secondary market.

72. When a mortgage transaction involves warehousing, this refers to a
    a. mortgage broker using a short-term loan to fund a mortgage loan.
    b. lender packaging several loans together and selling them on the secondary market.
    c. lender providing loan servicing for a variety of other lenders.
    d. lender using a short-term loan from a bank to fund mortgage loans.

73. Acme Mortgage sold a number of loans with normal recourse on the secondary market. This means that
    a. Acme must repurchase the loan if the borrower defaults.
    b. Acme must repurchase the loan if the default is due to faulty underwriting.
    c. the buyer of the loan must take responsibility for the default.
    d. Acme is not required to repurchase the loan if the buyer defaults.

74. Pierre has signed a contract offering full price on a lakefront property in Orlando. He is paying $745,000 for the property with a $55,000 down payment. The contract indicates Pierre may be able to assume the seller's mortgage, but he will need another mortgage for at least $125,000 more. If Pierre cannot find financing,
    a. the contract is enforceable but Pierre will need to find another lender.
    b. the sales contract is voidable.
    c. Pierre's time limit for finding financing is extended five business days.
    d. Pierre can roll the additional $125,000 into the assumable mortgage.

75. In most transactions, the mortgagee's title insurance will be paid for by the
    a. lender.
    b. buyer.
    c. seller.
    d. broker.

76. A borrower obtains a mortgage for $325,500 at 6.75 percent for 15 years. The lender would like to get a return of 7.375 percent. How many points should the lender ask the borrower to pay?
    a. 0.625
    b. 7.375
    c. 5
    d. 3

77. Alice would like to use first-time homebuyer status in order to buy a house. To do this, the lender will need to confirm that Alice
    a. never owned a home.
    b. had no ownership interest in a home for at least three years.
    c. had no ownership interest in a home for at least four years.
    d. has been prequalified for a starter home.

78. An appraiser has been called to estimate the value of a townhouse located two blocks from a shopping center on a major highway. Most likely the appraiser will use which of the following to determine the value of the property?
    a. Income capitalization
    b. Lot and block
    c. Sales comparison
    d. Cost depreciation

79. Susie Smith received her mortgage broker license on May 15. With regard to her continuing education requirements, Susie
    a. will need to complete the CE requirements that same year if she received her license in an odd-numbered year.
    b. will not need to complete a CE course because she is exempt in her first licensing period.
    c. will need to complete the CE requirements that same year if she received her license in an even-numbered year.
    d. need only pay the renewal fee and not take the CE course.

80. As a wedding gift, Mr. Schwartz is buying and guaranteeing the financing on a condo for his daughter and her new husband. All three names will appear on the deed. Mr. Schwartz
    a. must also sign the promissory note.
    b. need not sign the promissory note if he, his daughter, and her husband become joint tenants on the property.
    c. need not sign the promissory note because his daughter and her husband are a tenancy by the entireties.
    d. cannot take title to the property under this arrangement.

81. The requirement that lenders provide borrowers with the CHARM booklet is part of
    a. TIL.
    b. RESPA.
    c. F.S. 494.
    d. HOEPA.

82. In order to avoid inactive status, a mortgage brokerage business must renew its license within
    a. 30 days of the expiration date.
    b. 60 days of the expiration date.
    c. six months of the expiration date.
    d. 90 days of the expiration date.

83. The clause in a mortgage contract that allows a borrower to avoid foreclosure by paying all expenses and overdue payments is called the
   a. exculpatory clause.
   b. open-end clause.
   c. right of redemption clause.
   d. defeasance clause.

84. Jason closed on a single-family home in Sebring on July 15. His first mortgage payment will be due
   a. August 1.
   b. August 15.
   c. September 1.
   d. 30 or 31 days after the mortgage is recorded.

85. Mrs. Alameda wants a mortgage in which taxes and insurance payments are not escrowed. With regard to escrowing tax and insurance payments, Fannie Mae would allow Mrs. Alameda's lender to
   a. make these payments each month.
   b. waive the requirement if the seller of the property agrees.
   c. waive the requirement but reinstate it if the borrower is not making the payments.
   d. determine withholding requirements because Fannie Mae regards escrowed payments as a matter between the borrower and lender only.

86. A wraparound mortgage can be a type of
   a. deed of trust.
   b. purchase-money mortgage.
   c. buy-down mortgage.
   d. deed-in-lieu mortgage.

87. Fred missed the second payment on his mortgage. What will most likely be the lender's response?
   a. Notify Fred of foreclosure
   b. Cancel Fred's mortgage
   c. Seek reimbursement through the mortgage insurance policy
   d. Accelerate Fred's payments

88. An example of abusive lending would be when a
   a. lender looks to a homeowner's equity rather than his or her income to repay a loan.
   b. borrower's loan allows interest rates to rise a certain percentage every year.
   c. lender accepts only interest payments so that a homeowner cannot build up equity in his or her home.
   d. mortgage has a prepayment penalty clause.

89. Richard can afford the monthly payment on a property, but he cannot afford the $35,000 down payment, nor can he qualify for a mortgage loan. Richard may still be able to buy the property if he can arrange a(n)
   a. wraparound mortgage.
   b. deed-in-lieu.
   c. deed of trust.
   d. open-end mortgage.

90. The mortgage department of First Bank has decided not to make loans on properties in a poor, crime-ridden area of the city. From a legal perspective, First Bank may be found guilty of
    a. violating the Florida Fair Lending Act.
    b. adverse action.
    c. violating Regulation Z.
    d. violating HMDA.

91. Matthew works as a short-order cook and earns $6.75 per hour. His job requires him to work 37.5 hours a week. What is his annual income?
    a. $12,632.50
    b. $12,150.00
    c. $13,162.50
    d. $12,656.25

92. What is the maximum fee a broker can charge on a net loan of $150,000?
    a. $15,000
    b. $10,000
    c. $8,500
    d. $15,250

93. Melissa bought a home by paying $35,000 as a down payment and by acquiring new financing for $172,000. What is her loan-to-value ratio?
    a. 80 percent
    b. 83 percent
    c. 66 percent
    d. 77 percent

94. Rick arranged a loan of $155,000 for 30 years at 6.75 percent interest. Monthly payments are $1,005.33. What is Rick's interest payment in the second month of the loan?
    a. $871.12
    b. $871.88
    c. $875.22
    d. $888.13

95. Colleen agrees to a 30-year mortgage for $140,000 at 7.25 percent with three points. What is the approximate yield to the lender on this loan?
    a. 7.55 percent
    b. 7.25 percent
    c. 7.625 percent
    d. 10.25 percent

96. Sharon's monthly housing expense is $850, she has car payments of $145, and student loan payments of $135. She earns $37,000 per year. What is her front-end ratio?
    a. 28 percent
    b. 31 percent
    c. 37 percent
    d. 41 percent

97. Rita bought a new home for $212,500. She made a down payment of $45,000 and financed the rest by assuming a mortgage for $15,000 and by arranging a new mortgage to cover the balance of the purchase price. In a typical real estate transaction, what are the total taxes owed by Rita?
   a. $2,378.75
   b. $586.25
   c. $835.00
   d. $891.25

98. If the tax rate is 12 mills, taxes on Jared's $450,500 home will be
   a. $540.60.
   b. $5,400.00.
   c. $5,455.00.
   d. $5,406.00.

99. Vicki Short sold her luxurious home on Lake Okechobee for $770,250. The buyer made a down payment of $212,500 and acquired new financing for the rest. Documentary stamp taxes on deed for this sale will be
   a. $5,392.10.
   b. $743.75.
   c. $1,952.13.
   d. $1,115.50.

100. If Claire makes a monthly payment of $155.24 principal, $658.22 interest, $78 taxes, and $65 insurance, and pays her conventional mortgage late, how much will her late fee be?
   a. $7.76
   b. $44.57
   c. $47.82
   d. $40.67

ANSWER KEY

ANSWERS TO CHAPTER QUIZZES

Chapter One

1. d
2. c
3. b
4. a
5. b
6. c
7. b
8. a
9. d
10. a
11. a
12. c
13. b
14. d
15. c
16. c
17. b
18. d
19. a
20. d
21. d
22. c
23. c
24. b

Chapter Two

1. a
2. d
3. b
4. b
5. a
6. d
7. a
8. c
9. c
10. d
11. c
12. c
13. a
14. b
15. d
16. d
17. b
18. b
19. d
20. c
21. c
22. d
23. d
24. c
25. b
26. b
27. d
28. d
29. b
30. a
31. b
32. d
33. d

Chapter Three

1. c
2. b
3. a
4. d
5. a
6. a
7. d
8. c
9. b
10. c
11. c
12. b
13. d
14. d
15. b
16. c
17. d
18. a
19. c
20. c
21. d
22. d
23. b
24. d
25. b
26. c

Chapter Four

1. d
2. d
3. d
4. a
5. c
6. c
7. d
8. c
9. b
10. a
11. d
12. a
13. c
14. b
15. c
16. b
17. b
18. a
19. c
20. a
21. c
22. a
23. b
24. c
25. a
26. d

Chapter Five

1. b
2. b
3. a
4. c
5. b
6. a
7. a

8. c
9. a
10. c
11. d
12. b
13. b
14. a
15. d
16. a
17. d
18. b
19. c
20. a

Chapter Six

1. d
2. c
3. c
4. c
5. a
6. b
7. a
8. c
9. b
10. c
11. a
12. d
13. b
14. d
15. c
16. c
17. a
18. b
19. d
20. b
21. b
22. a
23. b
24. c
25. b
26. d
27. c
28. d
29. c
30. b

Chapter Seven

1. a
2. c
3. c
4. d
5. b
6. b
7. c
8. d
9. b
10. d
11. b
12. d
13. c
14. a
15. a
16. b
17. c
18. b
19. b
20. a
21. b
22. c
23. b
24. d
25. b

Chapter Eight

1. a
2. d
3. b
4. d
5. d
6. d
7. d
8. b
9. a
10. a
11. b
12. a
13. c
14. c
15. c
16. b
17. a
18. c
19. c
20. c
21. c
22. a
23. c
24. b

Chapter Nine

1. a
2. d
3. d
4. b
5. b
6. c
7. d
8. c
9. b
10. d
11. c
12. b
13. c
14. b
15. d
16. d
17. c
18. a
19. a
20. c
21. b
22. d
23. b
24. a
25. d

Chapter Ten

1. b
2. a
3. a
4. d
5. b
6. c
7. c
8. c
9. c
10. a
11. d
12. a
13. b
14. d

Chapter Eleven

1. a
2. d
3. c
4. b
5. a
6. d
7. d
8. d
9. d
10. b
11. b
12. d
13. c
14. d
15. c
16. d
17. b
18. a
19. d
20. d
21. b
22. c
23. d
24. d
25. a
26. d
27. d
28. d
29. b
30. a
31. c
32. a
33. c
34. d
35. a
36. a
37. b
38. b
39. b

CHAPTER ELEVEN MATH SOLUTIONS

3. ($350,000 – $40,000) ÷ $350,000 = 89%

4. House value × 0.10 = $30,000
   $30,000 ÷ 0.10 = $300,000

5. ($105,000 + $2500) ÷ 10 = $10,750

6. ($125,000 – $35,000 – $65,000) × 0.002 = $50

7. $235,500 × 0.002 = $4,710

9. ($175,000 + $2,500) ÷ 11 = $16,136.36

10. ($275,000 × 0.0645) ÷ 12 = $1,478.13
    $1,729.15 – $1,478.13 = $251.03

11. $275,000 – $251.03 = $274,748.97
    $274,748.97 × 0.0645 = $17,721.31
    $17,721.31 ÷ 12 = $1,476.78
    $1,729.15 – $1,476.78 = $252.37

12. $975 ÷ 12 = $81.25

13. ($215.15 + $622) × 0.05 = $41.86

14. ($5,775 + $2,500) ÷ 11 = $752.27

18. $850 ÷ $2,500 = 0.34

19. ($850 + $225 + $125) ÷ $2,500 = 0.48

23. $1,200 ÷ 365 = $3.29
    $3.2876712 × 120 days = $394.52 debit

25. ($155,125 × 0.0725) ÷ 365 = $30.81
    $30.812501 × 9 days = $277.31

26. $675 ÷ (150 × $8.25) = 0.55

31. ($220,000 ÷ 100) × 0.70 = $1,540

32. ($220,000 – $45,000) ÷ 100 = $1,750
    $1,750 × 0.35 = $612.50

33. $20,000 × 0.002 = $40

36. $3,345 ÷ 365 = $9.16
    $9.1643835 × 152 days = $1,392.32

37. ($212,000 × 0.0675) ÷ 365 = $39.21 × 17 days = $666.57

38. ($182,300 ÷ 100) × 0.70 = $1,276.10

39. $2,125 × 0.97 = $2,061.25

ANSWERS TO PRACTICE EXAM

1. b
2. d
3. d
4. c
5. b
6. d
7. b
8. d
9. c
10. c
11. b
12. a
13. c
14. d
15. b
16. b
17. b
18. b
19. a
20. b
21. c
22. a
23. c
24. d
25. d
26. d
27. c
28. b
29. d
30. b
31. b
32. d
33. c
34. a
35. b
36. a
37. c
38. b
39. d
40. b
41. c
42. c
43. d
44. c
45. c
46. b
47. d
48. c
49. c
50. c
51. a
52. a
53. b
54. d
55. c
56. d
57. d
58. b
59. d
60. d
61. c
62. a
63. d
64. b
65. d
66. d
67. c
68. c
69. d
70. a
71. a
72. d
73. b
74. b
75. b
76. c
77. b
78. c
79. a
80. a
81. a
82. c
83. c
84. c
85. c
86. b
87. d
88. a
89. a
90. d
91. c
92. d
93. b
94. a
95. c
96. a
97. d
98. d
99. a
100. d

MATH SOLUTIONS—PRACTICE EXAM

2. $325,000 × 0.04 = $13,000

8. $200,000 × 0.78 = $156,000

50. ($6,200 + $2,500) ÷ 10 = $870

76. 7.375 – 6.75 = 0.625
    0.625 ÷ 0.125 = 5

91. $6.75 × 37.5 × 52 = $13,162.50

92. ($150,000 + $2,500) ÷ 10 = $15,250

93. $172,000 ÷ ($172,000 + $35,000) = 0.83

94. ($155,000 × 0.0675) ÷ 12 = $871.88
$1,005.33 – $871.88 = $133.45
$155,000 – $133.45 = $154,866.55
($154,866.55 × 0.0675) ÷ 12 = $871.12

95. 7.25 + 0.375 = 7.625

96. $850 ÷ ($37,000 ÷ 12) = 0.28

97. $212,500 - $45,000 = $167,500
($167,500 ÷ 100) × 0.35 = $586.25
$167,500 – $15,000 = $152,500
$152,500 × 0.002 = $305
$586.25 + $305 = $891.25

98. $450,500 × 0.012 = $5,406

99. Round $770,250 to $770,300. ($770,300 ÷ 100) × 0.70 = $5,392.10

100. ($155.24 + $658.22) × 0.05 = $40.67

GLOSSARY

A

abstract of title Written summary of all recorded documents affecting the title of real property.

acceleration clause Requires that entire balance of the mortgage be paid if the borrower defaults.

acknowledgment Legal recognition that execution of an act is voluntary and signature is genuine.

act as a mortgage broker For compensation or gain, or in the expectation of compensation or gain, either directly or indirectly, accepting or offering to accept an application for a mortgage loan, soliciting or offering to solicit a mortgage loan on behalf of a borrower, negotiating or offering to negotiate the terms or conditions of a mortgage loan on behalf of a lender, or negotiating or offering to negotiate the sale of an existing mortgage loan to a noninstitutional investor.

actual age Age based on when a property was built.

actual notice Notice given when the owner acts in the role of owner by physically possessing and maintaining property, paying taxes, preventing trespass, etc.

adjustable-rate mortgage (ARM) A mortgage in which the lender can adjust the interest rate charge on a loan to reflect economic conditions.

adjustable-rate mortgage (convertible) An ARM with the option to convert to a fixed-rate mortgage.

adjustment cap The maximum amount a loan's interest rate can increase.

ad valorem According to value.

ad valorem taxes Taxes based on the value of real property.

adverse action Denial of an individual's loan application.

alienation clause Allows lender to call loan due and payable if the borrower sells the property.

Alt-A program Low documentation loan program.

Amendment I An amendment approved by Florida voters in 2008 that increased the homestead exemption on residential property, allowed partial transfer of the Save Our Homes benefit to another home, and limited future assessments on non-homesteaded property.

amortization (positive) The systematic payment of a loan and its interest over a specified period of time.

annual percentage rate (APR) The true annual cost of borrowing funds, including interest, mortgage insurance premiums, origination fees, discount points, and other costs.

anti-coercion statement A form signed by the borrower at closing stating that the lender did not require the borrower to obtain hazard or property insurance from a particular insurance company.

appraisal An opinion of a property's value.

arbitration clause A method of dispute resolution where a third party renders a binding decision.

arrears The end of a period when a payment is due.

assessed value Value placed on real property for purposes of taxation.

assets Things of value.

assignee Person who has received rights assigned by another.

assignment of mortgage Transfer or selling of a mortgage.

assignor Person who has assigned his or her rights to another.

associate A person who is required to be licensed as a mortgage broker and is employed by or acting as an independent contractor or a mortgage brokerage business or a person acting as an independent contractor of a mortgage lender or correspondent mortgage lender.

assumption of mortgage Agreement to pay mortgage debt incurred by another person.

attorney-in-fact Person who holds power of attorney.

automated underwriting system Computer program that analyzes an individual's loan application with information that exists in a database of loan portfolios to determine risk and fit with lender's criteria.

B

back-end ratio An applicant's total monthly expenses divided by gross monthly income.

balance sheet Statement showing an individual's assets, liabilities, and net worth as of a specific date.

balloon mortgage A mortgage that requires a lump sum payment due at the end of a specified period.

balloon payment A lump-sum payment due at the end of a specified period.

bankruptcy Situation in which an individual has surrendered all assets in order to pay debts and is relieved of further liability.

bargain and sale deed Transfers title but allows only limited warranty regarding the title.

basis point A unit of measurement used to describe yield; equal to 1/100th of 1 percent.

biennial Happening every two years.

biweekly mortgage Mortgage requiring half the monthly payment every other week for an annual total of 13 full payments rather than 12.

blanket mortgage A mortgage that covers more than one property.

branch broker Person in charge of any branch office.

bridge mortgage loan According to the Florida Fair Lending Act, a loan with a maturity of less than 18 months that requires only the payment of interest.

brokerage fees Total compensation paid for services performed by the mortgage broker on behalf of either the borrower or lender.

build-up Percentage of parcels that have been improved.

bundle of rights Rights that come with property ownership.

business day Any calendar day except Sunday or a legal holiday.

buydown mortgage Mortgage where buyer or seller of a property pays the lender an up-front fee in order to lower the interest rate on the mortgage loan.

C

capital Cash used to generate a return.

capitalization rate A number that reflects an investor's total rate of return on a property.

CAPS (payment caps) The highest level to which an interest rate can rise either during an adjustment period or over the life of the loan.

cash flow Cash receipts minus cash payouts.

cash-out refinance Refinance in which borrower uses new loan to pay off first loan plus new loan closing costs and borrower is entitled to take any remaining cash as he or she chooses.

Certificate of Eligibility Issued by the Department of Veterans Affairs to persons who want to apply for a VA loan.

Certificate of Reasonable Value (CRV) An appraisal of the value of a property by a VA appraiser.

certified appraisal An appraisal by a licensed appraiser; required in all federally related loan transactions.

chattel mortgage A mortgage that uses personal property as security for a loan.

closing The process in which a seller delivers title to real property to the buyer and the buyer assumes responsibility for repaying the lender for the mortgage loan.

closing agent Individual with responsibility for making sure all documents are ready for the closing, ensuring the accuracy of all documents, and collecting and disbursing all funds associated with the transaction.

closing costs Expenses paid at the time ownership of a property is transferred from seller to buyer or the mortgage is refinanced.

cloud on the title A question about the title that may limit the right of the property owner to sell the property.

combined loan-to-value (CLTV) Total value of all loans divided by the value of the property.

commitment The terms under which a lender will make a loan to a borrower.

commitment fee Fee charged by lender for a future commitment of funds.

commitment letter A written statement of the terms under which a lender will make a loan to a borrower.

comparables Recently sold properties in the same market area with similar characteristics as the subject property used for comparison in a sales comparison appraisal.

competence of parties Requirement that parties to a contract be of legal age and not suffering from mental impairment.

completion escrow Money put in escrow to cover postponed or unfinished improvements on a newly constructed home.

conflict of interest Situation that occurs when a licensee or the licensee's relative provides additional products or services to the borrower, owns 10 percent or more of the firm that provides the additional products or services, or is an officer of a firm providing services.

conforming loan A loan that meets all the requirements of Fannie Mae and Freddie Mac.

consideration Something of value given by one party to another in a contract.

constructive notice Legal transaction recorded in the public records.

contract A promise to perform some act.

contract for deed Arrangement where a buyer takes possession of a property but the seller retains title until a certain amount of the purchase price is paid.

controlling interest Power to direct the management or policies of a company.

control person A person who has the power to direct the management or policies of a company.

conventional mortgage loan A loan that is not insured or guaranteed by a government agency.

conveyance An instrument such as a deed that transfers title from one person to another.

correspondent mortgage lender A lender that may make mortgage loans but can service a mortgage loan for no longer than four months after the date the mortgage loan was made or acquired.

cosigner A person who accepts responsibility for payment of a debt along with another person.

cost depreciation An approach to valuing property where appraisers estimate the cost of reproducing an already existing property.

credit score A single number derived from a large mathematical model that rates an individual's likelihood of honoring a new debt obligation.

credit score repositories The agencies that keep credit scores on consumers.

D

debt Money owed.

debt service The periodic payment of principal and interest on a loan.

debt-to-income ratio Total monthly obligations divided by total monthly income.

deed An instrument (document) that transfers ownership right and title of a property from one party to another.

deed-in-lieu of foreclosure Situation where a borrower avoids foreclosure by surrendering title to the property to the lender, thereby giving up all interests in the property.

deed of trust Situation where a trustee holds the title to a property on behalf of a lender.

deed restrictions Clause in a deed that controls certain future use of a property.

default Occurs when a property owner fails to make payments on a mortgage or live up to some aspect of the mortgage agreement.

defeasance clause Gives assurance that the lender will release the borrower from the pledge of his or her property upon payment of all monies owed to the lender.

deficiency judgment A judgment against a borrower when a foreclosure sale fails to produce enough funds to pay the mortgage in full.

depreciation A loss in value.

Desktop Underwriter® The automated underwriting system used by Fannie Mae to evaluate mortgage applications.

Direct Endorsement underwriting The program where a lender is eligible to fund an FHA or VA loan directly.

direct investor funding The process of investors or lenders working directly with borrowers.

discount points Fees charged by lenders at closing to borrowers to lower the interest rates and increase the yield on their loans.

disintermediation The flow of funds out of savings institutions resulting in a decrease in funds available for real estate financing.

documentary stamp tax on deeds A Florida state tax charged on the total purchase price of real property.

documentary stamp tax on notes A Florida state tax charged on the value of all mortgages recorded.

down payment The part of the purchase price paid by borrower.

due-on-sale clause Requires that as soon as a borrower sells a property, proceeds from that sale will be used to pay off the balance of the mortgage. Same as alienation or nonassumption clause.

DVA Department of Veteran Affairs.

E

easement A right to use or interest in property that belongs to another.

effective age Age of property considering actual depreciation.

egress The right to exit a property; required for a property to be marketable.

eminent domain The right of government to acquire property for public use.

employee A natural person engaged in the service of another for salary or wages and subject to withholding, FICA, and other lawful deductions, and under the control of an employer.

encroachment The unauthorized use of another's property.

encumbrance A question about the title that may impair the right of the property owner to sell the property; can be physical or financial in nature.

enforceable contract A contract made by competent parties, with mutual assent, legal purpose, in writing and signed, and offering consideration.

Equal Credit Opportunity Act (ECOA) Legislation designed to ensure that firms that extend credit to consumers do so fairly.

equitable ownership Ownership of a property by someone who does not hold title.

equity The value of a property that exceeds the amount of the mortgage.

escheat Reversion of property to the state when the owner dies without a will and no known heirs.

escrow A special account for accumulating borrower's funds—such as property taxes—until payment date.

escrow account An account for accumulating a borrower's payments; also known as an impound account in some states.

estate for years Tenancy of a property using a written lease for a specified period of time that does not convey title.

estoppel letter A statement of any outstanding balances due at the time of a real estate closing.

exculpatory clause Releases a borrower from personal responsibility for repaying a loan.

external depreciation Loss in value due to factors beyond the property lines.

F

Fair and Accurate Credit Transactions Act (FACT Act) Law requiring credit reporting agency disclosures and prompt action to improve accuracy and confidentiality of credit information.

Fair Credit Reporting Act (FCRA) Legislation that regulates what credit reporting agencies may do with the information they have about individuals.

Fair Isaac Corporation (FICO) Company that provides credit scoring models that predict borrower behavior.

Fannie Mae Federal National Mortgage Association.

fee simple The most complete type of property ownership, allowing the owner to use or dispose of the property however he or she chooses.

felony A serious legal offense; first-degree felonies are the most serious; third-degree less so.

FEMA Federal Emergency Management Agency.

FHA Federal Housing Administration.

FHLMC Federal Home Loan Mortgage Company; Freddie Mac.

FICO Acronym for Fair Isaac Corporation, the company that provides credit scoring models.

financing concessions (IPC related) Contributions from an interested party (IPC) to a mortgage transaction used to reduce the interest rate, lower the borrower's monthly payment, or cover other expenses.

fixed-rate mortgage Mortgage where the interest rate does not change and borrowers repay a fixed amount each month for the term of the loan.

Flexible 97® A loan that requires a 3 percent down payment and contribution toward closing costs.

Flexible 100® A no down payment loan that requires the borrower to pay 3 percent of the purchase price toward closing costs.

flood certification fee The cost of the assessment to determine if a property lies in a flood zone.

flood insurance Insurance on properties that lie within a FEMA-designated flood zone.

flood zone An area designated by FEMA as having a 1 percent or greater flood risk in any given year.

Florida Fair Lending Act A Florida law passed in 2002 intended to reduce incidents of abusive mortgage lending.

Florida Mortgage Brokerage and Lending Act Title XXXIII, Chapter 494 of the Florida Statutes.

FmHA Farmer's Home Administration, now known as the Rural Housing Service of the Department of Agriculture.

FNMA Federal National Mortgage Association; Fannie Mae.

forbearance The practice of not foreclosing on a mortgage in default in the expectation that the borrower will resume payments.

foreclosure The process of selling real property pledged as security for a debt in order to repay the debt, usually triggered by nonpayment of the debt or violation of the mortgage contract.

Freddie Mac Federal Home Loan Mortgage Association.

freehold estate A tenancy without an expiration date.

front-end ratio An applicant's monthly housing expense divided by gross monthly income.

FTC Federal Trade Commission.

functional depreciation Loss in value due to changing consumer preferences.

funding fee An up-front charge to the borrower for a VA loan.

G

general warranty deed Guarantees that the grantor (seller) can convey clear title and that the grantor will forever help defend the buyer's right to clear title.

gift letter Letter required by lender when a loan applicant plans to use a gift to help purchase a home.

Ginnie Mae security A security that is guaranteed by Ginnie Mae based on pools of FHA, VA, and FmHA mortgages.

GNMA Government National Mortgage Association; Ginnie Mae.

good faith estimate Estimate of total closing costs and amount of cash needed for closing.

government survey system System for locating property that uses certain latitudes and longitudes known as principal meridians and base lines.

graduated payment mortgage (GPM) Mortgage that allows borrowers to start at a lower payment in the first years of a loan; same as GEM.

grantee The party who receives title in a real estate closing.

grantor The party transferring title in a real estate closing.

gross loan The total amount of a loan including certain lender and mortgage broker fees.

growing equity mortgage (GEM) A mortgage that allows borrowers to start at a lower payment in the first years of a loan; same as GPM.

guarantor Person who guarantees an obligation.

H

hazard insurance Insurance purchased by the borrower to protect a property from loss from fire or other damage.

HELOC Home equity line of credit.

high-cost home loan A loan with an interest rate that is more than ten percentage points above the yield on Treasury securities or points and fees that exceed the greater of 8 percent of the loan amount or $400.

highest and best use The most profitable, physically possible, legal use of real property.

home equity loan An open-ended adjustable-rate loan that operates as a line of credit.

Home Mortgage Disclosure Act (HMDA) Federal legislation that collects demographic information from loan applications to determine if needs of the community are being met.

Home Ownership and Equity Protection Act (HOEPA) Act that protects consumers from unfair lending practices on subprime loans.

Homeowners Protection Act Act that allows homeowners to cancel their private mortgage insurance policy when the mortgage balance reaches 80 percent of the property's value.

homestead tax exemption A Florida tax law that allows registered homeowners to deduct a standard amount from their assessed value to reduce their taxable value.

housing expense ratio (HER) Monthly housing expense divided by monthly income; also known as the front-end ratio.

HUD Department of Housing and Urban Development.

HUD-1 Settlement Statement The uniform settlement statement required by the Real Estate Settlement Procedures Act (RESPA).

hypothecation To pledge property as security for a debt without giving up possession of the property.

I

income capitalization Approach to valuing properties that create a revenue stream to the owner.

independent contractor A person who contracts with another to perform a service where this person is not directed or controlled by the other person or is required to maintain separate records regarding his or her contract for services in respect to, but not limited to, accounting and taxes.

index Some general economic measure of the cost of borrowing funds.

ingress The right to enter a property; required for a property to be marketable.

institutional investor A state or national bank, state or federal savings and loan association or savings bank, real estate investment trust, insurance company, real estate company, accredited investor, business, or other business entity that invests in mortgage loans, including a secondary mortgage market institution.

intangible tax on new mortgages A Florida tax paid on new mortgages.

interest A cost associated with borrowing money.

interested party contributions Contributions to a transaction made by an interested party to lower certain costs to the borrower.

intermediation Consolidation of small accounts to make large investments.

investor funding The process of investors or lenders working directly with borrowers.

involuntary lien A claim against real property without the consent of the owner.

J

joint and several liability Situation in which a party who loses a judgment can pursue other parties for a contribution toward their share of the liability.

joint tenancy Estate where owners have undivided possession but equal interest in the property.

judgment Court ruling in favor of one party or another.

judgment lien A lien secured by a judgment.

junior mortgage A mortgage that is subordinate to another.

L

late fee Fee assessed if a mortgage payment is late.

leasehold estate An estate with a definite period of duration.

legal description A system for describing the exact location of a property.

legal form Requirement that contracts have a legal purpose to be enforceable.

legal purpose Requirement that real estate contracts must be in writing and signed to be enforceable.

lender's title insurance policy Policy that protects the lender by guaranteeing the amount of the mortgage loan.

leverage Use of borrowed money to increase return on an investment.

liabilities Debts or obligations.

lien A claim against a property.

lien theory Legal doctrine where title to a property stays with the borrower and the mortgage given to the lender constitutes a lien on the property.

life estate Estate owned by an individual during his or her lifetime that reverts to the original owner or a designated third party known as a remainderman upon the death of the individual.

limited cash-out refinance Allows borrower to pay off existing loans, cover closing costs, and take the lower of $2,000 or 2 percent of the loan amount in cash.

lis pendens Pending legal action.

loan closing The process by which a lender offers and a borrower accepts a loan.

loan commitment A statement by the lender setting forth the terms and conditions by which the lender is willing to make a mortgage.

loan originator Being employed by a mortgage lender or correspondent mortgage lender for compensation or gain to negotiate or offer to negotiate the making of a mortgage loan.

Loan Prospector® Freddie Mac's automated underwriting system.

loan servicing Collecting a borrower's monthly payments and disbursing payments for taxes and insurance, handling mailings to parties with an interest in the loan, monitoring liens or encumbrances on a property, making certain that a homeowner has sufficient insurance to protect the lender's interest, and handling a foreclosure when necessary.

loan-to-value ratio (LTV) Calculated by dividing the loan amount by the price or appraised value of a property.

lock-in agreement A promise on the part of a lender that the mortgage loan will carry a specific interest rate, regardless of the prevailing rates when the loan is closed.

loss payable clause A clause in an insurance policy authorizing payment to someone other than the insured.

lot and block description The most common method of describing property when parcel is part of an approved subdivision.

M

margin Amount that covers the expenses of the lender and provides a profit.

marketability of title Evidence that a property can be conveyed without questions regarding the title.

marketing time Average time a property stays on the market.

market value The most likely price based on informed buyers and sellers acting in their own best interests and a reasonable marketing period.

mechanic's lien A lien against a property filed by a person who has improved the property.

metes-and-bounds description A method used by surveyors to locate property.

mill One-thousandth of one dollar.

millage rate A rate used by government agencies to determine property taxes.

mortgage The pledge of real property as security for a loan.

mortgage-backed securities (MBSs) Debt instruments similar to bonds secured by a pool of mortgages.

mortgage banker Lender who may fund and service the loans he or she originates after the loan transaction has closed.

mortgage broker An individual who connects potential borrowers with potential lenders.

mortgage brokerage fee Compensation paid for services performed by a mortgage broker.

mortgagee The party who grants a loan in exchange for a mortgage.

mortgagee clause A clause in an insurance policy stating that the mortgage will be paid.

mortgage contract Contract pledging real property as security for a loan.

mortgage fraud Misstatement or misrepresentation regarding a mortgage transaction that results in harm to another.

mortgage insurance premium (MIP) Payment required of the borrower to fund the federal government's insurance program on FHA loans.

mortgage lender Individual who may fund the loans he or she originates and may continue to service the loan after the transaction has closed.

mortgage lending The process by which individuals or groups who want to buy property borrow money from other individuals or institutions by offering the property as security for the loan.

mortgage loan application Submission of financial information in anticipation of a credit decision.

mortgage loan officer An individual who works for a bank or other financial institution; may or may not hold a mortgage broker license.

mortgagor The party who offers a mortgage in exchange for a loan.

mutual assent The willingness of parties to enter into a contract.

N

National Flood Insurance Act (NFIA) Created an insurance program through which homebuyers could purchase insurance against damage from floods in special flood hazard areas.

natural person An individual; not a corporation, general partnership, limited partnership, or other legal entity.

negative amortization Situation where monthly payments are not sufficient to cover interest payment.

net loan The actual amount of funds provided by the lender at closing.

net worth Total assets minus total liabilities.

net yield Combination of stated interest rate and discount points that creates the investor's annual interest earned as a percent of the net loan amount provided.

nonassumption clause Requires that the lender be paid as soon as the property is sold.

nonconforming loans Loans that do not meet Fannie Mae or Freddie Mac guidelines with regard to underwriting or appraising or exceed the conforming loan limit set by Congress.

note The borrower's personal promise to repay the debt.

notice of noncompliance Notification that a person has violated an administrative rule that is classified as a minor offense.

novation Substitution of a new party on an existing obligation.

O

obsolescence A loss in value due to design, the age of the property or its fixtures, changes in consumer tastes, or other factors.

open-end clause Allows a borrower to reborrow any principal already repaid.

open-end mortgage Mortgage that gives the borrower the right to borrow back any principal already paid.

opinion of value An estimate of what a property is worth not performed by a certified appraiser.

origination fee Paid by the borrower to the lender as an additional up-front fee at loan closing.

Office of Thrift Supervision Federal agency that oversees savings institutions and Freddie Mac.

overimprovement Occurs when the cost of an improvement is greater than the value it adds.

owner's title insurance policy Issued for the amount of the purchase price and cannot be transferred.

P

package mortgage A mortgage that covers both real and personal property.

partial-release clause Clause that allows mortgagor to sell part of a mortgaged property and pay part of the mortgage without requiring payment in full.

participation An aspect of the secondary market that offers investors the opportunity to have different levels of ownership of mortgages.

participation certificates Securities backed by mortgages sold to investors.

participation loan A mortgage originated by two or more lenders.

pattern of misconduct Three or more violations of the Florida Mortgage Brokerage and Lending Act and Regulations or the Rules Regulating Mortgage Brokerage during a one-year period or any criminal conviction for violating these laws.

payment abatement A incentive to the buyer, usually provided by a party interested in the transaction.

personal property Property that is not real property.

physical depreciation Loss in value due to normal use.

PI Principal + interest.

PITI Principal + interest + taxes + insurance (included in a typical mortgage payment).

plat book (plat map) A record showing land subdivided into lots.

point of beginning (POB) The starting point in a metes-and-bounds legal description of a property.

prepayment penalty clause States that prepaying the mortgage will result in certain monetary penalties.

prepayment privilege clause Defines the conditions under which the borrower can prepay a mortgage, usually without financial penalty.

prequalification Submission of financial information in anticipation of a credit decision without identification of a specific property.

primary market The market where mortgage loans are originated.

principal broker Person responsible for the operation of the mortgage company's principal place of business and all branch offices.

principal representative Manages the business operations of a mortgage lender or correspondent mortgage lender.

principle of conformity Principle holding that properties that fit with their neighborhood will have higher value.

principle of substitution Principle holding that no reasonable buyer will pay more for a property than what the buyer would pay for a comparable property.

private money Money loaned from a noninstitutional investor.

private mortgage insurance (PMI) Insures the portion of a mortgage loan that exceeds 80 percent of the property's value.

profit and loss statement Statement of the income and expenses of a business.

prohibited practices Practices related to the mortgage lending business prohibited by F.S. 494 and Rule 69V-40.

promissory note The borrower's or guarantor's personal promise to repay the debt associated with the purchase of real property.

proration The process of identifying expenses shared by the buyer and seller.

public records Documents maintained by government.

purchase-money mortgage An arrangement where a buyer obtains a loan to buy property with the seller holding a mortgage, usually for the amount of the down payment.

Q

qualifying The process of the applicant providing financial information so the lender can assess the risk associated with making a mortgage loan.

Quarterly Report Transmittal Form Report submitted to the DFS listing each person employed by a mortgage brokerage firm.

quitclaim deed Allows a grantor to relinquish all rights in a property without providing any warranty regarding the title.

R

Real Estate Settlement Procedures Act (RESPA) Legislation designed to ensure that lenders inform buyers of any charges they will be expected to pay at closing.

real property Land, improvements on the land, and the rights that come with ownership.

reconciliation The process by which appraisers determine a final value for a property using several valuation methods.

recording Filing legal notice of the details of a transaction.

recourse Requirements regarding the repurchase of a loan. *Full recourse* means that the seller must repurchase the loan if the buyer defaults; loans sold *without recourse* do not require the seller to repurchase the loan in case of default; *normal recourse* means that the seller is required to repurchase the loan if the buyer defaults due to faulty underwriting.

redlining Intentionally excluding certain urban areas from consideration for mortgage loans based on illegally discriminating against the protected classes of familial status (size of family), race, sex, disability, color, religion, or nationality.

refinancing The process of obtaining new financing on a property a borrower already owns.

Regulation B The Equal Credit Opportunity Act.

Regulation X Real Estate Settlement Procedures Act.

Regulation Z Requires lenders to disclose the annual percentage rate (APR) after considering all interest and finance charges within three business days of accepting a borrower's loan application.

representative credit score A score derived from credit information from more than one company.

Request for Verification of Deposit Form used to verify applicant has sufficient funds for down payment and closing costs.

Request for Verification of Employment Form used to verify applicant's income and work history.

residual income A set of adjustments used by the VA based on the number of family members and the area where the property is located.

restrictive covenants Requirements for the use of a property common to all parcels in a particular subdivision.

reverse mortgage Mortgage in which older homeowners can borrow against the equity they have built up in their property.

right of redemption Allows a borrower to reinstate a mortgage by paying all indebtedness and penalties.

right of rescission A consumer's right to cancel certain loan transactions.

right of survivorship Allows members of a tenancy to divide equally the share of a member when that member dies, preventing transfer of ownership to anyone outside the ownership group.

S

sales comparison A valuation method based on comparing similar properties to the subject property and adjusting the comparable property's price to reflect superior and inferior features relative to the subject property.

satisfaction of mortgage Certificate issued by a lender when a mortgage is paid in full.

secondary mortgage market Investors who buy already existing mortgages.

second mortgage A mortgage that is subordinate to the first mortgage.

security holder (Ginnie Mae) Person or entity who holds a security guaranteed by Ginnie Mae.

self-employed Owning 25 percent more of a business where one works.

servicing released Sale of mortgage where seller releases mortgage servicing.

servicing retained Sale of mortgage where seller retains mortgage servicing.

setback line An indication of the distance that cannot be encroached.

shared appreciation mortgage Mortgage where a lender charges the borrower an interest rate below market value in exchange for ownership in a certain percentage of the property.

simultaneous issue The issuing of owner's and lender's title insurance at the same time.

special warranty deed Provides limited warranty in that the grantor guarantees that he or she has done nothing to create a cloud on the title.

standard eligibility criteria The standards used by Fannie Mae to determine an applicant's eligibility for a loan.

standby commitment A promise from a different lender to make funds available under certain conditions; used in situations where the borrower may be uncertain that his or her initial application will be approved.

statute of frauds Law stating that real estate contracts must be in writing and signed by both parties to be enforceable.

statute of limitations A law that sets time restrictions for enforcing legal rights.

subject property The property being purchased or sold in a sales comparison appraisal.

subject to the mortgage Occurs when a buyer purchases property and may make payments on the mortgage but the buyer does not take responsibility for the note.

subordination Practice of making one mortgage inferior to another in terms of priority of repayment.

subpoena duces tecum A subpoena that requires the subpoenaed to produce all documents related to a transaction.

subprime loans Loans involving higher risk to the lender because the borrower usually has poor credit history and scores.

survey Procedure used to identify the exact location and size of a property.

sweat equity A purchaser's willingness to improve the value of a property by doing work on the property.

T

table funding The practice of a lender closing a loan in the lender's own name.

taxable value Assessed value minus any exemptions.

tax discounts Factors such as homestead exemptions that lower taxes on a property.

tenancy at sufferance Occurs when a tenant who has had lawful possession of a property continues at that property after his or her period of legal possession has ended and without the owner's permission.

tenancy at will A situation where an individual has tenancy for an unspecified period with the permission of the owner, who retains title.

tenancy by the entireties Ownership between a legally married husband and wife; similar to joint tenancy.

tenancy in common A relationship in which any number of people can be owners of a property, can have acquired their ownership at different times, and can hold different percentages of ownership.

term The period over which a mortgage will be paid.

term mortgage Mortgage requiring payment of interest only during the term of the mortgage.

third-party fee account Account for holding fees in escrow for refundable application fees, credit reports, appraisals, or third parties prior to a lender making a written commitment.

title Legal concept signifying ownership of real property.

Title 18, U.S. Code, Section 1001 Prohibits making false statements or representations.

title insurance Insurance designed to protect the owner and the lender from financial loss caused by defects of record in the title.

title search Process to determine whether a seller has the right to transfer title of a property.

title theory The legal doctrine where the lender receives title to a property through a mortgage deed or a third party holds a deed of trust and retains title until the mortgage is paid.

total obligations ratio (TOR) Calculated by dividing the sum of all fixed monthly obligations by monthly income; also known as the back-end ratio.

triggering term Financial information in an ad that requires full disclosure of terms of financing.

Truth-in-Lending Act Requires lenders to disclose all costs associated with a loan.

U

underwriting Process by which lenders analyze the risk associated with a loan.

Uniform Residential Appraisal Report (URAR; Fannie Mae 1004) Appraisal form preferred by most lenders.

Uniform Residential Loan Application (Fannie Mae 1003) Application form required by most lenders.

Uniform Settlement Statement (HUD-1) Settlement statement preferred by most lenders.

Uniform Underwriting and Transmittal Summary (Fannie Mae 1008) Form that summarizes information about the borrower and property, the mortgage, underwriting information, seller, contract, contact information, and delivery data.

up-front mortgage insurance premium (UFMIP) Insurance to protect the lender from default on the part of the borrower.

USA Patriot Act Law requiring lenders to collect a federal tax ID from borrowers as well as information about their ethnicity.

usury A contract for repayment of a debt at a rate higher than allowed by law.

V

VA The Department of Veterans Affairs.

VA loan A loan with partial guarantees from the DVA.

Verification of Deposit Form (Fannie Mae 1006) Used to verify an applicant's assets.

Verification of Employment Form (Fannie Mae 1005) Used to verify the applicant's gross earnings, overtime or bonus pay, and the likelihood of a pay increase.

Verification of Mortgage Form Used during the application process to verify the terms of an applicant's current mortgage.

voluntary lien A claim against property made with the consent of the owner.

W

warehousing The practice of a lender or correspondent lender using a short-term loan from a commercial bank to fund its loan commitments. Also known as warehouse lending.

with full recourse Requirement that seller must repurchase a loan if the borrower defaults.

with normal recourse Requirement that seller must repurchase a loan if the borrower defaults and the underwriting was faulty.

without recourse A loan that does not require repurchase in case of borrower default.

Wood Destroying Organism (WDO) Report Report assessing the presence and damage done by wood-destroying organisms such as termites.

wraparound mortgage Mortgage where a seller or other party agrees to pay the mortgage on a property while lending money to the buyer at a higher rate of interest.

Y

yield The return to an investor on a mortgage loan.

yield spread premium A commission paid by lenders to mortgage brokerage businesses when a loan is funded based on the loan's interest rate and market conditions.

INDEX

W

Y